HAWAII KAI
COOKBOOK

HAWAII KAI COOKBOOK

BY

ROANA AND GENE SCHINDLER

Drawings by Carol Nelson
Photographs by Robert Dickstein

Hearthside Press Inc.
Publishers • New York

This book is dedicated to our three wonderful and tolerant sons, Stephen, Seth and Rafe—who lived on beans while their parents wrote an exotic cookbook.

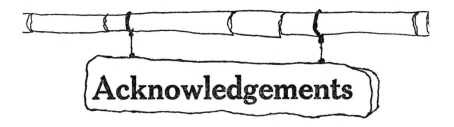

Acknowledgements

Our deepest gratitude to

Joe Kipness and Irving Karter, owners of the Hawaii Kai Restaurant for giving us *carte blanche* to use the extensive facilities, incomparable menu, festive drinks and the famous name of the restaurant.

Master Chef K. K. Pang or, as he is affectionately called by the staff, Haku Billy Pang—the "gentleman" in the kitchen; the organizing genius who supervises 14 chefs and produces over 10,000 meals per week.

Manny "Blackie" Andal, chief mixologist who, like all Island bartenders, jealously guards the secrets of his native concoctions, but nevertheless contributed them to our book.

Kaz Yamashita of Orchids of Hawaii International, whose first-hand knowledge of everything Hawaiian was invaluable.

Allan Gascoyne for his constant encouragement, ideas and help in research.

Our neighbors in Brower Hill: Bob Dickstein, photographer, for his fine camera work in reproducing the glamour of our native dishes; Carol Nelson, who did the charming drawings; Marilyn Barlaz and Jean Haagmans for typing and proofreading.

Mimi Jasse, our official taster, for her many kindnesses and unflagging support.

Alana Weinerman, Elaine Eisenberg and Tyana Reade for their culinary inspirations.

Cousin Arthur, who first introduced us to Hawaii.

Nedda Casson Anders, our editor and new friend—the best thing that could have happened to two neophytes. Her interest, guidance, counsel, exuberance and "know-how" made us believe we were writing the best cookbook ever!

CONTENTS

DESCRIPTIONS OF THE COLOR PLATES

(Between pages 96 and 97)

I. Fun Food. Lomi Lomi Salmon in sea shells (p. 29); Lemon Rosettes (p. 170); Waikiki Daiquiri (p. 20).

II. Lobster Buffet. Left to right: Rice with Ginger (p. 202); Lobster Aloha (p. 80); Fried Rice (p. 199); Waikiki Wontons (p. 50); center bowl, Fried Noodles (p. 49). Plum Brandy Sauce (p. 182) in the foreground.

III. An Edible Table Decoration. Luau Fruit Decoration with Crème de Menthe Sauce (p. 237).

IV. Garden Luau. Bottom row, left to right: Barbecued Roast Pork (p. 54); Hibachi Shrimp and Pineapple (p. 35); Waikiki Coconut Shrimp (p. 77). Second row: Bean Curd Appetizer (p. 28); Pickled Mushrooms Hilo (p. 175). Third row: Waikiki Wontons (p. 50); Fried Noodles (p. 49); Bean Sprout Vinaigrette (p. 181); Pickled Rose Radishes (p. 174). Fourth row: Teriyaki Beef Puu Puu (p. 31); Flaming Tahitian Beef Brochettes (p. 149). Fifth row: Meatballs Bali Bali (p. 162); Noodles Ono Loa (p. 203); Shrimp Momi Kai (p. 72). Sixth row: Corn from the Islands (p. 189); Lion's Head Shrimp Balls (p. 34); Spareribs Alii (p. 56). Seventh row: Pickled Cucumbers and Carrots, Japanese Style (p. 180); Luau Fruit Decoration (p. 237). The drinks are Pina Passion Cocktail (p. 17) and Coco Loco Cocktail (p. 21).

V. Come to a Hoolaulea. Clockwise, beginning at top: Lion's Head Shrimp Balls (p. 34); Native Mustard (p. 181); Plum Brandy Sauce (p. 182); Spareribs Alii (p. 56); Waikiki Coconut Shrimp (p. 77); Noodles Ono Loa (p. 203); Meatballs Bali Bali (p. 162); Barbecued Roast Pork (p. 54).

VI. Cornish Hen Platter. Cornish Hens Miko Moko on pineapple halves (p. 113), Spiced Crabapples and Kumquats. Cinnamon-Nut Rice (p. 201) in the center, with Orange Sweet Potato Rosettes (p. 206) between each hen. Hawaii Kai Swizzles (p. 21) and ti leaves around the border.

Shrimp Curry on the jacket. Top row, left to right: Coconut Rice (p. 201); Island Mandarin Oranges (p. 224); Macadamia Nuts; Cucumber Wedges; Mushroom Caps. Second row, left to right: Pineapple Cubes, Saffron Rice (p. 202), Shrimp Curry (p. 165). Cherry tomatoes at the bottom.

INTRODUCTION
TO FEASTING,
HAWAIIAN STYLE

On a pearl- and ruby-encrusted throne high above a cloud-drenched mountain on the island of Maui sits the great Polynesian god, Lono. Though he is revered by his people as a just and benevolent god, legend tells us that he had the power to cause all the Islands of Hawaii to disappear into the sea as miraculously as he made them appear some 20,000 years ago.

Now we seriously doubt if this fable is solely responsible for the customary good behavior of the Hawaiian people. But one thing is certain, if the mighty Lono should ever decide to carry out his ominous threat, the world would lose the most fascinating cultural conglomerate known to man. For in reality the five major Islands of Hawaii, occupying an area smaller in size than New Jersey with a total population less than that of Boston, represent the world's most polyglot community of national and international types . . . a blend of Polynesian, Japanese, Chinese, Filipino, Korean, Spanish, Portuguese and mainland American cultures. From this melting pot of people has come one of the most exciting and extensive of cuisines.

In that other "melting pot of the world", New York City, some half a million people feast each year on the exotic dishes of the Islands at a "little bit of paradise" called the Hawaii Kai Restaurant. As its Executive Director, Gene has had unlimited access to a profusion of recipes, menus and accumulated culinary wisdom. Here, amongst the pots and pans of a noisy, bustling grand galley, we have been free to touch and taste, sniff and smell, poke and pick from an incomparable Hawaiian treasure chest. We have made a selection from hot dishes and cold ones, spicy foods and bland, pungent and delicate, nutty and fruity, chewy and flaky—a total of some 300 recipes, with hundreds of suggested variations. Not all of the recipes are from the restaurant files; many come from our personal collection, but all have been made virtually failure-proof by consistent use.

Every dish meets two criteria: it is practical to use in mainland kitchens (ingredients available, procedures not overly complicated, etc.); and it has popular taste appeal. (Several recipes such as *poi* are so representative of Hawaiian cookery that to exclude them would be unthinkable, but we have cautioned the reader that mainland diners often find them unpalatable.)

Variations on a Theme

Roana, a long-time cooking teacher and food demonstrator, knows how puzzling the language of cookbooks can be to beginning cooks, so she has tried to anticipate any doubts that the reader might have.

Can I use mushrooms? Omit the tomatoes? Use canned pineapple instead of fresh? Replace the spinach? These are some of the questions asked her by new cooks. To answer these questions, sections following the recipes labeled *Kamailio* (Hawaiian for "talk" or "conversation") have been included.

Ingredients

Most ingredients are easily obtained. Even the supermarket now stocks canned water chestnuts, bamboo shoots, soy sauce, duck sauce, and frozen snow peas. At the back of the book you'll find a list of some of the more exotic ingredients, with mail-order sources suggested.

Cooking ahead (Liu Liu):

At the Hawaii Kai Restaurant expert chefs cook everything to order and nothing is reheated; but for home use, it is often practical to cook and store delectable dishes for later use. Remember to under-cook foods that will be frozen—cooking will be finished when the dish is reheated.

For party dishes, a good way to proceed is to line the company casserole with foil, cook the food in this foil-lined dish, freeze it, then remove foil from casserole and store in freezer. When it's party time, slip the foil back into the casserole and reheat as directed.

The Hawaiian term *Liu Liu*, literally "to make ready", appears throughout.

Number of Servings

Obviously the number of servings (unless otherwise stated, recipes serve 6) that any recipe will yield depends on such unknown (to us) factors as the size of the diner's appetite and the addiction to the food in question. We have given amounts based on whether the food is to be served as an hors d'oeuvre or as an entree (a term which in classic cuisine referred to a dish served just before the main course, but in the United States usually means the principal course).

Food Presentation

The menus, ideas for food presentation, and table decorations are based on the traditions of a people who have made the preparation and service of food an almost sacred part of their daily lives. But in temperate climates where taro leaves and mangoes, orchids and an-thuriums are not widely available, substitutions must be used and often are . . . in the informal spirit if not the actual style of Hawaii. With incomparable charm and grace the friendly Hawaiians seem to know instinctively how to use food and cooking not merely as a means to satisfy hunger but more importantly as a means towards a happier life. In a setting conducive to a cordial and relaxed mood they serve de-lectable food to welcome friends, to honor a guest, to celebrate a happy event, to lighten sorrows, to consummate a business deal, to enhance a love affair and even on occasions to propitiate the gods. And this is why you can be certain that the great god Lono would never make the Islands of Hawaii disappear. After all, where else can he find de-licious, mouth-watering, soul-satisfying luaus fit for a king . . . an emperor, or even a god.

2

EXOTIC SPIRITS
FOR
COCKTAIL
CONNOISSEURS

"Drink to me only with thine eyes"—this line from Ben Jonson's romantic poem is a pretty fair description of how the Hawaiians approach social drinking. This is not to say that Hawaii is a land of teetotalers . . . it's just that as a people they're basically gregarious and outgoing, so they seldom feel the need to put spirits down to keep theirs up.

The so-called Hawaiian Cocktail, as you may well have guessed, is a purely Western innovation. To make the tourist and visitor feel even more at home, the accommodating Hawaiians have come up with a number of appetizing libations with enough native ingredients to be honestly labeled "Hawaiian". As with most tropical drinks, the basis for these Island creations is usually Jamaican, Haitian or Barbadian rums. (Please note, however, that vodka, Scotch, Bourbon and other whiskies can be substituted for the rum.) The rum is proportionately blended with a variety of tropical fruit juices and then served chilled in a highly decorative fresh coconut or pineapple shell.

For those cocktail connoisseurs who will settle for nothing less than the real thing—we suggest that you beg, borrow, steal, or buy, if possible, a bottle of authentic, native Hawaiian brew—*Okolehao*. This is a potent and rather harsh liquor distilled from the ti plant. No luau or celebration is complete without it. Incidentally, *Okolehao* means, "iron bottom" . . . drink enough of these tropical tornados and you'll know why!

14

Wahini Cooler

1 can (6 oz.) frozen orange juice concentrate
½ cup sugar
1 can (12 oz.) apricot nectar
1 can (40 oz.) pineapple juice
1 can (6 oz.) frozen lemonade concentrate
⅛ cup grenadine or maraschino cherry juice
1 can (12 oz.) passion fruit nectar
4 ounces orgeat flavoring (see below)
ice cubes

In a large punch bowl or small barrel, dilute orange juice concentrate as label directs. Add sugar and mix until dissolved. Add remaining ingredients. Taste for additional sugar. (All this can be done one day in advance.) When ready to serve, add 2 trays ice cubes. Serve in Hawaiian mugs. 25 4-ounce servings.

(Orgeat is a non-alcoholic almond flavoring which can be bought in the fine food department of supermarkets and specialty stores.)

Heavenly Flower

A heavenly drink

1 can (6 oz.) frozen orange juice concentrate
3 cups pineapple juice
2 cups water
⅓ cup granulated sugar
⅓ cup lemon juice
1½ cups ginger ale

Combine all ingredients except ginger ale; stir to dissolve sugar. Add ginger ale. Pour into 8 tall ice-filled glasses. Garnish with an orchid and pineapple spear.

Outrigger Orange Flip

1 can (6 oz.) frozen orange juice concentrate
2 tablespoons lemon juice
2¼ cups cold water
2 eggs
3 tablespoons sugar
dash salt

Combine juices and water; beat with egg beater. Beat eggs with sugar and salt just until blended; add orange mixture; beat 5 to 10 seconds. Pour into 6 tall ice-filled glasses.

"Bird of Paradise"

(*Especially designed for youngsters*). *A swirl of exotic nectars blended with the mystic charms of Island paradise fruits; crowned with pineapple sherbet and a beautiful Bird of Paradise flower.*

> 1 ounce pineapple juice
> 1 ounce orange juice
> 1 ounce peach nectar
> dash of grenadine
> 1 scoop pineapple sherbet
> Bird-of-Paradise (strelitzia) flower

Pour all ingredients, except sherbet, over 1 cup shaved ice. Blend. Pour into 16-ounce glass and top with scoop of sherbet. Garnish with flower stuck in an 8-inch straw. Serves 1.

ALCOHOLIC

Fog Cutter

Even on a clear day, you will hear the sound of fog horns when you finish this.

> 2 ounces grapefruit juice
> 1 ounce lime juice
> ½ ounce passion fruit nectar
> ¾ ounce simple syrup or 1 teaspoon powdered sugar
> ½ ounce dry gin
> *½ ounce Lemon Hart rum or Demerara rum (86-proof)
> ½ ounce Port wine or Dubonnet red wine

Mix all ingredients except wine, into blending cup over 1 cup shaved ice. Whip. Pour contents over 2 to 3 ice cubes in a 15-ounce glass. Float wine. Garnish with pineapple spear skewered with red and green maraschino cherries, slice of orange, 8-inch candy-striped straw, and open paper parasol on tip of straw. (Make pineapple spear by cutting the core, lengthwise, into 4 pieces.) Serves 1.

---

* Or substitute whiskey of your choice.

Pina Passion

A romantic blend of light rums and lush tropical juices and spices, served in a fresh Kawai pineapple.

>   1 ounce lime juice
> ¾ ounce passion fruit nectar
> ½ ounce peach brandy
> ¾ ounce Demerara rum (86-proof)
> * ¾ ounce gold rum (80-proof)
>   1 pineapple slice, canned
> ¾ ounce honey
>   pineapple (#30 medium size)

Pour lime juice, passion fruit, brandy, both rums, pineapple slice and honey over half a cup of shaved ice in the mixing cup of a blender. Turn on blender. Pour mixture over ice cubes in pineapple. [To prepare pineapple, cut off half the leaves at a slight angle; cut off pineapple 1 inch below leaves, keeping the leafy part as the cover. Core out pineapple, leaving a ¾-inch shell to hold drink. Make a V-shaped notch to insert the straw.] Garnish with 8-inch candy-striped straw and parasol. Serve drink with leafy cover on. *Okolemaluna* (which means "bottoms up")! Serves 1.

Hawaii Kai Treasure

A reward all its own! An authentic pearl is your gift with this refreshing concoction of Martinique or Haitian rum.

>   2 ounces lime juice
>   1 ounce grapefruit juice
> ½ ounce light cream
> * 1½ ounces white rum
> ½ ounce green curaçao
> ½ ounce orgeat
> ½ ounce honey
>   15-ounce glass
>   8-mm. pearl; gardenia or cattleya

Blend all ingredients with cup of shaved ice. Whip. Pour over ice cubes in 15-ounce glass. Garnish with gardenia or cattleya flower. Insert pearl among petals; serve with an 8-inch candy-striped straw. *Kamau*—here's how! Serves 1.

---

* Or substitute whiskey of your choice.

Scorpion

You will feel it in the end! A tingling blend of Hawaiian or Tahitian rum, brandy, native nectar and liqueur, with a whisper of almond.

1½ ounces orange juice
1 ounce grapefruit juice
1 ounce pineapple juice
¾ ounce orgeat
1¾ ounces dry gin
¾ ounce brandy
¾ ounce white rum
  dash of almond extract
  fresh gardenia

Blend all ingredients, except almond extract, in mixing cup of blender with 1 cup shaved ice. Mix! Pour over cubed ice in tiki bowl. Add dash of almond extract; festoon with snowy-fresh gardenia and 10-inch straw. Serves 1.

Navy Grog

Landlubbers beware! This is a seaman's special, famous for its witch's blend of brew. Barbadian and Haitian rums.

¾ ounce Demerara rum (86-proof)
¾ ounce gold rum
¾ ounce grapefruit juice
½ ounce lime juice
 1 ounce passion fruit nectar
½ teaspoon sugar
½ ounce honey
  double old-fashioned glass

Pour all ingredients over ½ cup shaved ice in blender. Mix well! Pour over cubed ice in double old-fashioned glass. Garnish with pineapple spear skewered with green and red maraschino cherries, 8-inch straw and mini paper parasol. Serves 1.

Mai Tai

Mai Tai means the best! Every mixologist (bartender) in the tropics has his own secret recipe for this drink that symbolizes the picturesque Islands. Here's ours:

1½ ounces grapefruit juice
¾ ounce pineapple juice
¾ ounce orange juice
¾ ounce honey
½ ounce orgeat
1¾ ounces Demerara rum (86 proof)
1¾ ounces Bacardi amber

Mix all ingredients, in blender, over ½ cup shaved ice. Blend. Pour over ice cubes in 16-ounce glass. Garnish with pineapple spear skewered with green and red maraschino cherries, orange slice, mini parasol inserted in 8-inch candy-striped straw. Serves 1.

Sufferin' Bastard

A dirty stinker! This is also one of the favorite drinks and a spectacular blend of exotic potions.

1½ ounces lime juice
¾ ounce apricot nectar
¾ ounce papaya concentrate
½ ounce Falernum
¾ ounce simple syrup or 1 teaspoon powdered sugar
1½ ounces gold rum
1 ounce dark rum (151 proof)
dash of angostura bitters

Mix all ingredients, except angostura bitters, in blending cup over ½ cup shaved ice. Blend. Pour over cubed ice in 16-ounce Easter Island mug. Add dash angostura bitters. Garnish with sliced orange, green and red maraschino cherries, mini parasol stuck in 8-inch candy-striped straw. Serves 1.

Maiden's Downfall

Virgins beware! This arouses the beast in any man.

2 ounces grapefruit juice
1 ounce lime
¾ ounce orgeat
1 teaspoon sugar
1¾ ounces vodka
¾ ounce gold rum
½ cup shaved ice
dash of bitters

Mix all ingredients, except bitters, in blender over ½ cup shaved ice. Blend! Pour into 16-ounce glass over ice cubes. Add dash of bitters. Garnish with pineapple spear skewered with red and green maraschino cherries, ½ slice orange, and parasol placed into an 8-inch straw. Serves 1.

Waikiki Daiquiri

Does its own hula! Exciting cocktail with light rum, passion liqueur and fragrant limes. Served in a frosty igloo.

    5 ounce champagne glass
    1 ounce lime juice
    ½ ounce grapefruit juice
    1½ ounces white rum
    1 teaspoon sugar

Shave ice until it resembles snow. Form into a hollow mound in the champagne glass. Freeze overnight! Mix all ingredients in blender with ¼ cup shaved ice. Blend! Pour into cone of "frozen igloo". Garnish with 4-inch candy-striped straw and open parasol stuck on side of igloo. Serves 1.

shaved ice igloo

"Waikiki" Daiquiri

Coco Loco

A South Sea sneak! Fresh coconut filled with a devilish mixture of Martinique rum and coconut milk.

1½ ounces white rum
1 teaspoon sugar
1 teaspoon coconut powder (see index)

Mix in blender with 1 cup shaved ice. Pour over cubed ice in coconut. [To prepare coconut: use 1 medium-size coconut—with saw or bandsaw, cut off tip of coconut so that it can stand on the flat surface. Then measure 2 inches down from flat surface and cut off. Invert cut-off piece. That is your stand! Then set the coconut on top of the cut piece —the open end of the coconut will be facing up. Pour drink into it.] Garnish with 8-inch candy-striped straw and parasol. Serves 1.

Hawaii Kai Swizzle

Potent and palatable! Loaded with two distinct rums.

2 ounces lime juice
1 ounce orange juice
1 ounce grapefruit juice
1 ounce apricot nectar
½ ounce Falernum
1 teaspoon sugar
1 ounce gold rum
1 ounce Demerara (86 proof) rum
dash of angostura bitters

Mix all ingredients, except angostura bitters, over 1 cup shaved ice. Blend. Pour over cubed ice in a 16-ounce glass. Add dash of bitters. Garnish with pineapple spear, skewered with red and green maraschino cherries, 8 inch straw and paper parasol. Serves 1.

Tahitian Breeze

Enchanting touch of the Islands. An exotic blend of Tahitian passion nectar with Barbadian rum.

1 ounce lime juice
1 ounce maraschino cherry juice
1 ounce orange juice
1½ ounces white or gold rum
½ ounce grenadine
1 teaspoon sugar

Take 16-ounce footed glass—shave block of ice until it is as fine as snow—line inside of glass to ½ inch thickness with snow. Keep in freezer overnight (will not harm glass).

Mix all ingredients over ½ cup shaved ice. Blend! Pour into glass containing snow cone. Garnish with 8-inch straw and paper parasol inside tip of straw. Serves 1.

Headhunter Zombie

Renowned as the "walking dead"! Two is the limit!

1 ounce papaya nectar
1 ounce peach nectar
1 ounce lime juice
1½ ounces Demerara dark rum (86 proof)
1 ounce heavy dark rum (151 proof)
¾ ounce gold rum
¾ ounce honey
dash of angostura bitters

Pour all ingredients, except bitters, over ½ cup shaved ice. Blend! Pour mixture into 13-ounce frosted Zombie glass; add dash of bitters. Garnish with fancy pick, pineapple spear, red and green maraschino cherries, 8-inch straw, and paper parasol stuck in tip of straw. So here's mud-in-the-eye or, in graceful Hawaiian style, *lea lea kakou*—to happiness! And your response can be *Mahalo,* thank you or *likepuol* (the same to you). Serves 1.

AFTER-DINNER FAVORITES

Kona Koffee Grog

This wakes you up! Flaming rum and Hawaiian coffee blended with rare honey and cinnamon sticks, tangerine peels and served in a Headhunter's bowl.

1 cup black coffee, Kona coffee preferably
1 ounce honey or honey cream
dash of nutmeg and cinnamon
*1 lime cup, 1 ounce capacity
1 ounce heavy dark rum (151 proof)
1 cinnamon stick, 4 inches long

———

* Lime cup—cut a fresh lime in half and remove pulp. Dry skin overnight.

Pour coffee into Headhunter bowl. Mix with honey or honey cream, dash of nutmeg and cinnamon. Place lime cup on top, floating on coffee. Pour 1 ounce rum into cup. Set aflame. Put cinnamon stick into coffee; serve hot and flaming.

Tahitian Kooler

An enchanting, delicate drink. A favorite of the Island sweethearts.

    1 ounce pineapple juice
    ½ ounce orange juice
    1½ ounces milk or light cream
    ¼ ounce triple sec
    ¾ ounce dry gin
    dash of grenadine

Pour all ingredients into blending cup over ½ cup shaved ice. Blend. Pour finished drink into 10-ounce footed, frosted glass. Decorate with an 8-inch candy-striped straw with open paper parasol inserted into straw.

Hawaiian Russian

Hawaiian wedding of Kona liqueur and vodka.

    ½ ounce pineapple juice
    ½ ounce dark crème de cacao
    ¾ ounce vodka
    1 ounce heavy cream

Pour ingredients into blending cup over ¼ cup shaved ice. Blend! Pour into 8-ounce rock glass over cubed ice. Garnish with an open paper parasol stuck into an 8-inch candy-striped straw.

O'Brien Hawaiian

Hawaiian version of Irish coffee.

    1 ounce Irish whiskey
    ¼ ounce green crème de menthe
    1 cup black coffee
    1 tablespoon whipped cream

Mix whiskey with crème de menthe. Set aside. Pour black coffee into Headhunter's cup. When ready to serve, add whiskey mixture and top with whipped cream.

King Ka-Meha-Meha

His royal sins are rolled into this devilish mixture of brandy laced with gin.

> 1 ounce passion fruit nectar
> 1 ounce pineapple juice
> ¼ ounce triple sec
> ¾ ounce dry gin
> ¾ ounce brandy

Blend all ingredients over ¼ cup shaved ice. Pour into 7-ounce highball glass. Garnish with slice of orange, red cherry, 6-inch candy-striped straw with paper parasol inserted.

Waikiki Sunset

A delicious pink taste treat of rum and suggestive passion fruits—the hula is a cinch after 2 drinks.

> ½ ounce pineapple juice
> ½ ounce lime
> 1 ounce white rum
> ¼ ounce maraschino liqueur
> dash of grenadine

Pour ingredients over ½ cup shaved ice in blender. Blend! Pour into 7-ounce highball glass. Garnish with slice of orange, green cherry, 4-inch straw, and paper parasol.

Humuhumunukunukuapuaa

(Hum Hum for short.) Intrepid ones love this innocent-looking concoction of coconut milk and gin whipped into a frenzy, then enhanced with the nectars of the romantic Island fruits.

> 1 ounce orange juice
> 1 ounce honey cream
> ½ ounce heavy cream
> 1 ounce dry gin
> 1 ounce white rum
> ½ ounce coconut milk (see index)

Pour ingredients over ½ cup shaved ice and blend. Pour into 10-ounce footed highball glass. Garnish with half a slice of orange, pineapple spear on pick with green and red cherries stuck on end of spear, 8-inch candy-striped straw, parasol open and in straw end.

3

HAWAIIAN FUN FOOD
Don't Puupuu It
Until You've Tried It

The Swedes have their famous Smörgasbörd—the French have their splendid hors d'oeuvre, and the Italians have their famous antipasto. But those happy, harmonious Hawaiians have their *puu puu* dish. And what a wonderful dish it is! From stem to stern it's a veritable potpourri of international delicacies that deliciously reflect the many ethnic influences so typical of Hawaiian cuisine.

Give or take a few goodies, the traditional Lealea Mea, or puu puu platter, consists of Chinese-style barbecued spareribs, butterfly shrimps, Japanese Kumaki on sticks, Korean meat balls, Hawaiian Lomi Lomi salmon, cherries, rum and sugar-glazed pineapple chunks, and fresh-roasted macadamia nuts.

The perfect puu puu tray should be served hot and kept hot over a small flame. If available, a hibachi stove is ideal. Served as an appetizer or on a hot buffet table, the many-flavored, colorful puu puu platter is your best way to say "Aloha!" . . . a snack sampler supreme.

Island Cheese Spread

1 cup creamy peanut butter
½ cup sherry wine
½ pound shredded Cheddar cheese
½ teaspoon nutmeg
½ teaspoon fresh ginger root, minced

Combine all ingredients. Refrigerate in plastic container. Can stay for 2 to 3 weeks. Serve with shrimp or lobster chips. Makes about 2 cups.

Honolulu Dip

½ pint sour cream
1 teaspoon hoisin sauce
1 tablespoon ketchup
1 tablespoon chili sauce

Stir together and refrigerate until ready to use. Serve with lobster or shrimp chips (see index).

Island Cocktail Dip

Good with lobster or shrimp chips, seafood, etc.

2 cups commercial sour cream
½ teaspoon Five Spices (see index)
½ cup unsalted peanuts, chopped
½ cup chopped chutney
3 teaspoons chopped onion

Combine all ingredients and mix well. Refrigerate. Will keep about 1 week in refrigerator. Makes 3 cups.

Lanai Dip

½ pint sour cream
1 tablespoon oyster sauce
1 teaspoon brown sugar
dash of fresh pepper

Refrigerate combined ingredients. Serve with lobster or shrimp chips (see index).

Sesame Seed Dip

    1 package (8 oz.) cream cheese
      mixed with 3 tablespoons sour cream to soften
    1 teaspoon hoisin sauce
    1 tablespoon ketchup
    1 teaspoon sesame oil
    2 tablespoons toasted sesame seeds

Combine all ingredients and refrigerate. Will keep in refrigerator
1 week. Good with lobster and shrimp chips.

Shrimp or Lobster Chips

*These are dehydrated cylinder-shaped thin chips made of shrimp or
lobster meat, maize flour, salt and baking powder. They come in white,
or a magnificent array of pinks, purples, yellows, greens and oranges.
When cooked, they resemble flower petals and have a delicate texture
and a delicious shrimp or lobster taste.*

    1 pound shrimp or lobster chips (see index)
    oil for deep frying

Heat 3-4 cups oil in a large skillet until it smokes. Add the chips,
a handful at a time and turn down the heat a little. The chips will
blow up to five times their size and turn into graceful petal shapes.
They are finished when they float to the top. Remove with a slotted
spoon and drain on paper toweling. Stop when you have made enough
chips. But we warn you, "nobody can stop at one".

Liu Liu:

Prepare them in the morning and store in an airtight container.
Your guests can warm them over a hibachi, if you wish, as we do at
the Hawaii Kai.

Coconut Delight

    1 package (8 oz.) cream cheese
    2 tablespoons Plum Brandy Sauce (see index)
    dash of salt
    flaked coconut

Soften cream cheese at room temperature and mix with Plum
Brandy Sauce and salt. Chill and shape into tiny balls. Roll in coconut.
Makes about 24.

Macadamia Hors D'Oeuvre

1 package (8 oz.) cream cheese
¼ cup chopped macadamia nuts
dash of cinnamon sugar
flaked coconut

Soften cream cheese at room temperature and mix with chopped nuts and cinnamon sugar. Chill and then shape into bite-size balls. Roll in coconut. Makes about 24.

Pickled Mushrooms

2 teaspoons sesame oil
1 cup water
½ cup tarragon vinegar
1 teaspoon salt
¼ teaspoon fresh pepper
2 garlic cloves, minced
1 tablespoon onion powder
2 tablespoons sugar
½ pound, tiny white, fresh mushrooms, stems removed
    or 1 can mushroom caps, drained and rinsed

Combine sesame oil, water, vinegar, salt, pepper, garlic, onion powder and sugar in a large jar. Add mushrooms and marinate them at room temperature for 24 hours. Refrigerate—can be kept 1 month. Drain to use.

Bean Curd Appetizer
Very okoa (*translation: different*).

4 or 5 bean curd cakes (see index), cut into 1-inch cubes
parsley sprigs or chopped lettuce
3 tablespoons soy sauce
2 tablespoons oyster sauce(see index)
dash of fresh pepper
sesame oil
1 scallion, chopped fine

Arrange bean curd cubes on an attractive dish covered with parsley or chopped lettuce. Mix soy sauce with oyster sauce, pepper and sesame oil. With a teaspoon, drizzle this mixture over bean curd cubes. Sprinkle with chopped scallion. Put a fancy pick through each cube and serve cold.

Lomi Lomi Salmon

A luau favorite.

¾ pound fresh or frozen salmon
1½ tablespoons salt
6 tablespoons lemon or lime juice mixed with 1 teaspoon sugar
4 ripe tomatoes, peeled (see index) and chopped
4 scallions, chopped

Wash salmon (salted cod and mackerel are also used), dry and rub with salt. Sprinkle lemon or lime juice and sugar on both sides. Cover and place in refrigerator for 12 to 24 hours. Turn occasionally. The lemon or lime juice will "cook" the salmon (salted salmon, if used, should first be soaked in water overnight). Remove bones and skin from the fish and cut into ¼-inch pieces or shred with fingers. This way you'll be able to feel any small bones. Combine chopped tomatoes and scallions with fish and a little juice. Serve cold in small sea shells over cracked ice. It can be refrigerated for another day or so. Serves 6 to 10.

Kamailio:

1. You can substitute lox or smoked salmon for the fresh salmon, if you wish, but don't marinate it. Just combine with chopped tomatoes and scallions.

2. Chopped green pepper can be added with tomatoes and scallions.

3. Lomi Lomi Salmon can be served in scooped-out tomato halves on a bed of watercress or salad greens. Combine chopped tomato pulp with the rest of the ingredients and heap into tomato shells. Chill.

Sashimi

Raw fish, Japanese fashion

A Hawaiian delicacy served as a first course or as a puu puu. In the Island waters where fish are profuse, albacore, marlin, swordfish, sailfish and tuna are just a few that are used.

1½ pounds filleted red snapper, sea bass, halibut
    or other firm, white saltwater fish without too many small bones
2 slices fresh ginger root, minced
1 cup soy sauce (shoyu)
1 cup shredded lettuce, watercress, grated *daikon* (Japanese radish),
    and/or cucumber

Cut fish diagonally into strips 1½ to 2 inches long, ½-inch wide and ⅛-inch thick. Refrigerate. Combine ginger root with soy sauce and place in a pretty bowl. Arrange the fish strips on a bed of shredded lettuce, watercress, diced daikon or cucumber or combination of these. The pieces of fish are dipped into the sauce as they are eaten. Sometimes the fish slices are wrapped around a small amount of the shredded or sliced vegetable and skewered with a toothpick. Serves 10-12.

OTHER DIPPING SAUCES

1. 1 cup soy sauce combined with grated daikon (see index) or white radish.

2. 1 cup soy sauce combined with 1 tablespoon dry mustard mixed with 1 tablespoon water.

3. 6 tablespoons soy sauce, 2 teaspoons sugar, 3 tablespoons vinegar, minced garlic cloves and 1 teaspoon finely chopped chili pepper.

Tahitian Fish (Poisson Cru)

1½ pounds fresh halibut, swordfish, red snapper
    or other white-flesh fish
1 teaspoon coarse salt
juice of 6 lemons or limes
3 tablespoons grated onion or chopped scallions
1½ cups coconut milk (see index)

Cut fish into cubes. Sprinkle with salt, lemon or lime juice and onion. Cover and refrigerate overnight. Turn occasionally. Drain fish, add coconut milk and chill for 2 to 3 hours. Serve in small clam shells on a bed of rice. (Can be used as the first course.) Serves 10 to 12.

Korean Meatballs

Wan-Jah Juhn

1 pound chopped meat
1 tablespoon sesame oil
2 tablespoons soy sauce
½ teaspoon salt
2 scallions, chopped fine
1 garlic clove, minced
3 tablespoons sesame seeds, pulverized (see index)
dash of fresh ground pepper
2 tablespoons cornstarch
2 eggs, beaten with 1 tablespoon soy sauce
½ cup flour mixed with 1 tablespoon paprika
oil for frying

Mix the first nine ingredients together in a bowl. Shape into small meatballs. Dip in egg mixture, then roll in flour and paprika. Heat oil in skillet and brown evenly on all sides. Serve with Vinegar-Shoyu Sauce (see index). 25-30 meatballs.

Kamailio:

You can serve these meatballs with other sauces (see index). They can be presented in a chafing dish, skewered with fancy picks. For browning large amounts, follow the procedure given under Meat Balls Bali Bali. The meatballs can be refrigerated for 2 days or frozen for several weeks and reheated in a 375° oven.

Teriyaki Beef

Puu Puu

1 pound prime fillet of beef, cut into pieces
    ½-inch thick, 1 inch by 1½ inches

MARINADE

½ cup soy sauce
4 tablespoons brown sugar
1 tablespoon honey
1 can pineapple chunks (15 ounces) drained
1 large garlic clove, minced
2 slices fresh ginger root, minced
1 tablespoon sesame oil

18 bamboo skewers, 6-inch length

In a large bowl, combine all marinade ingredients. Add meat and toss to coat well. Place pineapple chunks on top and drain off a little marinade from bowl to coat them also. Cover and marinate 2 to 3 hours at room temperature or overnight in refrigerator. Remove from marinade and skewer the meat and pineapple alternately on bamboo sticks using 3 meat pieces and three pineapple cubes. Broil in oven 3-4 inches from flame for 3 minutes and turn. Broil additional 3 minutes. At the Hawaii Kai Restaurant, these are served with Plum Brandy Sauce combined with Native Mustard (see index).

Kamailio:

1. Marinade may be heated and used as a sauce. Thicken with 1 tablespoon cornstarch mixed with 2 tablespoons water.

2. Although the Hawaii Kai uses prime fillet of beef for the Teriyaki hors d'oeuvre, you can substitute any lean, tender steak.

3. If you have a small hibachi, your guests will enjoy warming their skewered Teriyaki on the flame.

4. Marinade can be frozen and reused. Add additional garlic and ginger root, since freezing tends to lessen flavor.

5. For a change of flavor, add drained pineapple juice to the marinade.

6. Teriyaki can be broiled over hot charcoal. Watch for charring.

7. Cut steak into long thin strips 1 inch by 5 inches, and thread two strips, accordion-fashion, on skewer with pineapple in between. Proceed with recipe.

8. Follow recipe but broil meat until rare. Reserve marinade. Refrigerate for 1 to 2 days. Prior to serving, remove from refrigerator, brush with marinade and keep at room temperature for 1 hour. Preheat oven to 375° F. and reheat Teriyaki or broil 3 to 4 inches from flame, turning once. Watch for charring.

TERIYAKI BEEF

pineapple cubes

bamboo skewer

Baked Clams Kai

Although the Hawaii Kai uses fresh cherrystone clams in this savory appetizer, we recommend the canned type as being sweet, delicious . . . and expedient! You can get clam shells by visiting a local clam bar or seafood restaurant and politely asking for a bagful of shucked shells. They're only too glad to be rid of them. No local clammery? Try the department stores for man-made containers.

⅜ pound butter (1½ sticks)
4 large garlic cloves, minced
1 can (10 oz.) minced clams
1 small can (5 oz.) water chestnuts, drained, rinsed and chopped fine
½ cup coarse bread crumbs
salt and fresh ground pepper to taste
paprika

Melt butter in a skillet and sauté garlic until golden. Place clams in a large bowl and remove half the juice (reserve). Add all but 2 tablespoons garlic butter to clams. Add and combine water chestnuts, bread crumbs, salt and pepper. Mix well. Let rest 5 minutes to thicken. Mixture should be soft and pliable. Spoon into clam shells and sprinkle with paprika. Combine reserved clam juice with remaining garlic butter and drizzle over clam mixture. Broil in oven until hot, bubbly and brown. Serve with lemon rosettes (see index). Allow 2 to 3 small shells per serving for hors d'oeuvre. Enough for 12-15 clam shells.

Kamailio:

1. I find that the clam shells are easier to handle if they are first placed in a muffin tin or shallow baking pan then filled with mixture and broiled.

2. Water chestnuts can be omitted and chopped green pepper or bacon or both, can be added. Sauté the pepper with the butter and garlic. Bacon should be cooked separately, crumbled and drained of fat, then added to clam mixture.

3. *Advance preparation:* any one of the mixtures can be made in advance and refrigerated or frozen. Or the clams can be filled, broiled and refrigerated for 2 days or frozen until needed. Broil only until lightly golden. Reheat thoroughly in oven at 350° F.

4. To take up less space in freezer, freeze clams on a tray, then pop into a plastic bag and seal.

5. Remember that seasonings in frozen foods have a tendency to dissipate; retaste and compensate for garlic loss.

Shrimp Fingers

1 pound fresh shrimp, shelled, cleaned and deveined
3 slices fresh ginger root, minced
1 large onion, chopped
salt and fresh pepper to taste
1 egg
6 slices day-old white bread, crusts removed, and cut vertically
    into 3 or 4 strips each
corn flake crumbs
2 inches oil for deep frying

Chop shrimp fine and combine with minced ginger root and chopped onion. Add salt, pepper and egg. Mix well and spread over bread fingers. Sprinkle fingers with corn flake crumbs and deep fry at 375° F. until golden brown. Drain on absorbent paper. Makes 18 to 24 fingers. [Fingers can be prepared in advance, refrigerated or frozen (wrapped, labeled and sealed), and reheated in a 325° F. oven until piping hot.]

Lion's Head Shrimp Balls

An adaption of a famous old Chinese recipe.

½ pound ground pork
½ pound cooked shrimp, minced fine
1 egg, beaten with 1 teaspoon sherry wine
1 scallion, chopped fine
1 teaspoon fresh ginger root, minced
1 tablespoon soy sauce
1 can (5 oz.) water chestnuts, drained, rinsed and chopped
cornstarch
4 tablespoons oil

Combine all ingredients except cornstarch and oil. Mix thoroughly and shape into tiny balls. Roll in cornstarch and then sauté in the oil using a large skillet. Cook slowly until browned, turning constantly. Keep hot in preheated oven and when all balls are browned, drain on absorbent paper. Serve hot on cocktail picks with Plum Brandy Sauce and Native Mustard or other sauces (see index). Makes about 25 shrimp balls.

Kamailio:

This dish can be made in a chafing dish and kept hot over the water pan, or it can be made in advance and transferred to a chafing dish for buffet service. It can also be made in advance and refrigerated or frozen, then reheated in a preheated oven at 325° F.

A variation of this dish is to roll balls in finely chopped rice flour noodles (see index) instead of cornstarch, and deep-fry. The noodles turn white and puff up when fried.

Hibachi Shrimp and Pineapple

   2 large pineapples
   ½ cup soy sauce
   ¼ cup honey
   1 slice fresh ginger root, minced
   1 large can frozen pineapple juice concentrate, thawed
   1 tablespoon sugar
   2 pounds shrimp, cooked

Hollow out pineapples for use as hibachis (see index). Cube fruit and reserve. In a saucepan heat soy sauce, honey, ginger, pineapple concentrate and sugar together and simmer for 3 to 5 minutes. Prepare bamboo skewers by threading 1 shrimp between 2 pineapple cubes. Put pineapple hibachis in center of a large tray covered with ferns or parsley (artificial leaves are fine too). Pour sauce into a pretty bowl and place on the tray. Surround tray with skewered shrimp and pineapple, inserting a few into pineapples also. Place sterno cans into pineapple hibachis and light. Guests dip the skewered shrimp and pineapple into the sauce and then heat over the fire. *Kupaianaha* (translation: marvelous)!

Kamailio:

If necessary, use a small custard cup to elevate the sterno can set in the pineapple.

Shrimp Nui

1½ pounds (about 25) large fresh shrimp,
　cleaned and butterflied (see index)

MARINADE

3 tablespoons soy sauce
1 tablespoon sherry wine
½ teaspoon garlic powder
1 teaspoon sesame oil
dash of fresh white pepper

Put shrimp in a shallow pan or bowl. Combine all marinade ingredients and sprinkle over shrimp. Toss shrimp to coat well. Let stand 1 hour or refrigerate overnight.

BATTER

¼ cup cornstarch
1⅓ cups water
2 eggs
2 cups flour
1½ teaspoons baking powder
1 teaspoon sherry wine
½ teaspoon garlic powder
1 teaspoon sesame oil (optional)
½ teaspoon sugar
1 teaspoon salt
oil for deep frying

In a large bowl, mix cornstarch with water. Add eggs and beat well. Gradually add flour and the remainder of the ingredients beating until batter is smooth. Heat oil in a large skillet and, holding each shrimp by the tail, dip in batter to coat. Add shrimp to hot oil one by one (do not crowd). Reduce heat to medium and when shrimp are golden brown on both sides and float to surface, they are done (4 to 5 minutes). Drain well on paper towels. Serve with Plum Brandy Sauce or Native Mustard (or the sweet and sour sauce given under Flaming Pork Ipo).

Liu Liu:

Shrimp Nui recipe can be completed, wrapped in foil and refrigerated for 2 days or frozen. The shrimp must be fried only until faintly golden brown. When ready to serve, they can be refried or reheated in a 325° F. oven on a foil-lined shallow pan. We cover them with foil loosely for 5 to 10 minutes and then remove foil for browning and crisping.

Chinese Chicken Wing Clubs

Fang Guy Yick

12 chicken wings
¼ cup soy sauce
   dash of garlic powder
⅛ teaspoon hoisin sauce
2 inches oil for frying

Cut off and discard tip of wing. Sever wing at joint. You now have two wing sections. Take the smaller section and with fingers and a small knife, scrape and push skin and meat down to form a ball at end of bone (like a small drumstick). Take the wing section that has 2 bones and cut the smaller bone loose at top and bottom. Remove

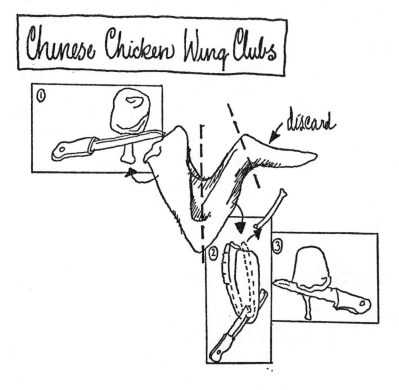

and continue as with the first section. You will have 24 small chicken clubs. Place in a shallow dish; combine soy sauce, garlic powder and hoisin sauce and sprinkle over wings. Toss and turn to coat. Marinate 2 to 3 hours or overnight. Heat oil in a large skillet. Dip chicken clubs into batter (below) and deep fry. Serve with Plum Brandy Sauce and Native Mustard or other sauces (see index).

BATTER

1 cup flour
1 teaspoon salt
½ teaspoon sugar
2 teaspoons baking powder
1 egg, beaten
⅔ cup water
¼ cup sesame seed or pine nuts

Combine flour and salt, sugar and baking powder. Add egg and then the water. Stir until smooth. Add sesame seed or pine nuts and mix well.

Liu Liu:

Chicken clubs can be shaped in advance and refrigerated. Chicken can be dipped into batter, pre-fried lightly in the morning and then reheated thoroughly on a shallow baking pan in preheated oven, 375° F.

Chinese Chicken Wings

An Oriental delicacy

12 chicken wings
1 garlic clove, minced
2 scallions, chopped
¼ cup soy sauce
1 tablespoon sherry wine
½ cup water
¼ cup honey
2 tablespoons sugar
3 tablespoons oyster sauce (see index)

1. Chop off and discard bony tip of chicken wings. Cut each wing into two parts. Place all ingredients in a large pan, stir and combine well. Add chicken wings; bring to a boil and simmer covered 30-40 minutes. Shake pan and baste occasionally. Uncover pan and simmer for an additional 15 minutes, stirring and basting frequently. Remove wings from pan and reserve liquid.

2. When ready to serve, place under broiler flame, sprinkle with reserved liquids and broil until brown and crisp. Turn once. Serve with Plum Brandy Sauce or any other sauce (see index). Allow 2-3 pieces per person.

Kamailio:

An inexpensive but delicious hors d'oeuvre. They can be arranged on a chafing dish surrounded by several different sauces (see index). A half teaspoon of hoisin sauce can be substituted for the oyster sauce.

The recipe can be completed through step 1. The wings can then be refrigerated or frozen. Reheat in preheated oven until warm and then broil until brown and crisp. Serve as directed.

Chicken Puu Puu

    2 breasts of chicken, skinned and boned
    ½ cup oil
    ¼ cup soy sauce
    2 tablespoons vinegar
    1 tablespoon honey
    ½ teaspoon hoisin sauce (see index)
    1 garlic clove, minced
    ½ pound small button mushrooms

Cut chicken breasts into 1-inch squares. Combine oil, soy sauce, vinegar, honey and garlic. Marinate chicken squares and mushrooms for 2 to 3 hours or refrigerate overnight. Drain and thread chicken and mushrooms alternately on small bamboo skewers. Broil about 4 inches from heat, about 3 to 4 minutes on each side, or until chicken loses pinkness. Makes about 15 hors d'oeuvre. (Marinade may be heated and used for sauce. Thicken with 2 tablespoons cornstarch mixed with ¼ cup water.) May be served with other sauces.

Manu Chix

1 pound cooked white meat chicken
1 can (5 oz.) water chestnuts, drained and rinsed in cold water
1 egg, beaten
1 scallion (white and green part), minced
1 garlic clove, minced
1 tablespoon sherry wine
2 tablespoons soy sauce
1 teaspoon sugar
½ teaspoon salt
dash of freshly ground pepper
1 tablespoon cornstarch mixed with 2 tablespoons water
oil for deep frying

Mince or grind chicken and water chestnuts. In a bowl, combine remaining ingredients except oil and mix thoroughly. Wet hands and shape mixture into small balls the size of walnuts. Do not pack too heavily. Using a large, deep skillet, heat oil for frying and add the Manu Chix balls a few at a time. Do not crowd. Reduce heat when skillet is full. Turn balls occasionally and fry until golden. Remove with slotted spoon and drain on paper toweling. Keep hot in 350° F. oven. Repeat until mixture is depleted. Reheat oil each time. Serve on fancy picks wtih Plum Brandy Sauce and Native Mustard or other sauces (see index), or on a bed of shredded lettuce as an entrée. Makes 18 to 24.

Kamailio:

1. In lieu of deep-fat frying, the chicken can be sautéed in a small amount of oil or chicken fat and browned lightly, 3 tablespoons chicken broth added and cooked, covered, over medium heat for about 10 minutes. Turn several times.

2. There are hundreds of variations of this recipe. Shrimp, crab meat, turkey, chicken roll, pork or beef can be used in place of chicken. You can add or substitute bamboo shoots, mushrooms and celery.

3. After shaping the Manu Chix, they can be dipped in flour, then in an egg beaten with 2 teaspoons water, and then in flour mixture again. (Bread crumbs can be substituted for flour.)

4. *Advance preparation:* To use within 2 days, complete recipe and cool. Cover and refrigerate. To keep longer, freeze in foil. To serve, preheat oven to 325° F. and spread Manu Chix on a baking sheet until thoroughly heated.

Tahitian Tidbits

   1 pound small pork sausages
   2 garlic cloves, minced
   ¼ cup soy sauce
   ¼ cup honey
   ¼ cup chicken stock
   salt and pepper to taste
   3 tablespoons rum (151 proof)

Brown sausages on all sides in a large skillet with the garlic. Drain fat. Add soy sauce, honey, chicken stock, salt and pepper and cook covered, over low heat for 10 minutes. Stir often to coat sausages. Remove cover and simmer until sauce thickens. Transfer to chafing dish and flambé with warm rum (see index). Serve with cocktail picks or bamboo skewers. Can be made a day or two in advance and then reheated in a chafing dish and flambéed. Serves 8-10.

Aloha Puu Puu

   8 fillets of dolphin, sole or salmon
   1 can (15 oz.) pineapple chunks,
      or 1 fresh pineapple, peeled and cut into cubes

   MARINADE

   ¼ cup soy sauce
   2 tablespoons brown sugar
   1 tablespoon lemon juice
   ¼ cup pineapple syrup or juice

Cut each fillet in half lengthwise, and slightly on a bias. Marinate the fillets for at least an hour, turning occasionally. Drain and wrap each fillet around one pineapple chunk and secure with toothpick. Dip into the batter below and fry in deep fat. Serve with Plum Brandy Sauce or other sauces (see index).

   BATTER

   1 cup flour
   2 tablespoons cornstarch
   2 teaspoons baking powder
   1 teaspoon salt
   ⅔ cup water

Combine all ingredients and stir until the batter is smooth.

Liu Liu:

The entire recipe can be made in advance and refrigerated for two days or frozen. Reheat on tray covered with foil in 375° F. oven until thoroughly heated. Remove foil to brown and crisp the fillets.

Mushrooms Lelani

    1 pound (about 25) fresh medium-size mushrooms
    3 scallions
    2 tablespoons oil
    ½ pound ground pork
    2 garlic cloves, minced
    ½ cup corn flake crumbs
    2 tablespoons soy sauce
    2 teaspoons sugar
    ½ teaspoon salt
    dash of fresh pepper
    1 teaspoon sherry wine
    3 water chestnuts, chopped
    1 egg, beaten with 1 tablespoon water
    ½ cup chicken broth (scant)

(1) remove sliver from bottom if mushroom wobbles

(2) form meatballs with wet hands... meatball should be large enough to fill entire cavity

Mushrooms Lelani

place stuffed mushrooms in baking dish

(3)

Rinse mushrooms with cold water in a colander and dry on paper towels. Snap off stems and reserve caps. Chop stems together with scallions very fine. Remove ¼ cup of this mixture and reserve. Heat oil in skillet and sauté ground pork and garlic until pork turns white. Add mushroom and scallion mixture and sauté along with pork for 3 minutes. Remove from heat and add all remaining ingredients. Mixture should be soft and pliable. If necessary add a little more broth. Adjust seasoning. When cool enough to handle, wet hands and form into small plump balls. Place these into mushroom caps.

FOR PAN

1 cup chicken broth
2 tablespoons soy sauce
2 teaspoons sugar
salt and pepper to taste
dash of paprika
reserved mushroom and scallion mixture

In a heatproof serving dish, mix chicken broth, soy sauce, sugar, salt, pepper, paprika and reserved mushroom and scallion mixture. Place stuffed mushrooms in dish, cover with foil and bake for 15 minutes in moderate oven (325° F.). Remove foil, baste with pan juices and bake for additional 10 minutes. Plan on 2 to 3 mushrooms per serving, or 1 if you use very large mushrooms.

Liu Liu:

Baked mushrooms can be refrigerated 2 to 3 days or frozen. Bake only for 15 minutes in advance preparation to prevent mushrooms from becoming too soggy when reheated. However, do not freeze more than 1 month because most of their flavor is lost after that time.

Tim San

These are light, dainty, steamed meat dumplings that are wrapped in a flour leaf dough and served on the flaming Puu Puu tray. You can buy the ready-made wonton skins or wrappers in any oriental shop and cut them into 3-inch rounds (see Sources of Supply). Or make your own (recipe follows); it will resemble a cupped leaf, hence its name.

24 3-inch-round skins or wrappers

HOW TO STEAM Tim San

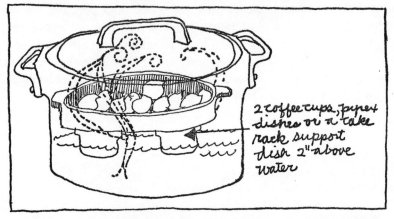

2 coffee cups, paper dishes or a cake rack support dish 2" above water

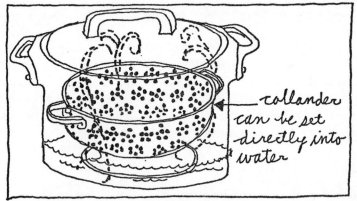

collander can be set directly into water

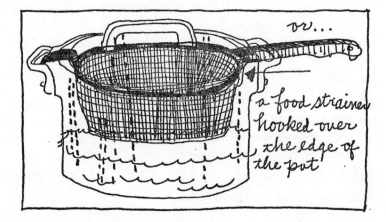

or...

a food strainer hooked over the edge of the pot

FILLING

2 stalks celery, trimmed
1 pound boneless pork, finely ground
1 tablespoon sherry wine
1 tablespoon soy sauce
1 teaspoon salt
1 tablespoon sugar
½ can water chestnuts, drained, rinsed and finely chopped
1 tablespoon cornstarch

Dry celery thoroughly and chop fine. Extract as much of the moisture from celery as you can by rolling in a clean towel and squeezing tightly. Combine remaining ingredients with the celery in a bowl. Wet hands and shape the mixture into small meatballs (about a heaping tablespoon). Place a skin in palm of left hand and cup palm. Insert a meatball into the center of the skin. With the right hand gather the sides of the skin around the filling as if pleating it. Pinch in the centers of the sides of the skin and fit skin firmly against the filling. Tap the bottom of the completed dumpling on a flat surface, so that it can stand by itself. After wrapping and filling the first few dumplings you'll be amazed how simple it really is because no matter how much you handle the dough in shaping, it can't be damaged. Place the dumplings on a greased heatproof platter that is a little smaller than the pot in which you plan to steam dumplings.

TO STEAM DUMPLINGS

Pour boiling water into the lower part of a steamer (see below). Place plate of dumplings on the rack of the steamer and keep water boiling. Cover the pan and steam for 30 minutes. Keep boiling water on hand to refill steamer when needed. Serve with Plum Brandy Sauce and Native Mustard, as we do at the Hawaii Kai. See other sauces in Index.

HOMEMADE STEAMER

Use a large Dutch oven or roasting pan with well-fitting cover. Fit bottom with raised trivet, cake rack or 2 small custard cups. Fill bottom with boiling water, to come within an inch of the rack, etc. Place your plate of dumplings on this and follow steaming directions (there must be enough space around the plate to permit the steam to circulate). At home we have even filled a large pan with several inches of water, hooked an aluminum colander over the edge, filled it with **Tim Sans**, covered it and let it steam away.

Tim San Skins or Wrappers

1 cup flour
¼ teaspoon salt
1 egg, beaten with 2 to 3 tablespoons cold water

Sift flour and salt together into a bowl. Make a well and pour egg and water into it. Wet fingers and knead mixture into a smooth elastic dough. Divide dough in half and on a lightly-floured surface roll out the halves, one at a time, into thin sheets 14 inches by 14 inches. Roll dough away from you until it is thin and semi-transparent. Don't worry about overdoing the rolling or kneading. Handling doesn't hurt the dough. (Although the skins are easy to make, it takes lots of energy to knead the dough until it is elastic and rolls out thinly.) Use a 3 inch cookie cutter to cut the rounds. Cover with a damp cloth until ready to use. To refrigerate or freeze stack between individual layers of wax

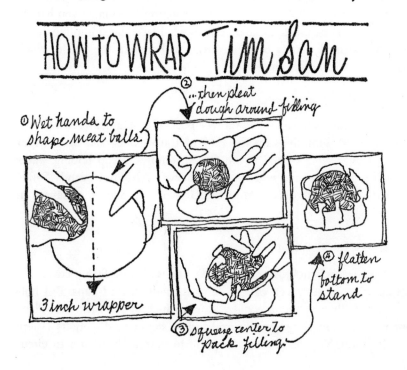

HOW TO WRAP Tim San

① Wet hands to shape meat balls.

② ...then pleat dough around filling

③ squeeze center to pack filling.

④ flatten bottom to stand

3 inch wrapper

paper or Saran wrap and sprinkle with cornstarch between each skin. Cover well.

Kamailio:

You can make a double recipe of skins and refrigerate them for about two weeks. Be sure they are wrapped well. They can also be frozen and thawed before use (see under Egg Rolls for storing information).

A pound of skins makes 60 to 70 squares and costs about fifty cents. They are sometimes sold in 9-inch sheets from which you can make the rounds—about 4 or 5 rounds per sheet.

Leftover pieces of skins can be cut in small strips and fried in deep fat; they are delicious in soup or just for nibbling.

The entire recipe can be prepared, except for steaming, and refrigerated for 2 days, or wrapped in foil and frozen; when ready to serve, do not thaw but bring water to boil in steamer and heat tim sans until thoroughly cooked (about 40 minutes).

Egg Rolls Ami Ami (Served on the Flaming Puu Puu)

This looks complicated but it isn't and it is well worth the little effort it takes. Like the Tim Sans, the egg roll skins can be purchased easily (see Sources of Supply) or made at home in a few minutes. Either way they can be refrigerated or frozen. More about this under Liu Liu.

    2 cups celery, minced (with leaves)
    3 tablespoons oil
    1 cup roast pork (see index), cut into ½-inch strips
    1 cup cooked shrimp, chopped
    1 teaspoon salt
    1 teaspoon sugar
    2 tablespoons soy sauce
    1 can (5 oz.) water chestnuts, drained, rinsed and minced
    1 can (5 oz.) bamboo shoots, drained, rinsed and minced
    5 scallions, minced
    ½ teaspoon freshly ground pepper
    24 egg roll skins (6½ inches square); see recipe on page 49.

With paper towels, squeeze celery tightly to remove moisture. Heat oil in large skillet and add celery. Sauté for 2 minutes and add pork, shrimp, salt, sugar and soy sauce. Stir briskly and sauté for a minute or two. Add remainder of ingredients and stir again. Taste for additional seasoning. Transfer to colander and drain. Cool for 30 minutes in refrigerator. It is important that the filling be as dry as possible to prevent tearing of the skin when filling.

FILLING AND FOLDING THE EGG ROLLS

For sealing them, make a mixture of 1 egg beaten with 2 tablespoons water to which you add 2 tablespoons cornstarch or flour. Place skin so that one point of the square is nearest you and the skin resembles a diamond shape. Put a heaping tablespoon of filling slightly below center of skin. Fold the bottom point up and over the filling to cover filling completely. Now fold both sides to the center, one overlapping the other. Roll over to top point and brush inside of top edge with the sealing mixture. Press as if sealing an envelope flap.

AND NOW THE FINAL TOUCH:

In a large skillet, heat 3 to 4 cups of oil to high heat (about 375° F.). Place egg rolls in the hot oil (do not crowd); lower heat a little and deep fry them until golden brown and crisp on both sides. Lift with slotted spoon and drain on paper towels. Continue with next batch in same fashion. If you are planning to eat them at once, preheat oven to about 325° and keep egg rolls warm, until all are completed. Otherwise, see below. Serve with Plum Brandy Sauce and Native Mustard (see index).

Kamailio:

1. We have given you the filling used at the Hawaii Kai; however, there are many other fillings—use what you have on hand. For the

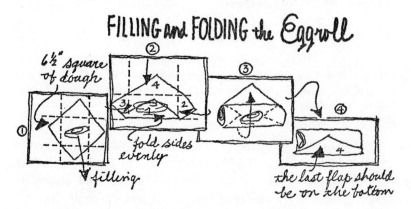

FILLING and FOLDING the Eggroll

shrimp, cooked lobster and crab meat can be substituted. Cooked chicken and ham, mushrooms, cabbage, bean sprouts or spinach are equally delicious (bean sprouts, however, will lose their crispness if egg rolls are frozen).

2. When you have leftovers, that's the time to think of the egg rolls. A little of this and that and you have the filling.

3. Store-bought skins cost about 35¢ a pound.

Liu Liu:

1. Whether purchasing ready-made skins, or making them yourself, they can be kept for two weeks in refrigerator if wrapped well (a damp towel is good), or they can be frozen (thaw before using). Homemade skins should be sprinkled lightly with cornstarch between each layer to prevent sticking together, or use wax paper or Saran wrap between each one. The bought ones are sold prepared in this fashion.

2. Cooked egg rolls can be kept up to 3 days in refrigerator or frozen and reheated in a slow oven until heated thoroughly.

3. Do not stack hot egg rolls one on top of the other until cooled.

4. Any leftover or torn skins can be cut into uneven strips and deep fried. You will have delicious, crisp noodles. Refrigerate or freeze for soup or snack.

Egg Roll Skins

    4 cups flour
    1 teaspoon salt
    2 eggs, beaten well
    1¼ cups ice water

Sift flour and salt together in bowl and make a well. Add eggs and ice water. Wet fingers and knead the dough until smooth and elastic (5 minutes). Cover bowl and refrigerate for half an hour. Divide dough in half and roll out the halves, one at a time, on a lightly-floured surface. Roll it away from you until it is paper thin (no more than 1/16 of an inch thick). Cut into 6½-inch squares (about 24). These can be stacked between layers of wax paper, or Saran wrap, or sprinkled with cornstarch in between each skin. Cover well with Saran wrap or damp towel so that they don't dry out, if they are to be refrigerated. To freeze, wrap in foil.

Easy Egg Roll Dough

    2 eggs, beaten
    3 cups water
    4 cups sifted flour
    oil

Put beaten eggs in a bowl and add water. Add flour gradually, stirring until you have a smooth batter. Use a 6- or 7-inch frying pan or skillet. Grease the pan thoroughly with oil and heat until very hot. Put a small amount of batter into pan, pick the pan up and tilt and turn to spread batter into a thin layer. Excess batter can be poured back from the pan into bowl. When the pancake is slightly brown, turn and heat the other side until dry. Turn out on paper towels. Repeat until all of the batter is used up. You can stack them, one overlapping the other. Make cornstarch and water sealer as done in Egg Rolls Ami Ami recipe above. Place a tablespoon of filling in center of pancake. Take the bottom edge of pancake (nearest you) and fold over filling. Brush edges with cornstarch paste and fold left and right sides toward center. Roll up and close securely.

Waikiki Wontons

    ½ pound crabmeat, fresh cooked, frozen or canned (7½ oz.)
    1 package (8 oz.) cream cheese (softened at room temperature)
    1 egg, beaten
    dash of garlic powder
    dash of onion powder
    dash of freshly ground pepper
    1 teaspoon soy sauce
    oil for frying
    48 wonton skins (bought or homemade, see index)

Drain crabmeat and pick over, carefully removing cartilage. Reserve. In a large bowl, combine remaining ingredients until well mixed. Add crabmeat pieces to mixture and fold in gently. Follow directions on How To Fill Wontons and see diagram, page 94.

TO FRY

Heat oil to a depth of 1 inch in a large skillet. Maintain heat at moderately hot. Fry wontons until golden brown (do not crowd). Turn once while frying. Drain on absorbent paper. Serve hot with Plum Brandy Sauce or other sauces (see index).

Five-Spice Chicken Livers

    1 pound chicken livers
    ½ cup soy sauce
    ½ cup water
    2 tablespoons sherry wine
    1 tablespoon sugar
    2 scallions, chopped
    2 slices fresh ginger root, minced
    dash of fresh ground pepper
    ¼ teaspoon Five Spices (see index)

Combine all ingredients and simmer for 10 minutes or until chicken livers are done. Cool and cut chicken livers into bite-size pieces. Serve on fancy picks, hot or cold.

Kumaki

Lots of people call this Rumaki but we prefer Kumaki since there's no R in the Hawaiian alphabet. There are many variations of this hors d'oeuvre in the Islands, and because of their popularity and ease of preparation, we thought you'd enjoy knowing how to make more than one. You can serve an assortment at your next party on a puu puu tray, and have guests reheat their own over the flame of the hibachi.

The Hawaii Kai chef, Mr. K. K. Pang, makes this delicious tidbit using a whole chicken liver, but for home use this seems too much of a good thing; each hors d'oeuvre in the recipe below requires only half a chicken liver. In the Islands, we have had Kumaki made from livers divided into three or four pieces. So—decide for yourself. You can also make Kumaki using sardines, nuts and olives in place of the chicken livers. Decisions, decisions!

    ½ cup soy sauce
    ¼ cup brown sugar
    dash of pepper
    12 chicken livers, cut in half
    12 water chestnuts, drained, rinsed and cut in half
    12 strips of bacon, cut in half (precook until just soft, if desired)

Combine soy sauce, brown sugar and pepper in a shallow dish; add chicken liver halves and toss to coat well. Marinate at room temperature 2 to 3 hours or overnight in refrigerator. Remove livers and drain. Reserve marinade. Place a chicken liver half on the edge of a bacon strip, a water chestnut half on the liver and roll bacon around these firmly. Secure with a toothpick. Dip into reserved marinade and place on a rack over a foil-lined pan. Bake in a hot, preheated oven (400° F.) about 20 to 30 minutes, until bacon is crisp. Turn once. If you wish, you can broil the Kumaki in the same fashion but it bears more watching. Replace toothpick with fancy pick. Serve with Plum Brandy Sauce and Native Mustard. Makes 24 kumaki.

Liu Liu:

It's nice to know that you can prepare the Kumaki in advance, and refrigerate it unbaked for a day or so, and then bake it as directed. Or you can bake it lightly, for about 10-12 minutes, refrigerate or freeze, and reheat without defrosting in a preheated oven set at 325° F. Test to see that they're heated thoroughly before serving with the recommended sauces.

Chicken Kumaki

    2 tablespoons soy sauce
    1 teaspoon hoisin sauce
    1 tablespoon sherry wine
    dash of salt and fresh pepper
    ½ teaspoon sesame oil
    2 cups chicken cut into 1-inch cubes (cooked or raw)
    ¾ pound bacon slices, halved (precook until just soft, if desired)
    2 eggs beaten with ½ cup water
    1 cup flour
    oil for deep frying

Combine soy sauce, hoisin sauce, sherry wine, salt, pepper and sesame oil in a bowl. Add cubed chicken and toss and turn to coat well. Marinate for 2 to 3 hours or overnight in refrigerator. Drain chicken cubes and wrap one bacon strip around each cube. Fasten with toothpick. Mix eggs with flour to make a batter. Dip Kumaki into batter and coat evenly; if batter is too thick, thin with water. Heat 2 inches oil in large skillet. Add Kumaki cubes and fry over medium heat. Do not crowd. When golden on both sides, drain on absorbent paper. Remove toothpicks and replace with fancy picks. Serve with Plum Brandy Sauce and Native Mustard or other sauces (see index).

Lychee Kumaki

    1 can (10 oz.) lychee fruit
    ½ cup peanuts, coarsely chopped
    15 bacon slices, cut in half
    ¼ cup soy sauce
    ½ cup brown sugar

Drain lychee fruit very well (there will be about 30 lychees) and reserve syrup. Fill the cavity of each lychee with coarsely chopped peanuts. Wrap bacon slices around each filled lychee and secure with toothpicks. Dip into soy sauce mixed with an equal amount of reserved syrup, and roll in brown sugar. Place on a rack over a foil-lined pan and bake in a hot preheated oven 400° F. for 20 to 30 minutes until bacon is crisp. *E malama* (translation: watch carefully)! Replace toothpick with fancy picks before serving. Serve with Plum Brandy Sauce (see index). Makes 30 kumaki.

Kamailio:

1. Kumquats can be used instead of lychees.
2. Apricots can be substituted for the lychees and filled with chutney instead of peanuts. (You will need whole bacon slices for the apricots.)

Oyster Kumaki

    1 small can (8 oz.) oysters, drained
    1 can (5 oz.) water chestnuts, drained, rinsed, and cut in half
    ¼ pound bacon slices, cut in halves

MARINADE

    ¼ cup sherry wine
    ½ cup soy sauce
    ¼ cup oil (sesame preferably)
    4 tablespoons ketchup
    2 tablespoons brown sugar
    2 tablespoons vinegar
    2 garlic cloves, minced
    dash of pepper

Combine sherry, soy sauce, sesame oil, ketchup, brown sugar, vinegar, garlic, and pepper and marinate oysters 2 to 3 hours or overnight. Remove from marinade and place half a water chestnut on oyster. Wrap bacon slice around oyster and water chestnut and skewer with toothpick. Bake on a rack over a foil-lined pan in 375° F. oven or broil 4 inches from flame, turning occasionally until bacon is crisp. Watch carefully. Replace toothpick with fancy pick before serving. Heat marinade and use as sauce.

Pineapple Kumaki

> 1 fresh pineapple, peeled, cored and cut into 1-inch cubes
> ¾ pound bacon slices, halved

> MARINADE:

> ½ cup soy sauce
> ¼ cup pineapple juice
> 3 tablespoons brown sugar
> 1 tablespoon vinegar
> 1 slice fresh ginger root, minced

Wrap each pineapple cube with half a slice of bacon and secure with a toothpick. Place in a shallow pan and cover with marinade, tossing and turning them to coat well. Marinate for 3 hours at room temperature or overnight in refrigerator. Prior to serving, roll in additional brown sugar. Bake on a rack over a foil-lined pan in a 375° F. oven, or broil 3 to 4 inches from flame, turning until bacon is crisp. Replace toothpicks with fancy picks before serving. Prepare the pineapple shell as a hibachi (see index) and have guests warm their Kumaki over the fire. Banana chunks can be substituted for the pineapple.

Barbecued Roast Pork

A people-pleasing hors d'oeuvre served on a sizzling steel platter.

> ½ cup soy sauce (light preferably)
> 1 tablespoon honey
> 2 tablespoons sherry wine
> 2 garlic cloves, minced
> 1 tablespoon tomato coloring (see index)
> ¼ cup sugar
> ¼ cup chicken broth
> 1 tablespoon oyster sauce
> dash of fresh ground pepper
> 1 loin of pork, boned

In a shallow pan, combine all ingredients and marinate loin of pork for 2-3 hours at room temperature, or preferably overnight in refrigerator. Turn occasionally. Drain, but reserve marinade. Preheat oven to 425° F. and place meat on a grill, rack or trivet over a shallow baking pan containing an inch or two of water; or suspend "imu fashion" (see index) from two hooks. Roast for 10 minutes and reduce heat to 375° F. Turn meat (if not suspended) and brush with marinade. Roast for 30 minutes more, basting occasionally. Cut pork loin into thin slices against the grain. Serve hot with Plum Brandy Sauce and Native Mustard.

Kamailio:

1. At the Hawaii Kai, only the choice loin of pork is used. However, we heartily recommend tenderloin, a shoulder of pork or pork butt which can be boned, all fat removed and cut into rectangular strips 2 inches wide by 2 inches thick and 5-6 inches long. The shoulder or butt will yield 3 to 4 strips, which can all be roasted at the same time and the unused strips wrapped in foil and frozen. Reheat in foil without defrosting and use for the many other recipes requiring roast pork.

2. The roasted pork can keep about 4 to 5 days in refrigerator and is *ono loa* (delicious) eaten cold or reheated in oven. Just brush with leftover marinade or 3 tablespoons chicken broth combined with 3 teaspoons soy sauce and 1 tablespoon honey.

3. Try barbecuing a pork strip on your charcoal grill for 15 to 20 minutes on each side, basting at intervals (see Roast Suckling Pig for barbecuing information).

4. For a change of flavor, add any of the following ingredients to marinade or combine several: 1 teaspoon minced ginger root, 1 teaspoon hoisin sauce, 1 teaspoon brown bean sauce (mashed) or a pinch of Five Spices (see index).

5. You can heat marinade with additional broth and ¼ cup honey and use as a dipping sauce for barbecued pork.

6. We always have a strip or two of barbecued roast pork in the freezer. When company drops in it takes just a few minutes to heat pork until it can be sliced down and then brushed with a little soy sauce, honey and broth until sizzling. There's nothing so delicious!

Spareribs Alii

*At the Hawaii Kai Restaurant, only the choice sections of the spareribs
are used. The ribs themselves are small and meaty. Gene designates
them as "2 and under", meaning that one rack weighing between 1⅞
and 2 pounds yields 11-13 ribs. The chefs remove the back flap of meat
and the fat; then chop away the gristle and bone from the top and
sides and trim the rack so that all the ribs are uniform in size (the
trimmed away meat can be frozen and used for soup and other pork
dishes requiring ground or shredded pork).*

> 4 pounds pork spareribs (25 ribs)
> 5 tablespoons hoisin sauce (see index)
> 5 tablespoons soy sauce
> 1 teaspoon sherry wine
> 3 tablespoons brown sugar
> 3 garlic cloves, minced
> 1 teaspoon tomato coloring (see index)
> 1 tablespoon brown bean sauce
> pinch of Five Spices (see index)
> 1 pastry brush or small paint brush

With a sharp knife make tiny slits between each rib (not clear
through), to permit marinade to penetrate. Combine all ingredients
well and with brush, paint or rub this thick marinade on the ribs. Marinate 3 to 4 hours at room temperature or overnight in refrigerator.
When ready to bake, preheat oven to 350° F. and place ribs on a rack
over a pan filled with two inches of water and roast for 1½ hours,
turning occasionally. Or, suspend ribs by 2 hooks, like a hammock (imu
fashion, see index), from the top rack of the oven, over a pan filled
with 2 inches of water. The suspended ribs need no turning. If ribs
dry out too quickly, baste with a mixture of 2 tablespoons soy sauce,
3 tablespoons chicken broth and 2 tablespoons honey. Turn up heat to
425° F. to crisp the ribs during the last 10 minutes of roasting. Slice
ribs completely through before serving with Plum Brandy Sauce and
Native Mustard (see index).

ABOUT BARBECUING RIBS:

Ribs are delicious when barbecued outdoors. However, care must
be taken to prevent charring. Prepare twice the amount of marinade
used in Spareribs Ali so that you can baste frequently. The grill must

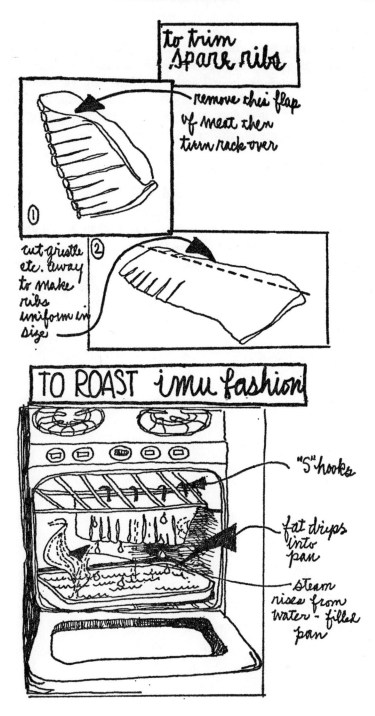

to trim
Spare ribs

① remove this flap of meat then turn rack over

cut gristle etc. away to make ribs uniform in size

②

TO ROAST *imu fashion*

"S" hooks

fat drips into pan

steam rises from water-filled pan

be as far from the coals as possible and no coals directly under the ribs. Use a drip pan. Slow cooking is best, so plan on about 50 to 60 minutes. Turn frequently. If you have an electric rotisserie, thread the ribs in the center through the rod and use a drip pan. For family use you may not wish to trim the racks of ribs as closely as the chefs do at the Hawaii Kai—no harm done. You can chop the individual ribs in half, to make tiny pieces of ribs for hors d'oeuvre.

Liu Liu:

1. Ribs can be partially roasted for 1 hour and refrigerated 2 to 3 days or frozen. When ready to serve, turn oven to 375° F. and reheat covered with foil. Uncover to brown (about 30 to 45 minutes).

2. If we're in a hurry to reheat the ribs, we cut them apart into individual ribs and roast them; that shortens the cooking time considerably.

4

THE WONDERFUL FISH
OF
HAWAII

Every country has its fishermen and, naturally, wherever there's a fisherman there's sure to be a fish story. The Hawaiians are no exception. Ask a Polynesian fisherman "how's the fishing" and he'll very likely say, "we Hawaiians don't have to fish because the fish know we cook them so well that they happily jump out of the sea and beg to be served in one of our luaus."

The jumping-out-of-the-sea part is obviously the figment of some fisherman's imagination but take our word for it—the cooking part is absolutely true. Hawaiians can do more things with more types of fish than any other people we know. Making no bones about it, they expertly know how to bake it, fry it, broil it, stew it, barbecue it, and if they're in a Japanese mood they'll serve and eat it raw.

In addition to mullet and mahimahi, a real Hawaiian fish and seafood menu is very likely to include: lobster, shrimp, albacore, yellow fin, tuna, marlin, sea bass, red snapper, halibut, swordfish and deep sea turtle.

Though most Hawaiians are fond of fish (served raw or cooked, and frequently with a sauce), they seldom prepare a one-fish meal as we do. With more than 100 varieties of fish abounding in the neighboring seas and lakes, the Hawaiians prefer to serve a mixture of fishes with their meals, rather than make a complete meal of one kind.

Weight watchers take note, for a low-calorie, high-protein diet, you can't beat a wholesome meal of fresh fish. And if by chance one jumps out of the Pacific and says "Aloha"—grab it. That's an authentic *mahimahi* (dolphin to you), as indigenous to Hawaii as the hula.

Fish for All Purposes

(*You can make substitutions for any of the fish recommended in the recipes by following this guide.*)

For Steaming—sea bass, black bass, bluefish, carp, flounder, halibut, mackerel, mullet, perch, salmon, red snapper, whitefish (whole fish are best).

Boiling—whitefish, bluefish, sea bass, cod, halibut.

Deep-Frying—bluefish, carp, halibut, haddock, red snapper, sea bass, smelts, trout, whitefish, yellow pike, mullet, flounder, sole, dolphin (mahimahi).

Sautéeing—flounder, swordfish, bluefish, salmon, trout, sea bass, haddock, sole, cod, halibut.

Baking—dolphin (mahimahi), swordfish, carp, salmon, sea bass, mackerel, whitefish, red snapper.

Broiling—albacore, dolphin (mahimahi), swordfish, red snapper, marlin, trout, sole, sea bass, mackerel, mullet, bluefish, cod.

Raw—mullet, swordfish, halibut, sea bass, tuna, albacore, red snapper, marlin, flounder, sole, whitefish.

Abalone and Chicken

 1 can (15 oz.) abalone
 2 tablespoons oil
 1 garlic clove, minced
 1 slice ginger root, minced
 3 chicken breasts, cut in cubes
 1 cup chicken broth
 1 tablespoon sherry
 2 tablespoons oyster sauce
 1 teaspoon oil (sesame preferably)
 1 tablespoon soy sauce
 1 teaspoon sugar
 1 can water chestnuts (5 ounces), rinsed and sliced
 1 tablespoon cornstarch mixed with 3 tablespoons water

Drain abalone and cut into small cubes. Reserve liquid. Heat oil and sauté garlic, ginger root and chicken cubes until chicken loses its pinkness. Add abalone and sauté *only* for one minute. Add chicken broth, sherry, oyster sauce, oil, soy sauce, sugar and abalone liquid. Combine well and heat quickly. Add water chestnuts and gradually add cornstarch mixture and cook until thickened. Serve hot with rice. (Do not overcook abalone or it will toughen.) Serves 6.

Stuffed Fish Rolls

 1½ pounds fish fillets [mullet, sole, flounder, dolphin (mahimahi)]
 3 tablespoons soy sauce
 1 teaspoon fermented black beans, soaked, rinsed and mashed
    (see Index)
 1 slice fresh ginger root, minced
 ½ pound fresh spinach, washed, stems removed, and chopped,
    or ½ package frozen chopped spinach
 1 cup ground cooked pork, shrimp or ham
 1 garlic clove, minced
 1 egg, beaten
 1 cup flour
 ½ cup water
 salt
 2 tablespoons sesame seeds
 oil for deep frying

Sprinkle fish fillets with soy sauce, black beans and ginger root. Toss to coat well. Blanch spinach in boiling water and drain. Combine with pork, shrimp or ham and add minced garlic. Spread this mixture on the fish fillet and roll like a jelly roll. Fasten with toothpicks. Make a smooth batter of the egg, flour, water and salt. Spread sesame seeds thinly over a sheet of wax or foil paper. Dip fillets in batter, then coat with sesame seeds. Fry in deep fat until golden. Serve with a sauce, if desired (see index). Serves 6.

Island Fish in Shrimp Sauce

      3 pounds dolphin (mahimahi), cod steak, swordfish or similar type
         cut ¾ inch thick
      3 tablespoons lemon or lime juice
      ¼ cup butter, melted
      ½ teaspoon salt
       dash of fresh pepper
      1 can frozen cream of shrimp soup
      ½ cup mayonnaise
      ½ cup very small shrimp
      2 scallions, chopped

Wash, dry and cut fish into 6 serving size pieces. Place in an ovenproof serving dish. Sprinkle with lemon or lime juice and allow to marinate for 1 to 2 hours. Drain and pour melted butter over fish. Sprinkle with salt and pepper. Broil for 10 minutes, 3 inches away from flame, and remove from heat. Baste with juices from the pan and cool. Mix soup and mayonnaise together and spoon over each piece of fish. Thirty minutes before serving, bake in oven preheated to 350° F. until

fish is flaky. Five minutes before serving, top with little shrimp and bake only until shrimp are hot. Garnish with scallions. Serves 6.

Liu Liu:

Recipe may be completed in advance up until fish is ready to be baked. Allow 40 minutes baking time if fish has been refrigerated.

Island Fried Fish with Pineapple Sauce
Batter fish with a golden crust.

2 pounds fish fillets (sea bass, flounder, etc.)
½ cup soy sauce
1 teaspoon garlic powder
½ cup flour
½ cup cornstarch
⅔ cup milk
1 egg
2 teaspoons baking powder
1 teaspoon salt
dash of pepper
1 can pineapple tidbits (30 ounces)
½ cup sugar
1 tablespoon cornstarch mixed with 2 tablespoons water
oil for deep frying

1. Wash and dry fish. Cut into 1½ inch squares. Marinate in soy sauce and garlic powder for 1 hour. Turn occasionally. Make a smooth batter of the flour, cornstarch, milk, egg, baking powder, salt and pepper.

2. Heat pineapple tidbits with syrup and sugar in a large saucepan, slowly until sugar is dissolved. Simmer for 10 minutes; thicken with cornstarch mixture. Cover and keep hot.

3. In a large skillet, heat oil and when hot, remove fish from marinade; using tongs dip fish into batter and fry (do not crowd). When fish are golden brown, remove and drain on absorbent paper. Keep hot in 325° F. oven while doing the next batch. Serve with the pineapple sauce. Serves 6.

Liu Liu:

The entire recipe can be made in advance and reheated in 375° F. oven when ready to serve. Omit cornstarch mixture from sauce and add only just before serving.

Japanese Broiled Fish in Teriyaki Sauce
Sakana No Teriyaki

6 swordfish steaks or fish fillets

MARINADE

1 cup soy sauce
⅓ cup sugar
1 garlic clove, minced
1 slice fresh ginger root, minced
2 tablespoons sake or sherry wine (optional)

Combine all ingredients and pour over fillets. Marinate for 2 hours. Drain and reserve marinade. Broil fish in a pan (not on a grill) 3 to 4 inches from flame. Baste once with marinade, but do not turn fillets. Fish is done when it flakes easily. Heat marinade and use as a sauce for the fish. Serves 6.

Kamailio:

1. The above marinade is called Teriyaki Sauce. It's delicious when used with chicken, spareribs, hamburger steaks, roasts and skewered steak bits. It can be thickened with cornstarch.

2. You can broil, sauté, bake or charcoal grill, using it as a marinade and to baste with.

3. It can be made up in a double quantity, refrigerated and used over and over again.

4. To make a Teriyaki Roast Beef, marinate overnight and use some of the sauce to roast beef in and to baste with.

5. Chicken parts or slices can be marinated overnight and broiled, basting with sauce; or sautéed in a pan with a little oil. Add sauce while sautéeing and thicken and glaze by permitting it to cook down.

6. Hamburgers can be marinated in sauce for 30 minutes and broiled. Brush with more sauce when turning them over.

7. Thread marinated steak slices, or chicken pieces, on bamboo skewers. Broil; baste occasionally. Turn once.

8. One or two chopped scallions can be added to marinade.

Steamed Fish Chinese Style

For steaming, a whole 2 to 3 pound fish, or the equivalent in fish steaks, is best. Steaming allows the fish to cook in its own juices and remain moist. Black bass, sea bass, bluefish, mullet, salmon, red snapper and whitefish are good. Allow ½ pound per person.

1 whole fish, 3 pounds, cleaned but with the head and tail remaining
salt (coarse)
1 tablespoon fermented black beans, soaked and mashed (see index)
1 garlic clove, minced
1 teaspoon sesame oil
2 tablespoons soy sauce
1 teaspoon sugar
1 large slice fresh ginger root, shredded
1 scallion, cut in 2-inch lengths

Rinse the fish in cold water and dry. Score fish ¼ inch deep in 3 or 4 places on each side (not too close to the tail). Rub fish with salt, inside and out. Place in a heatproof platter. Combine black beans, garlic, sesame oil, and sugar, and spread over fish. Arrange shredded ginger and scallion on top of fish.

Steam (see below) until done (about 20 to 30 minutes). Fish is done when the meat at the thickest part shows white, not pink, and translucent.

Serve fish at once on its own steaming platter. Garnish with parsley sprigs and lemon rosettes. Serves 6.

TO STEAM FISH:

If you do not have a fish steamer, use a wide pot with a tight fitting lid; a roaster or Dutch oven is good. Add a few inches of boiling water (2 to 3 inches). Place a rack in the pot large enough to hold the fish platter (a cake rack is fine). Or, the fish platter itself can be set directly into the large pot containing boiling water to a depth of ¾ the height of the platter. Cover tightly. Water should not be permitted to boil down during steaming. Add more occasionally to maintain the necessary level. (See index for other steaming procedures.)

Mullet in Orange Sauce
One of the Island favorites.

3 pounds mullet, cleaned, or similar fish (sea bass, red snapper, bluefish)
¼ cup melted butter
2 cloves garlic, minced
3 scallions, chopped fine
2 tablespoons soy sauce
½ cup ketchup
3 tablespoons orange juice
dash of fresh pepper

Score or slash fish in 3 places on each side of fish. Combine all ingredients. Place fish on greased, foil-lined, shallow pan and pour ½ the sauce over fish. Broil on one side, 3 inches from flame. With the help of the foil and a spatula, turn fish to other side and pour remaining sauce over it. Broil until fish flakes easily. Serve with Orange Rice (see index). Serves 6.

Sea Bass with Pine Nuts

    2 sea bass, filleted and boned
    1 teaspoon salt
    dash of fresh pepper
    ¾ cup cornstarch
    3 tablespoons oil
    4 tablespoons pine nuts
    1½ cups chicken broth
    ¼ cup brown sugar
    3 tablespoons vinegar
    1 cup green and red peppers, diced
    1 can grapefruit sections (16 ounces), drained
    ¼ teaspoon sesame oil
    2 tablespoons oyster sauce
    1 tablespoon soy sauce
    3 tablespoons cornstarch mixed with ¼ cup water

Cut fillets into quarters, sprinkle with salt and pepper. Dip into cornstarch, which has been spread out on wax paper, and coat well. Heat oil in large skillet and sauté fish only until golden on both sides. Remove to a heatproof serving dish and keep hot in preheated oven. Toast pine nuts at the same time, in a shallow pan, until they begin to brown.

In a saucepan combine chicken broth, sugar and vinegar. Heat and add green and red pepper, grapefruit sections, sesame oil, oyster sauce and soy sauce. Simmer for 5 minutes. Mix cornstarch with water and gradually add to saucepan until mixture thickens. Remove fish from oven and pour sauce over fillets. Sprinkle with pine nuts. Serve with hot boiled rice or fried rice (see index). Serves 6.

Liu Liu:

The fish can be sautéed in advance and refrigerated. The sauce can be prepared but without the cornstarch mixture. Reheat fish in oven and add cornstarch to thicken sauce before serving.

Dolphin (or Flounder) with Shrimp and Scallops

Fresh dolphin is incomparable, but frozen dolphin is almost as good, and can now be found all over the mainland in many fine fish markets. If you wish, you can substitute other fish in the following recipes for dolphin. Any firm fish will do.

¼ pound butter, clarified preferably (see index)
¼ pound fresh mushrooms, sliced lengthwise
2 scallions, chopped
1½ pounds dolphin (or flounder), cubed
½ pound fresh shrimp, cleaned
½ pound bay scallops
1 teaspoon salt
freshly ground pepper
1 cup dry white wine
½ cup chicken broth
⅓ cup medium cream
2 tablespoons cornstarch mixed with 4 tablespoons water
fine bread crumbs
paprika

In a large skillet, heat ⅓ of the butter and sauté mushrooms and scallions. When mushrooms become tender (but not soft) remove to a platter. Put remainder of butter into skillet and add mahimahi, shrimp and scallops. Toss to coat and sauté until shrimp turns pink. Add salt, pepper, white wine and broth. Stir and simmer for 10 minutes. Add cream. Return mushrooms and scallions to skillet and simmer until thoroughly heated (do not boil). Mix cornstarch and water and add gradually, stirring until thickened. Fill buttered scallop shells with mixture and sprinkle with bread crumbs and paprika. Drizzle with butter and place under broiler until golden brown. Serves 6.

Kamailio:

Seafood mixture can be prepared as above and placed into a large casserole dish instead of individual scallop shells. Broil as recipe indicates.

Almost all seafood dishes are good served with rice.

Liu Liu:

Recipe can be prepared in advance up until thickened with cornstarch. Prior to serving, continue with recipe.

Dolphin (or Flounder) in Nut Sauce

*2 pounds dolphin (or flounder) fillets
1 teaspoon salt
flour
5 tablespoons butter, clarified preferably (see index)
1 cup chicken broth
¼ cup wine vinegar
1 teaspoon fresh ginger root, minced
¼ cup brown sugar
3 tablespoons soy sauce
2 tablespoons cornstarch
½ cup chopped macadamia nuts or unsalted toasted peanuts

Season dolphin (mahimahi) fillets with salt and dredge with flour. Melt butter in a large skillet and sauté fish until golden. Remove to oven and keep hot.

Combine remaining ingredients except nuts in a saucepan and heat. Simmer for 10 minutes until hot and thick. Pour sauce over fish fillets and sprinkle with chopped nuts. (Other sauces can be used, too.) Serves 6.

Dolphin (or Flounder) in Coconut Milk
Samoan Style

*2 pounds dolphin (or flounder) fillets
1 teaspoon salt
flour
5 tablespoons butter, clarified preferably (see index)
2 cups coconut milk (see recipe)

Season fish with salt and coat with flour. In a large skillet, melt butter and sauté fish quickly, until golden. Add coconut milk and simmer, covered, for 10 minutes, or bake in preheated oven at 350° F. for 15 minutes. Serves 6.

Kamailio:

In the Islands octopus (squid) is a favorite dish and is often cooked in the above manner. Fish may be sautéed in advance and refrigerated. Twenty minutes prior to serving, continue with recipe.

Dolphin (or Flounder) with Sesame Seeds

1 cup flour
2 teaspoons salt
dash of fresh pepper
*2 pounds dolphin (or flounder) fillets
2 eggs beaten with 2 tablespoons water
1 cup sesame seeds
¼ pound butter (clarified preferably)
3 bananas
3 lemons

Combine flour, salt and pepper. Dip fish fillets in seasoned flour; then with tongs dip into eggs and into sesame seeds (spread out sesame seeds thinly on wax paper). In a large skillet, heat butter and fry until golden on both sides. Drain on absorbent paper. Arrange on a heatproof serving dish. Keep hot in oven.

Halve 3 bananas lengthwise and then cut each half in two. Roll bananas in remaining sesame seeds. Sauté *wickiwicki* (quick quick) in the same skillet and arrange on platter with fish. Serve with lemon rosettes (see index). Chopped nuts are a good substitute for the sesame seeds. Serves 6.

Liu Liu:

You can do all of this ahead, and reheat in a 325° F. oven. However, it's an uncomplicated recipe, even for last-minute cooking.

----

* Frozen dolphin is sold at many mainland stores. If it is not available, use any firm fish. (See Fish For All Purposes at beginning of chapter.)

Tahitian Seafood Mélange

½ pound mushrooms, cleaned and sliced
1 onion, chopped fine
¼ pound butter
1 cup chopped tart apple (peeled)
2 pounds fresh small shrimp, cleaned
½ pound lobster meat, cut bite size
½ pound crab meat or bay scallops
2 teaspoons salt
dash of fresh pepper
1 slice fresh ginger root, minced
2 teaspoons sugar
3 cups chicken broth
2 cups coconut milk or cream (milk or light cream can be substituted)
3 tablespoons cornstarch mixed with 6 tablespoons water
2 tablespoons lemon juice
paprika

In a large skillet sauté mushrooms and onion in half the butter until translucent. Add apple and cook until tender. Remove to platter. Add remaining butter and sauté shrimp, lobster and crabmeat for 5 minutes; or until shrimp and lobster turn red. Return mushrooms, onions and apple to skillet. Add salt, pepper, ginger root and sugar and mix thoroughly. Add chicken broth and coconut milk. Stir and heat (do not boil). Mix cornstarch and water and add gradually to mixture, stirring until thickened. Turn off heat and stir in lemon juice. Sprinkle with paprika before serving. Serve over hot, boiled rice. Serves 6.

Kamailio:

Frozen seafood may be used, although we prefer fresh. An attractive way of serving the seafood is in halved coconut shells (see index) or from a chafing dish.

The entire recipe can be prepared in advance up until the cornstarch and water are added. This must be done prior to serving, since cornstarch thins out when reheated.

Medley I A (Fish Medley)

1 pound bay scallops
¼ cup sherry wine
4-5 tablespoons oil
1 large onion, chopped
½ pound lobster meat, uncooked, cut into bite-size pieces
1 pound jumbo shrimp, cleaned and butterflied, tails removed
2 cloves garlic, minced
2 teaspoons fermented black beans, soaked and mashed (see index)
3 stalks bok choy, or celery cut into 1½-inch julienne strips
   with some greens
½ pound mushrooms, sliced lengthwise
3-4 cups chicken broth
3 teaspoons soy sauce (light preferably)
1 teaspoon sugar
dash fresh pepper
½ teaspoon sesame oil (optional)
3 tablespoons cornstarch mixed with ¼ cup water
1 can (5 oz.) water chestnuts, sliced
1 can (5 oz.) bamboo shoots

Bay scallops have a much more delicate and subtle flavor than sea scallops; however, if bay scallops are not available, sea scallops may be cut into four pieces and used.

Sprinkle scallops with sherry. Toss and let stand 15 to 30 minutes. Drain and discard all but 3 teaspoons of sherry.

In a large skillet, heat oil and add onion and garlic. Sauté until golden. Push to one side and add lobster chunks, shrimp and scallops. Sauté until lobster and shrimp turn red. Remove to a platter and keep warm. If necessary, add more oil to skillet and heat. Add mashed black beans and cook for 2 minutes; add bok choy or celery and cook for another two minutes. Toss in the mushrooms and stir. Cook only until mushrooms begin to wilt. Add chicken broth, sherry, soy sauce, pepper and sesame oil. Mix well and bring to boiling point. Return sea food, onion and garlic to skillet. Simmer for 5 minutes. Stir cornstarch mixture and add gradually, stirring all the time until thickened. Add water chestnuts and bamboo shoots. Mix well and heat thoroughly. Turn off heat, cover and let rest 2 minutes. Serve with fried rice. If you like, add some fresh ginger root (2 slices minced) while you are sautéeing onion and garlic. Serves 6.

Liu Liu:

You can cook the entire recipe up to (but not including) adding the cornstarch mixture to the skillet. This must be done just before serving; the water chestnuts and bamboo shoots must be crisp so they too are put in only at the end.

About Shrimp

Fresh shrimp can be kept for several days in the coldest part of your refrigerator, if left unshelled and covered with lemon slices.

Some restaurants parboil their shrimp and keep them in a lemon juice and water mixture for a week. This is done so that they have cooked shrimp on hand at all times.

The size of the shrimp is a matter of choice, not an indication of better quality.

Gene buys jumbo fresh white, headless, premium Panamanian shrimp, 15 and under (that is, 15 or less to the pound) for one of the house specialties, Shrimp Momi Kai.

He also uses jumbo shrimp for butterflying. Large shrimp yield 22-25 per pound.

Allow 6 jumbo shrimp per person if you are using them for an entrée; 2 shrimp per person for an appetizer or hors d'oeuvre.

Shrimp Momi Kai

Jumbo shrimp are served at the Hawaii Kai in a handsome footed compote dish, on a mound of shredded lettuce. The tails are placed pointing upward and circle the bowl, forming a crown. A small crystal bowl of exotic red sauce in the center of dish adds color.

1½ pounds large shrimp (about 22 to 25) cleaned and butterflied (see index) with tails left intact
25 three-inch bacon strips
¾ cup cornstarch (spread on wax paper)
3 eggs
3 tablespoons water
1 tablespoon soy sauce (light preferably)
½ teaspoon sugar
dash of fresh pepper
oil for deep frying

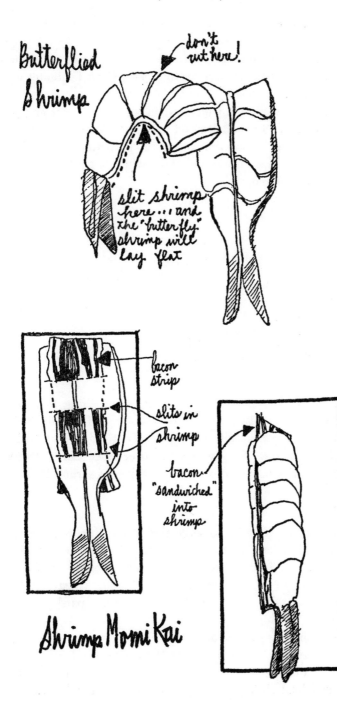

Butterflied Shrimp

don't cut here!

slit shrimp here . . . and the "butter fly" shrimp will lay flat

bacon strip

slits in shrimp

bacon "sandwiched" into shrimp

Shrimp Momi Kai

1. Center one strip of bacon on inside of each butterflied shrimp.

2. Lift each shrimp and bacon strip by the tail end with tongs and dredge lightly with cornstarch. Place on platter. When all shrimp are dredged, refrigerate for 15 minutes to 1 hour. (This facilitates working with the shrimp and bacon.)

3. Beat eggs well with water; stir in soy sauce, sugar and pepper.

4. When ready to cook, heat oil in a large skillet. Stir egg mixture and, using tongs as before, dip shrimp in egg batter. Fry until golden brown. Drain on paper towel and serve with the following sauce and fried rice. Serves 4 to 6.

EXOTIC RED SAUCE

½ cup ketchup
¼ cup chili sauce
  dash Tabasco sauce
2 tablespoons lemon juice or vinegar
3 tablespoons water
2 teaspoons brown sugar
2 teaspoons soy sauce
1 teaspoon fresh ginger, minced
1 garlic clove, minced
1 tablespoon honey

Mix all ingredients together in a saucepan. Bring to a boil and simmer for 5 minutes. Taste and adjust seasoning (if you like it sharper, add Tabasco). Serve hot or cold. Makes about 8 ounces. Can be kept covered in refrigerator for 2 weeks. Leftover sauce can be frozen and used as a dip with other foods such as chicken or shrimp balls.

Kamailio:

You may find it easier to serve this recipe "family style", that is, using a handsome large platter or silver tray (make a mound of lettuce or rice in center). Surround with shrimp, tails standing up. Fill a small crystal dish with Exotic Sauce (or other dipping sauces) and wedge into lettuce mound. Decorate platter or tray with parsley and lemon rosettes dusted with paprika.

Shrimp may be completely cooked as per recipe and refrigerated for 1 to 2 days or frozen. However, they must be fried lightly, just until barely turning golden. When ready to serve, turn on oven to 325° F. and heat shrimp thoroughly on a foil-lined shallow pan.

For a Luau:

1. Make 2 or 3 slits through center of the butterfly shrimp and weave bacon strip in and out. Follow remainder of recipe.

2. Or, press strip of bacon between the two sides of butterfly shrimp (book fashion). Close and proceed with recipe.

Shrimp Pacifica

1 teaspoon fermented black beans (see index)
4 tablespoons oil
2 garlic cloves, minced
2 slices fresh ginger root, minced
½ pound ground pork
½ teaspoon salt
3 tablespoons soy sauce (white preferably)
1 tablespoon sugar
1½ pounds medium shrimp, shelled and cleaned
2 cups chicken broth
2 tablespoons sherry wine
2 tablespoons cornstarch mixed with 4 tablespoons water
2 eggs beaten with ¼ cup water
2 scallions, chopped fine

1. Soak the black beans in cold water for about 5 to 10 minutes and rinse to remove salt. Wipe dry and squash down with back of knife blade. Mince.

2. Heat oil and add minced black beans and garlic. Sauté for 1 or 2 minutes.

3. Add ginger root, ground pork and salt. Stir and with fork break up the pieces of pork. Cook until pork loses its pinkness. Add soy sauce and sugar; mix and push this mixture to one side of skillet.

4. Add shrimp and sauté until pink.

5. Add chicken broth and sherry; heat to boiling point. Turn heat down to medium and simmer for about 5 minutes.

6. Stir the cornstarch and water; add gradually to skillet, stirring until thickened; turn off the heat and slowly add the beaten eggs to this, stirring all the time. Add the chopped scallions.

7. Cover and let sit for 2 minutes. Serve with fried rice (see index). Makes 6 portions.

(This dish can be prepared in advance through step 5 and refrigerated for a day or two. When ready to serve, heat and continue with recipe.)

Shrimp Tempura

Tempura is actually another way of saying "fritters". Thin slices of vegetables, meat, fish, etc. are dipped in a batter, deep fried and served with a Tempura Sauce.

> ¾ cup flour
> ⅛ cup cornstarch
> 1 teaspoon baking powder
> ½ teaspoon salt
> 1 egg, beaten slightly
> ½ cup water
> oil for deep frying
> 2 pounds shrimp, cleaned
> 1 pound string beans, eggplant, carrots or asparagus
>   cut into 2- to 3-inch lengths

In a large bowl, combine flour, cornstarch, baking powder and salt. Stir in the beaten egg and mix well. Gradually add water until a smooth batter is obtained. Heat oil for deep frying in a large skillet. With tongs dip one shrimp at a time into the batter and deep fry until golden brown. Do not crowd. Drain on absorbent paper and keep hot in preheated oven. Vegetables are done in similar fashion. (Carrots and eggplant should be cut in fingers first.) Serve with Tempura Sauce. Serves 6.

1. TEMPURA SAUCE (E KAHI)

> ⅓ cup soy sauce
> 1 teaspoon sugar
> 1 cup water
> 1 tablespoon sake or sherry wine
> 1 cup grated daikon (see index) or white long radish

2. TEMPURA SAUCE (E LUA)

> ½ cup chicken broth
> ¼ cup soy sauce
> 1 tablespoon lemon juice

3. TEMPURA SAUCE (E KOLU)

Omit grated daikon from Sauce E Kahi and add 1 slice fresh ginger root, minced.

Combine ingredients in a saucepan and simmer for 10 to 15 minutes. Serve hot.

Liu Liu:

Sauce can be made in advance and kept in a covered container for several days. Tempura can be fried in advance, then refrigerated or frozen. Before serving, place tempura on a rack over a foil-lined pan and reheat thoroughly in a 325° F. oven. Always taste one to be sure it is heated through to the center before serving.

Waikiki Coconut Shrimp

 1½ pounds fresh shrimp, cleaned and butterflied (see index)
 2 tablespoons hoisin sauce
 1 tablespoon soy sauce
 1 slice fresh ginger root, minced
 1 teaspoon sesame oil
 1 tablespoon sherry wine

Put shrimp in a shallow dish. Combine all ingredients and sprinkle over shrimp. Toss and turn to coat well. Marinate for 2 hours or refrigerate overnight.

BATTER:

 2 cups flour
 ¼ cup cornstarch
 2 teaspoons baking powder
 1 teaspoon salt
 1 teaspoon sesame oil
 1 egg, beaten
 1⅓ cups water
 1 teaspoon hoisin sauce (see index)
 2 cups flaked coconut spread on wax paper or foil
 oil for deep frying

In a bowl combine the first four ingredients. Add sesame oil, egg, water and hoisin sauce gradually, beating until batter is smooth. Remove shrimp from marinade and, holding each shrimp by tail, dip into batter and then roll lightly in coconut. Press coconut into shrimp gently with fingers. Place on an oiled platter or one that has been covered with wax paper. Refrigerate for 15 to 30 minutes.

Heat 2 inches of oil in large skillet and holding shrimp by tail, place in skillet. Do not crowd. Reduce flame to medium and fry until golden on both sides. Drain on paper towels. Keep hot in oven until all are completed. Serve with South Sea Sauce (page 78). Serves 4-6.

SOUTH SEA SAUCE

Heat together ¼ cup soy sauce, 2 tablespoons each of honey and sherry, 1 can (13 ounces) crushed pineapple, 1 teaspoon lemon juice, salt and pepper to taste. Simmer 10 minutes and serve hot.

Kamailio:

1. The hoisin sauce in the recipe adds an almondy flavor to the shrimp. It can be omitted and oyster sauce or brown bean sauce substituted.

2. The entire recipe can be prepared in advance and refrigerated or frozen. However, shrimp should be fried only until lightly golden. Reheat covered in oven at 325° F., and then uncover to brown and crisp.

Sesame Shrimp

    2 cups flour
    1 can or bottle of beer (12 oz.)
    1 teaspoon salt
    ½ teaspoon sugar
    1 tablespoon soy sauce
    4 tablespoons sesame seeds, toasted (see index)
    1 teaspoon sesame oil
    1 teaspoon sherry
    1½ pounds fresh shrimp, cleaned and butterflied (see index)
    oil for deep frying

Combine all ingredients except shrimp and oil for frying, beating well until smooth and creamy. Let set for half an hour. Heat 2 inches of oil in large skillet. Hold shrimp by tail, dip into batter and then lower into oil. Do not crowd. Turn flame to medium. Fry until golden brown on both sides. Drain on absorbent paper. Serve with South Sea Sauce or any other sauce (see index). The Sesame Shrimp can be used as a hot hors d'oeuvre or main course. Plan on 2 or 3 as an hors d'oeuvre or 5 to 6 for the entrée.

Liu Liu:

Sesame shrimp can be completely done and refrigerated for 2 days or frozen. Fry only until lightly golden. Reheat in oven at 325° F. covered. Uncover for browning.

Fantail Shrimp and Vegetables

    2 egg whites
    ¼ cup cornstarch
    ¼ teaspoon salt
      oil for frying
    2 pounds large shrimp, cleaned and butterflied (see index)
    1 large onion, cut julienne style
    3 cups celery cabbage, cut julienne style
    ½ cup ketchup
    ½ teaspoon sesame oil
    1 slice fresh ginger root, minced
    1 teaspoon sugar
    1 tablespoon oyster sauce
    1 tablespoon soy sauce
      salt and fresh pepper to taste
    2 cups lettuce, shredded

1. In a large bowl, beat cold egg whites until stiff. Add cornstarch and salt. Heat 1 inch oil in a large skillet. Holding shrimp by tail, dip into batter and fry until golden brown on both sides. Do not crowd. Remove to heatproof platter and keep warm in oven.

2. Drain all but 2 tablespoons oil from skillet. Heat, add onion and celery cabbage and sauté until translucent only. Add remaining ingredients except lettuce. Combine well and simmer for one minute. Add lettuce and stir. As soon as lettuce is hot, remove from fire. Place vegetables on a serving platter and arrange shrimp around vegetables in a circle, tails pointing upward. Serves 6.

Liu Liu:

Step 1 can be done in advance. Reheat shrimp in 375° oven. If vegetables are cut in advance, the remainder of recipe takes only a few minutes.

About Lobsters

Gene orders only live lobsters weighing at least 1¼ pounds each with hard shells and two claws (smaller ones are not worth buying). One lobster per person is used. On the West Coast of the United States don't be surprised if you can't find claws when you order lobster, since crawfish are used and nature never gave them claws.

TO CUT UP LOBSTERS:

The chefs place the live lobster on its belly on a chopping board. With the left hand they hold the lobster firmly by the tail and with fingers of the right hand they pry and pull the shell of the head away from the body. The shell which contains the intestines and the lungs is discarded. With a cleaver, the large claws and legs are severed from the body. The claws are chopped at the joints and cracked with the flat side of the cleaver. The lobster is cut in half lengthwise across the back, and each half is chopped into 3 pieces. The gourmet's delight, the coral and tomalley are left intact.

Once you've tried it, you'll see how simple it really is.

You can keep lobsters alive in your own refrigerator for 2 to 4 days by putting them in a small box or bag lined with damp seaweed. Ask for seaweed at the fish store.

Lobster Aloha

The lobster is cooked in the shell, so you can do only two at a time in one large skillet, or to cook all four simultaneously use two skillets. Either way you'll have to divide the following mixture in half.

4 tablespoons oil
3 garlic cloves, minced
1 pound ground lean pork
3 tablespoons soy sauce (light preferred)
1 tablespoon sugar
4 lobsters (each 1¼ pounds), cut up
4 cups chicken broth
2 tablespoons sherry wine
salt and a dash of fresh pepper
3 tablespoons cornstarch mixed with ¼ cup water
4 eggs, beaten lightly with ¼ cup water
3 scallions, chopped fine

1. Heat oil in two large skillets and sauté garlic and minced pork until pork loses pinkness. Break up particles with fork.

2. Add soy sauce and sugar; mix well with pork and push aside. Add lobster pieces and sauté for a minute or two.

3. Add chicken broth, sherry, salt and pepper and heat to boiling. Turn heat down to medium. Cover and simmer for about 5 minutes. When done, the lobster shell will turn bright red, the lobster meat opaque white.

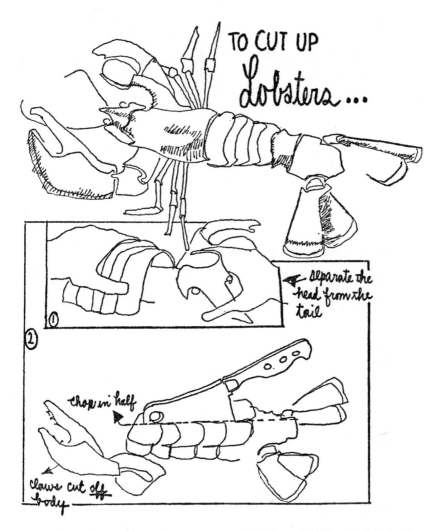

TO CUT UP Lobsters...

separate the head from the tail

chop in half

claws cut off body

4. Stir the cornstarch mixture and add gradually to the skillet, stirring until sauce is thickened; turn off the heat and stir in the beaten eggs. Mix well and add the chopped scallions. Cover and let rest for 2 minutes. Serve with fried rice (see index). Serves 4-6.

Kamailio:

1. The recipe can be prepared with the meat of the lobster only (shell discarded). To parboil live lobsters plunge them into boiling water; bring water back to boiling point and cook for 2 to 3 minutes.

This might be more convenient if you want to keep the lobsters a day or two, or to remove meat from shell. Lobster should then be added after step 3, only to heat thoroughly; do not let it boil.

2. If you like the taste of fresh ginger root, add two slices (minced fine) to the skillet with the garlic.

3. You can also add sliced water chestnuts or bamboo shoots at the same time the scallions are added.

Liu Liu:

For advance preparation, complete the recipe through step 3 (but omit the simmering direction), and refrigerate for 1 to 2 days. When ready to serve, heat slowly until piping hot and continue with step 4.

Lobster in Black Bean Sauce

Follow recipe for Lobster Aloha above, and in step 1 sauté 2 tablespoons fermented black beans (rinsed, soaked, and mashed), together with the garlic and pork. Continue with the recipe.

Lobster Song

Decorate with a garland of puffy rice flour noodles (see index).

10 black, dried mushrooms (see below)
2 pounds lobster meat (see *About Lobsters*)
4 tablespoons oil
2 garlic cloves, minced
½ pound ground lean pork
½ teaspoon salt
3 tablespoons soy sauce (light preferred)
2 teaspoons oyster sauce
1 tablespoon sugar
4 cups chicken broth
2 tablespoons sherry wine
dash fresh pepper
2 tablespoons cornstarch mixed with ¼ cup water
2 eggs beaten with ¼ cup water
3 scallions, chopped
1 can (5 oz.) water chestnuts, drained, rinsed and diced
1 can (5 oz.) bamboo shoots, drained, rinsed and diced

About black, dried mushrooms: they should be rinsed with cold water and then soaked in hot water to cover for 15-20 minutes. Drain (reserve liquid), and squeeze dry. Discard tough part of stem. Use reserved liquid as part of chicken broth.

Dice lobster meat. Heat oil in large skillet and quickly sauté lobster meat until it turns red. Remove to a platter. Sauté garlic until golden; add ground pork and salt and cook until pork loses its pinkness. Break up the clumps with a fork. Add soy sauce, oyster sauce, sugar, chicken broth, sherry and pepper. Mix well. Add soaked black mushrooms and lobster to skillet and bring mixture just to boiling point. Turn heat down and simmer for 5 minutes.

Stir the cornstarch mixture and add it gradually to the skillet, stirring constantly until sauce is thickened. Stir in the beaten eggs and turn off flame. Mix well and add the scallions, diced water chestnuts and bamboo shoots. Combine and cover skillet tightly. Let sit for two minutes. Serve over a bed of fried rice and garnish with rice flour noodles (see index). Serves 6.

Kamailio:

Black dried mushrooms can be omitted and fresh mushrooms used, but the former have a very unique taste which cannot be substituted by any other mushroom.

If all ingredients are cut and prepared in advance, the entire recipe should take about 15 to 20 minutes. However, it can also be cooked in advance up until the cornstarch mixture is added. When ready to serve, complete recipe.

Aloha Lobster Coconut Curry

2 onions, chopped
1 garlic clove, minced
4 tablespoons butter
1 tablespoon curry
2½ cups chicken broth
1 cup coconut milk (see index)
1 slice fresh ginger root, minced
1 teaspoon salt
1 teaspoon lemon juice
1 pound lobster meat, cut in serving pieces
2 tablespoons cornstarch mixed with ¼ cup water

In a large skillet, sauté onion and garlic with butter until soft. Add curry powder. Stir and cook for 1-2 minutes. Blend in chicken broth and coconut milk. Add ginger root and simmer (do not boil). Add salt and lemon juice to taste. Add lobster meat and simmer for 10 minutes. Mix cornstarch with water and add gradually to the skillet. Stir until thickened. Serve with boiled rice and sambals (see index). Serves 4-6, depending on rest of menu.

Kamailio:

If packaged coconut replaces coconut milk, add more lemon juice to compensate for its extra sweetness.

To make this dish a chef d'oeuvre (*he hana i pookela* as the Hawaiians would put it), prepare recipe in the blazer pan of a chafing dish and keep it heated over the hot water pan. Spoon into coconut shells at the table.

5

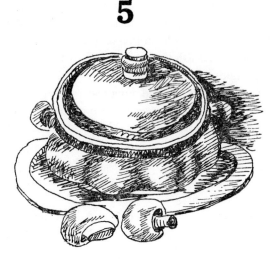

SOUPS ON--AND ON

A Hawaiian soup list starts where the Campbell soup list ends. And when you consider that the Hawaiians have ingeniously invented, borrowed, concocted, devised, combined and embellished more than 100 different soups from some 10 different countries, you can readily understand why we're not too impressed with Heinz's 57 varieties.

The Hawaiian family is especially fond of soup for many reasons. Made well as they invariably are, a tasty soup tends to stimulate the appetite and set the mood. They also have the advantage of being easy and quick to make, with on-the-spot improvisations when necessary.

Bora Bora (a favorite at the Hawaii Kai) is the number one of all Hawaiian soups and like Abalone Soup or Avocado Soup it is native to the islands. But for those who are looking for something more exotic —look no further—the Hawaiian menu can very likely offer you Tears of Snow Soup, Passion Fruit Soup, Celestial Nani Soup, Korean-style Vegetable Soup and many others.

Stock, Broth and Substitutes

At the Hawaii Kai Restaurant, stock is an integral part of the cooking. Many cooks feel that stock and broth are one and the same.

Actually, they're not. Our chefs, of course, are in a much better position to always have stock on hand to use for soups and sauces. They make it from pork bones with plenty of meat on them, chicken carcasses, backs, necks, gizzards and even chicken feet. (Beef is not used because of its pronounced flavor.) These are simmered in salted water for a long time until their natural juices are extracted. This is stock. The longer the stock cooks, the more concentrated it becomes. During the last 30 minutes of cooking, vegetables, additional salt and pepper are added (carrots, celery, leeks, onions, etc.). When done, the meat, bones and vegetables are removed. This full-bodied rich stock is then diluted and used as a basis for soups and broth, which are of a much thinner consistency.

Since the average homemaker may not have the time or inclination to keep her kitchen stocked with stock, our recipes will use chicken broth instead.

SUBSTITUTES FOR HOMEMADE BROTH:

Canned chicken broth, bouillon cubes and powdered chicken base can be used. We find that the canned broth although not comparable to the homemade broth, is the closest in flavor, and it is a timesaver.

Chicken Broth

Pork bones, chicken backs and necks are sold at the meat department of all supermarkets. If you don't see them, ask the butcher. We always have several packages in the freezer.

> 1 chicken (4 pounds), or 3 pounds chicken backs, necks, feet, plus
> 1 pound pork bones
> 12 cups water
> 1 tablespoon salt
> dash of fresh pepper
> 1 onion
> 1 carrot
> 1 celery stalk with greens
> 1 sprig parsley

Place chicken or chicken parts and pork bones in a saucepan with the cold water. Bring to a boil. When the impurities rise to the top, remove the scum. Reduce heat to simmer. If necessary remove scum again. Add salt and pepper and simmer for 2 hours. Add onion, carrot, celery with leaves and parsley. Simmer for ½ to 1 hour more. Adjust seasonings. If you are cooking a whole chicken, remove when tender, so that you can use it in sandwiches or recipes that call for cooked chicken. Strain through a fine mesh strainer to remove vegetables and bones. Cool and refrigerate. Yields 2½ quarts.

Kamailio:

The broth can be refrigerated for 5-7 days. The top layer of fat protects it from spoiling.

We prefer to freeze broth in 2 cup containers so that we can use it at a moment's notice. (Don't fill to top, leave 1 inch of room.)

If you're lucky enough to obtain chicken feet, immerse them in boiling water for a minute and the scaly skin will peel off like a tangerine. Add them to the water along with the other chicken parts.

Chicken Soup

To make a superb chicken soup, follow recipe for chicken broth (omit pork bones), and add 1 peeled parsnip, 1 peeled parsley root and 3 sprigs of dill along with other vegetables in the recipe. Continue with recipe. *Kamiko* (some flavor)!

Abalone Soup

    5 dried, black mushrooms (see index)
    2 tablespoons oil
    1 scallion, cut into 2-inch thin strips
    ½ pound lean pork, cut in thin strips
    1 slice fresh ginger root, minced
    1 can abalone, cut into thin strips
    8 cups chicken broth
    1 tablespoon soy sauce
    1 teaspoon sherry
    salt and freshly ground pepper to taste
    2 eggs beaten

Soak dried mushrooms in warm water for 1 hour (reserve water for soup). Drain and cut into strips.

Heat oil in a skillet and sauté scallions, pork strips and ginger root until pork loses its pinkness.

In a saucepan, combine liquid from mushrooms and from abalone with chicken broth. Heat to boiling point and turn down to simmer. Add mushrooms, pork, soy sauce, sherry, salt, pepper and ginger root. Simmer for about 15 minutes. Add abalone strips and taste for additional seasoning. Cook only for 1 or 2 minutes or abalone will toughen. Add beaten eggs and stir into soup. Turn off heat and let sit for 2 minutes covered. Serve *wicki wicki* (quickly)! Serves 6 or so.

Avocado Soup

    3 ripe avocados, peeled, seeded and cubed
    3 cups chicken broth
    1 teaspoon lemon juice
    1 slice fresh ginger root
    1 clove garlic, minced
    dash of salt and fresh pepper
    1½ cups medium cream
    ½ cup heavy cream, whipped
    ½ cup macadamia nuts, chopped coarse

In an electric blender, combine first six ingredients and purée until smooth and creamy. Turn into a large bowl and add medium cream. Stir and combine well. Chill thoroughly. When ready to serve, ladle into individual small bowls and top with a spoonful of whipped cream. Sprinkle with macadamia nuts and serve. Serves 6.

Liu Liu:

The soup can be prepared one day in advance and refrigerated. Garnish with whipped cream and nuts just prior to serving.

Bean Curd Soup

    8 cups chicken broth
    1 can (5 oz.) bamboo shoots
    ¼ pound fresh mushrooms, sliced lengthwise
    ¼ pound fresh spinach, cut into small pieces
    2 bean curd cakes (see index), cut into 1-inch cubes
    salt and fresh pepper to taste

Bring chicken broth to a boil. Add next three ingredients and simmer for 3-5 minutes. Add bean curds, salt and pepper and cook only until heated. Taste and adjust seasoning. Serves 6-8.

Bora Bora Soup

¼ pound Long Life Noodles (see index)
   (egg noodles may be substituted)
  boiling water
8 cups chicken broth
3 stalks celery cabbage, cut into ⅛-inch sections
¼ pound spinach, cut into small pieces
½ pound barbecued roast pork (see index), sliced thinly
  salt and pepper to taste
4 hard-boiled eggs, cut into wedges

Cook noodles in boiling water until soft. Rinse and drain. Reserve.

Heat chicken broth to boiling point and add celery cabbage, spinach, pork, salt and pepper. Simmer for 5-7 minutes. Return noodles to soup and cook only long enough to heat through. Serve soup in a tureen or individual bowls and float egg wedges on top. Serves 6-8.

Celestial Nani Soup

½ pound barbecued roast pork (see Kamailio)
8 cups chicken broth
2 scallions, cut into 1 inch sections
½ of 5-oz. can water chestnuts, drained, rinsed and sliced
12 to 18 wontons (see recipe on page 93)
½ cup shredded lettuce
  salt and pepper to taste
1 teaspoon soy sauce
3 hard-boiled eggs, each cut into 4 wedges

1. Slice pork into thin strips, julienne style (2 to 3 inches long, ⅛-inch thick).

2. Bring chicken broth to boiling point; add pork, scallions and water chestnuts and simmer for 2-3 minutes.

3. Add wontons and cook until heated throughout.

4. Add remainder of ingredients except egg wedges, stir and turn off heat; cover and let sit for two minutes. Serve in a tureen or individual bowls with egg wedges floating on top. Serves 6-8.

Kamailio:

Lean, fresh pork may be substituted for barbecued pork (one or two pork chops can be cut into thin julienne strips and sautéed in a little oil until all trace of pinkness is gone). Or, the pork strips can be cooked along with the broth. The soup can be prepared in advance but with the shredded lettuce and eggs omitted. These should be put in only when reheating soup for serving.

Cucumber Soup

    8 cups chicken broth
    2 tablespoons soy sauce
    1 teaspoon sugar
    1 tablespoon sherry
    ½ pound pork, cut into long thin strips
    2 cucumbers (medium)
    salt and fresh pepper

In a large saucepan, combine broth, soy sauce, sugar, sherry and pork strips. Bring to a boil and then simmer for about 10 minutes. Peel cucumber and cut in half, lengthwise. Scoop out seeds and slice. Add to soup and simmer only until cucumber becomes translucent. Taste and adjust seasoning with salt and pepper. Serves 8.

Korean Soups (Kook)

Most of the Korean soups have a basic stock from which many variations are made.

BASIC STOCK:

    ¼ pound chuck, sliced thinly into 1-inch squares
    1 tablespoon oil
    4 tablespoons soy sauce
    1 tablespoon pulverized sesame seed (see index)
    2 scallions, chopped
    1 teaspoon salt
    freshly ground pepper
    1 clove garlic, minced
    8 cups water

In a Dutch oven, sauté meat with oil until browned. Add remaining ingredients except water and cook at high heat for 3 minutes, stirring constantly.

Add the water and simmer until beef is tender. Serves 6-8.

SPINACH SOUP (SEE KUM CHEE KOOK):

To basic stock add ½ pound of washed spinach or 2 packages of frozen spinach and cook only until tender.

MUSHROOM SOUP (PUH SUT KOOK):

Sauté ½ pound sliced mushrooms together with meat and add to basic stock.

BEAN SPROUT SOUP (KONG NA MOOL KOOK):

Sauté 1 can drained and rinsed bean sprouts together with meat and add to basic stock (1 pound blanched fresh bean sprouts can be used also).

VEGETABLE SOUP (CHA SOH KOOK):

Add 1 cup of celery cabbage cut into 1 inch lengths, 3 carrots and 2 potatoes cut into julienne strips 1 inch long and 1 large onion thinly sliced, to the basic stock. Just before serving, beat one egg well and add gradually to the soup, stirring all the time.

OYSTER OR CLAM SOUP (GOOL KOOK OR CHO KAI KOOK):

Add ¾ pound fresh oysters or clams to basic stock (canned clams are good too; use broth for part of stock).

Papaya Soup

    1 onion, diced
    2 tablespoons butter
    1 large papaya, peeled and diced
    3 cups water
    2 sprigs watercress
    1 teaspoon salt
    2 cups milk
    1 cup light cream
    dash of fresh pepper
    1 tablespoon cornstarch mixed wth 3 tablespoons water

In a large saucepan, sauté the onion in butter only until golden. Add the diced papaya, water, watercress and salt. Simmer over low heat, covered for 1½ hours. Strain soup through a sieve and purée vegetables in blender. Return to soup; add 2 cups milk, 1 cup cream and a dash of fresh pepper. Simmer for 10 minutes but do not boil. Stir cornstarch mixture and add to soup slowly, stirring constantly until thickened. Garnish with watercress leaves and serve. Serves 6.

Passion Fruit Soup

Serve in crystal bowls embedded in crushed ice.

3 cans (10 oz. each) Passion Fruit Juice
1 teaspoon orange rind, grated
1 tablespoon cornstarch mixed with 2 tablespoons water
4 egg yolks, beaten well
1 cup white wine
3 ripe mangoes or peaches, peeled and diced (canned are good, too)
2 tablespoons Curaçao liqueur

In a saucepan, combine juice and orange rind and bring to a boil. Simmer for 5 minutes and add cornstarch and water, gradually. Mix egg yolks with wine and beat until smooth. Pour into saucepan and mix well. Cool and refrigerate. When ready to serve, add the mangoes or peaches and the Curaçao. Place a lemon wedge on rim of soup bowl. Serve with crisp crackers or macadamia nuts. Serves 6.

Tears of Snow with Eggs Paké Style

2 eggs
2 tablespoons sherry
dash of salt
8 cups chicken broth
2 stalks bokchoy or celery, diced
¼ pound fresh mushrooms, diced
2½ oz. (½ of 5 oz. can) water chestnuts, drained, rinsed and diced
1 teaspoon soy sauce (light preferably)
salt and pepper to taste
2 scallions minced (for garnish)

To make egg threads, beat eggs lightly with sherry and salt. Grease a skillet and heat.

Pour the egg mixture slowly into the skillet tipping the pan from side to side so that the mixture spreads thinly and evenly. Cook over low heat until set and edge curls away from pan. Invert on a plate and cool. Cut into narrow strips 2 inches long, ⅛ inch wide.

Heat chicken broth to boiling and add all the remaining ingredients except scallions. Simmer for 5 minutes. Taste for additional seasoning.

Pour soup into a large tureen or individual soup bowls. Garnish with egg threads and minced scallions. Serves 6.

Liu Liu:

1. The soup and egg threads can be prepared in advance; however, the egg threads and scallions must not be put into soup until ready to serve.

2. For storing and freezing see Chicken Broth. Note, however, that only the chicken broth can be frozen. Vegetables must be crisp and therefore should be added to broth just before serving.

Watercress Soup

¼ pound lean pork
8 cups chicken broth
1 onion, chopped
1 celery stalk, sliced thinly
1 teaspoon salt
dash of fresh pepper
1 bunch watercress (about 1-1½ cups), cut up (stems removed)

Cut pork into thin shreds. Heat chicken broth in a large saucepan; add pork shreds and simmer for 10 minutes. Add remaining ingredients except watercress and simmer for 10 more minutes. Add watercress and simmer only for 2 more minutes. Serves 6-8.

Wontons (for soup or hors d'oeuvres)

The wonton skins are made exactly like the Tim San wrappers (see index), but cut into 3-3½ inch squares instead of rounds. Or, they can be purchased in any gourmet or oriental shop (see Sources) very inexpensively. See Tim San recipe for storing information, etc. Egg roll skins or wrappers can also be used, if cut into 3-3½ inch squares (see recipe).

FILLING (for about 20-24 wontons):

½ pound ground pork
1 scallion, chopped fine
½ of a 5 oz. can water chestnuts, drained, rinsed and chopped
1 tablespoon soy sauce
dash of fresh pepper
dash of garlic powder (optional)
½ teaspoon sugar
1 egg beaten well
1 teaspoon cornstarch mixed with 1 tablespoon water

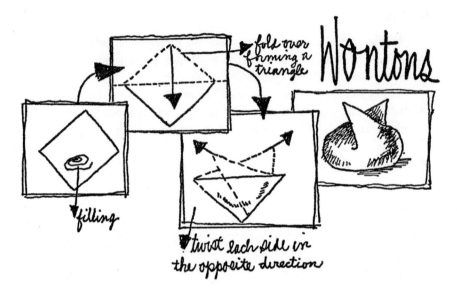

If pork is uncooked, it should be sautéed together with the scallion, using a tablespoon of oil. Cook until pork loses its pinkness. Break up meat particles with fork. Remove from heat and to the pork and scallions add water chestnuts, soy sauce, pepper, garlic powder and sugar. Mix. Add egg and cornstarch and combine well. Cool.

TO FILL WONTON:

1. Make a paste of 1 tablespoon cornstarch and 3 tablespoons water for sealing.

2. Place wonton wrapper on a flat surface, the points facing up and down (see diagram). Place about ½ to 1 teaspoon of filling slightly below the center of the skin.

3. Moisten edges of skin with cornstarch paste and fold the top half over to form a triangle. Press edges to seal.

4. With cornstarch paste, moisten the front of the triangles, right corner and the back of left corner.

5. With twisting movement, cross the right and left points by bringing them together on the opposite side of the fold from the point towards you. Press to seal.

6. If to be used for soup, drop the wontons into salted boiling water, one at a time, so that water is kept at boiling point and cook for 8-10 minutes. Remove with slotted spoon and add to soup.

FRIED WONTONS:

Wontons are delicious pan fried or deep fried, to be used as an hors d'oeuvres with Plum Brandy Sauce and Native Mustard, or as a side dish with an entrée. Heat oil for deep frying or pan frying and brown wontons on both sides. Boiled wontons can also be fried. Dry on absorbent paper and pan fry or deep fry until golden brown.

Liu Liu:

Boiled or fried wontons will keep for 2-3 days in refrigerator one layer deep. (Do not stack them or they will stick.) Cover well.

Fried wontons can be frozen, wrapped in foil and reheated (without thawing) in oven, 300° F., or refried for a short time.

Boiled or fried wontons can be put on a tray, placed in freezer uncovered until frozen, then removed from tray and tossed into a freezer bag. Reheat as in preceding directions.

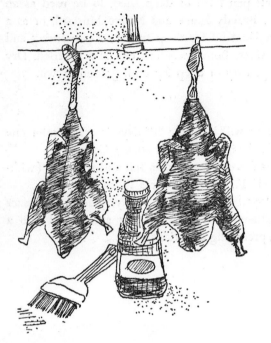

6
THOSE
EXOTIC
BIRDS
OF
HAWAII

Ok ... so you've struggled with a chicken fricassee and you've labored with a Duck L'Orange but ... have you ever tried a Manu Chicken marinated in a rare Polynesian sauce ... or a boned duckling baked with water chestnut flour ... or the famous Hawaii Kai's stuffed chicken breasts in succulent pineapple shells? Sounds absolutely great! ... They are indeed!

Now don't be chicken. *Mali Mali Moa Keiki* is not an exotic species of bird—it's just a Hawaiian chef letting his gustatory imagination take flight in the kitchen. These poultry dishes may seem difficult but they're not as complicated as they sound. So let's grease up the pans and put on the apron—tonight you're going to make something to crow about. And remember—don't worry about what came first "the chicken or the egg"; once you've tasted Bora Bora Soup and Chicken Hawaii Kai, you won't care!

I. Fun Food.

II. Lobster Buffet.

III. An Edible Table Decoration.

Descriptions of the color plates are on page 10.

IV. Garden Luau.

V. Come to a Hoolaulea.

VI. Cornish Hen Platter.

Chicken Hawaii Kai

This dish is a work of art—beautiful to behold and delightful to taste. You will be astonished to find it so simple to prepare. Use for company dinners or as an economical everyday meal. If small chicken breasts are not available, have butcher cut through center of each large half breast, to within ¼ inch of the end (butterfly fashion).

1 small whole breast of chicken per person,
    or ½ large breast, boned and skinned
1 slice hickory smoked ham, per person

BATTER:

2 eggs
1 cup water
1 teaspoon sesame oil (see index)
1¼ cups flour
2 teaspoons baking powder
1 teaspoon sherry
½ teaspoon salt
½ teaspoon garlic powder
    dash of fresh white pepper
    oil to cover 2 inches of skillet

Beat eggs with water in a large bowl. Add sesame oil, stir and gradually add flour and baking powder. Combine well and add the remaining ingredients except oil. Mix until batter resembles smooth heavy cream.

Fit one slice of ham evenly in between each small chicken breast and close. The ham should not be seen. If using the large chicken breast, fit ham in the same fashion. With tongs, dip breast in batter, coating evenly.

Heat oil in a large skillet and gently add chicken breasts (do not crowd in skillet). Fry only until golden brown, turning once. Transfer to heatproof serving dish. Continue browning all the breasts in this fashion, adding more oil if needed. Remove to preheated oven and bake for 20-30 minutes at 325° F. (Enough batter for 6-8 breasts.)

Meanwhile, prepare the sauce:

SAUCE:

3 tablespoons oil
½ pound mushrooms, sliced lengthwise
2 garlic cloves, minced
3 cups chicken broth
2 tablespoons soy sauce (white preferably)
1 teaspoon sugar
dash of freshly ground pepper
3 tablespoons cornstarch diluted with 4 tablespoons water
1 teaspoon sherry
1 can (5 oz.) bamboo shoots, drained and rinsed
2 scallions, cut in ¼-inch strips
½ pound fresh snow peas or ½ box frozen
¼ cup sliced toasted almonds (toast in oven while chicken is baking)

Heat oil in skillet and sauté mushrooms and garlic 3 to 5 minutes. Add broth, soy sauce, sugar, pepper and mix well. Simmer for 3 minutes. Stir cornstarch mixture and combine with sherry. Add to skillet gradually, stirring all the time, until sauce becomes thick and glazed. Turn off flame, add bamboo shoots, scallions and pea pods. Stir. Cover skillet and let set until ready to use. Enough for 6-8 breasts.

ASSEMBLY:

Now, remove chicken breasts from oven. If desired they may be cut into 3 slices per breast, so that the pink ham shows through. Place on a bed of rice and pour the sauce over them. Garnish with toasted almonds and you have a dish fit for the king in your house. Serves 6-8.

Kamailio:

1. Perhaps you have noticed that the vegetables went into the sauce last and that the flame was turned off. This is done to insure crisp vegetables, the essence of the sauce, and to prevent overcooking.

2. You can substitute or add sliced water chestnuts, canned mushrooms (which are not as mushroomy as fresh), green peppers, celery, turnips, rutabagas, string beans, carrots or cabbage. Cut the vegetables in thin strips.

3. The chicken breasts can be prepared and cooked until golden, then refrigerated up to two days, or wrapped in foil and frozen. To reheat, spread them on a flat baking pan and bake in a 325° F. oven until heated throughout (do not defrost).

4. The sauce can be prepared in advance, only up to the addition of cornstarch, since cornstarch will not act as a thickening agent if reheated. Also, if the vegetables are to be crisp and crunchy, they must be put into the sauce just a few minutes before serving.

Stuffed Chicken Breasts in Pineapple Shells

2 tablespoons oil
1 pound ground pork
1 small onion, minced
1 garlic clove, minced
1 scallion, chopped
½ cup corn flake crumbs
1 egg beaten with ¼ cup soy sauce
1 tablespoon sugar
1 can water chestnuts, (5 ounces), drained, rinsed and chopped coarse
2 tablespoons cornstarch
chicken broth
6 chicken breasts (small), boned and skinned

In large skillet, sauté pork, onion, garlic and scallion in oil 'til pork loses all trace of pinkness. Break up meat particles with fork. Remove from heat. Add remaining ingredients using enough chicken broth to make a soft pliable mixture. Divide stuffing into six parts and fold into chicken breasts. Fasten with toothpicks or white cord.

FOR THE PAN:

½ cup chicken broth
1 tablespoon honey
1 tablespoon soy sauce
dash of fresh pepper
4 tablespoons sesame seeds
3 small pineapples

In a large baking pan, mix chicken broth, honey, soy sauce and pepper. Place chicken breasts in this and bake for 35 minutes at 325° F., turning once. Split the pineapples in half lengthwise from crown to base (leaves remaining). Remove cores and slice meat into small cubes. Leave in shell. When chicken breasts are done, cut them on a flat surface with a sharp knife into 4 or 5 slices. Using a spatula, replace them intact on top of pineapple. Remove toothpicks or cord. Brush breasts with pan juices or with additional honey and chicken broth. Sprinkle top of chicken breasts with sesame seeds. Cover pineapple from crown to base with silver foil and bake in oven at 400° F. until brown and glazed. Remove foil and place pineapples on a bed of greens. Decorate with spiced crabapples, kumquats, etc. Serves 6.

Liu Liu:

Chicken breasts may be completely baked in advance, then refrigerated for 1 to 2 days or frozen. Defrost and proceed with recipe.

Chicken Breasts Tahiti

    6 small chicken breasts, skinned and boned (1 per person)
    2 scallions, chopped fine
    2 slices ginger root, minced (see index)
    3 tablespoons sherry wine
    ¼ cup soy sauce (light preferably)
    1 teaspoon sugar
    1 garlic clove, minced
    1 tablespoon sesame oil (see index)
    2 tablespoons cornstarch

1. Cut chicken breasts into rectangular strips, about ½-inch wide and 1½ inches long.
2. In a large bowl, combine all the ingredients except the cornstarch.
3. Add the chicken strips and toss and turn to coat well. Sprinkle chicken with cornstarch and marinate 1 to 2 hours or refrigerate overnight.

    SAUCE:

    3 tablespoons oil
    2 cloves garlic, minced
    3 stalks bokchoy or celery, cut diagonally, ⅛ inch thick
    2 tablespoons oyster sauce (see index)
    3 to 4 cups chicken broth
    dash of freshly ground pepper
    1 can (5 oz.) water chestnuts, drained, rinsed and sliced
    ⅓ pound fresh snow peas or ⅓ box frozen

Heat oil in large skillet and sauté garlic until golden. Add chicken pieces (do not crowd) and marinade, and cook until chicken is brown. Remove to a platter. If necessary, add additional oil to skillet and heat.

Sauté bokchoy or celery (stirring to coat with oil) for about 3 minutes. Stir in oyster sauce, chicken broth and pepper and bring to a boil. Return chicken pieces to skillet and simmer for 5 minutes. If gravy is not thick enough, mix 2 teaspoons cornstarch with 4 tablespoons water and add gradually, stirring well. Turn off heat and add water chestnuts and snow peas. Stir. Cover tightly and let sit for two minutes. Serve with fried rice. Serves 6.

Chicken and Cucumbers

    3 large chicken breasts, boned and cut into ½-inch cubes
    2 egg whites, beaten
    4 tablespoons cornstarch
    6 tablespoons oil
    2 scallions, cut into 1-inch sections
    2 slices ginger root, minced
    3 peeled cucumbers, cut into triangular wedges
    1 tablespoon sherry wine
    1 teaspoon sugar
    3 tablespoons soy sauce
    1 cup macadamia nuts

Dip chicken into beaten egg whites and then into cornstarch. Place on platter and refrigerate for 10 to 15 minutes. Heat oil and sauté scallions and ginger root with chicken and cucumber. Toss to coat well. When chicken turns white, add sherry, sugar and soy sauce and cook for 3 minutes. Add macadamia nuts. Mix well. Turn off heat and cover. Let sit for 2 minutes. Serve with white rice. [If additional sauce is desired, mix 2 tablespoons cornstarch with 2 cups cold chicken broth and add to pan with the soy sauce.] Serves 4-6.

Chicken Keo Keo

Served in a fresh coconut at the Hawaii Kai Restaurant.

    6 small chicken breasts, skinned and boned
    ½ cup soy sauce (light preferably)
    1 tablespoon sugar
    3 teaspoons sherry wine
    2 slices fresh ginger root, minced (see index)

Cut chicken into ½-inch cubes. In a bowl combine remaining ingredients and marinate chicken cubes for at least 1 hour at room temperature, or overnight in refrigerator. Toss and turn cubes to coat well. Drain chicken from marinade and dry on absorbent paper. Reserve marinade.

SAUCE:

    3 tablespoons oil
    2 cloves garlic, minced
    3 stalks bokchoy or celery, cut diagonally ⅛ inch thick
    ½ pound mushrooms, sliced lengthwise
    ½ pound fresh green peas
    3 to 4 cups chicken broth
    ½ teaspoon salt
      dash of freshly ground pepper
    3 tablespoons cornstarch mixed with ¼ cup water
    1 can (5 oz.) bamboo shoots, drained, rinsed and diced
    1 can (5 oz.) water chestnuts, drained, rinsed and diced
    ¼ pound almonds, toasted

Heat oil in large skillet and sauté garlic and cubed chicken (do not crowd) until chicken browns. Remove to a platter. If necessary, add additional oil to skillet and heat. Sauté bokchoy or celery for 3 minutes and add mushrooms. Sauté for 3 minutes. Push aside and add green peas. Cook for 2 minutes and stir in chicken broth and leftover marinade. Bring to a boil and then turn down heat to simmer. Add salt and pepper and taste for further seasoning. Return chicken cubes to skillet and simmer for 3 to 5 minutes. Stir together cornstarch and water and gradually add to mixture until thickened. Add diced bamboo shoots and water chestnuts. Stir, cover, and turn off heat. When ready to serve, pour into fresh coconut shells (see below) and decorate with toasted almonds. Serve with fried rice. Serves 6.

Kamailio:

The coconut used at the Hawaii Kai is large and oval rather than round. Laying it on its side, about an inch is sliced off with a bandsaw to make the opening for the chicken. A small sliver is also sliced off the bottom so that it sits well. The liquid is, of course, removed. Your butcher uses a bandsaw; perhaps he can cut the coconut for you. For the economical cook, coconuts may be reused by rinsing them well, then drying and freezing.

At the Hawaii Kai only the breasts of chicken are used. However, there is no reason why you can't substitute dark meat or even leftover chicken. However, cooked chicken should be marinated only and added at the very end of recipe to heat through.

Liu Liu:

The recipe (up until the cornstarch is added), can be completed in advance and refrigerated for one or two days. When ready to serve, reheat and continue with balance of recipe.

Tahitian Chicken

oil for deep frying
2 cups flour
¼ cup cornstarch
1 tablespoon baking powder
2 teaspoons salt
1⅓ cups pineapple juice
2 teaspoons sugar
6 small chicken breasts or ½ large chicken breast per person

Heat oil in a large skillet. Make batter by combining remaining ingredients and mix until smooth. With tongs dip chicken breasts into batter and deep fry in the hot oil until golden brown. Do not crowd. To keep cooked breasts hot, remove to preheated oven 325° F. Serve with Pineapple Coconut Sauce, below.

PINEAPPLE COCONUT SAUCE (*Halakahiki Niu*)

3 cups pineapple juice
½ cup sugar
2 teaspoons butter or margarine
1 can (13 oz.) crushed pineapple
dash of salt
2 tablespoons honey
½ cup flaked coconut

In a saucepan heat pineapple juice, sugar, and butter until sugar has dissolved. Add crushed pineapple, salt, honey and coconut. Bring to a boil and simmer about 5 minutes. Serve hot. Serves 6.

Liu Liu:

Chicken breasts can be fried, then refrigerated for 2 to 3 days, or frozen. Bake in preheated oven 375° F. (without defrosting if frozen), on a flat baking sheet, covered, for 10 minutes then uncovered and heated until piping hot. The batter in this recipe will remain crisp when reheated.

Pineapple Coconut Sauce can be made ahead and refrigerated for several days, but it takes only a few minutes to prepare—not much more than the time needed to reheat it.

Chicken Breasts Waikiki

    6 small chicken breasts, skinned and boned
    ½ cup soy sauce (white preferably)
    1 tablespoon sugar
    3 teaspoons sherry wine
    2 slices fresh ginger root, minced (see index)

Cut chicken breasts into rectangular pieces, roughly about ½ inch wide and 1½ inches long. In a bowl, combine remaining ingredients and marinate chicken strips for at least 1 hour at room temperature (or overnight in refrigerator). Toss and turn chicken at intervals to coat well. Drain chicken from marinade and dry on paper towels (reserve marinade). Serves 6.

    oil to cover 1 inch of skillet

    BATTER
    2 eggs
    ¾ cup water or milk (scant)
    1 tablespoon sesame oil
    1 cup flour
    1 teaspoon baking powder
    1 tablespoon sherry wine
    ½ teaspoon salt

Heat oil in skillet. Beat eggs with water or milk in a large bowl. Add sesame oil, stir and gradually add flour, baking powder, sherry and salt. Mix until batter resembles heavy cream. With tongs, dip chicken pieces into batter and then into hot oil. Do not crowd. Turn down heat to medium. Fry until golden brown and then transfer to a shallow baking pan. Preheat oven to 325° F. and keep chicken hot in oven. Continue until all pieces are done.

SAUCE:

3 tablespoons oil
½ pound mushrooms, sliced lengthwise
2 garlic cloves, minced
3 to 4 cups chicken broth
leftover marinade from chicken
dash of freshly ground pepper
3 tablespoons cornstarch mixed with 4 tablespoons water
1 can (5 oz.) bamboo shoots, drained and rinsed
1 can (5 oz.) water chestnuts, drained, rinsed and sliced
¼ pound fresh snow peas or ⅓ box frozen snow peas

Heat oil in skillet and add mushrooms and garlic; sauté for 3 to 5 minutes. Add broth, leftover marinade and fresh pepper. Heat thoroughly and taste for seasoning. Stir together cornstarch and water and add to skillet slowly, stirring all the time, until the sauce is thick and glazed. Add bamboo shoots, water chestnuts and snow peas. Combine well, cover and turn off flame. Let sit 2 minutes while you remove chicken nuggets from oven. Pour sauce on large platter and place nuggets of chicken on top. Serve with fried rice. Serves 6.

Kamailio:

At the Hawaii Kai Restaurant, only the breasts of chicken are used. However, dark meat is fine too. Cooked chicken can also be used. Vegetables can be varied to taste.

Liu Liu:

The chicken can be marinated, fried in batter and refrigerated for one or two days, or frozen. Heat in 375° F. oven until heated throughout. Cover with foil to prevent browning too quickly. Frozen chicken need not be defrosted.

The sauce can be prepared up until the cornstarch is added. The cornstarch and vegetables must be added at the last minute to insure crispness.

Luau Chicken (Chicken in Coconut Milk)

No native luau is complete without this dish, but Mainlanders often have to develop a taste for it . . . and some never do!

1 cup cornstarch
1 tablespoon salt (coarse preferred)
1 tablespoon garlic powder
1 tablespoon onion powder
fresh ground pepper
2½ to 3 pound fryer cut into 8 pieces
4 tablespoons oil
1 cup chicken broth or water
2 pounds fresh spinach (substitute for taro leaves), washed, stems
    removed and cut in half or 2 packages frozen spinach leaves
3 cups coconut milk (see index)

1. Combine cornstarch, salt, garlic, onion powder and pepper in a paper or plastic bag. Place 2 or 3 chicken pieces at a time in bag and shake to coat. Press pieces with fingers to secure coating.

2. Heat oil in a large skillet and sauté chicken until golden. Add chicken broth or water and simmer, covered tightly, until chicken is tender. Taste for additional seasoning. Keep hot.

3. Cook fresh spinach in only the water remaining on leaves. (Cook frozen spinach in ¼ cup water.) When tender, add 2 cups coconut milk and simmer for 1 minute.

4. To serve, arrange chicken pieces in center of a large deep casserole. Circle chicken with spinach in coconut milk. Heat remaining 1 cup coconut milk with the chicken broth (do not boil) and pour over chicken and spinach. Serves 4.

Liu Liu:

To prepare in advance, cook the chicken (steps 1 and 2). Cook spinach and prepare the coconut milk (do not combine with spinach). Store chicken, spinach and coconut milk separately in refrigerator. When ready to serve, heat chicken in oven, add 1 cup coconut milk to the spinach, and heat *malama pono* (that means "carefully"). Continue with step 4 of recipe.

Hidden Treasure Chicken

    6 chicken thighs
    6 chicken legs
    ½ pound ham, chopped fine
    ½ cup chopped almonds
    1 teaspoon sesame seed oil
    ¼ cup soy sauce
    1 teaspoon sugar
    dash of pepper
    ½ teaspoon hoisin sauce
    cornstarch
    oil for frying

Prepare chicken thighs and legs by carefully lifting the skin, starting at the cut edge. Mix ham and almonds together with sesame oil and insert this mixture between the meat and skin. Cover as much of the under surface as possible. Pull skin back so that mixture is invisible. If need be, fasten with toothpicks. Mix soy sauce, sugar, pepper and hoisin sauce in a bowl and sprinkle over chicken. Toss gently and marinate 1 hour or overnight in refrigerator. Spread cornstarch on wax paper and roll chicken pieces in it to coat well. Heat oil in a large skillet and brown chicken on all sides. Drain and remove to an oven-proof serving dish. Bake in a 350° F. oven for 30 to 40 minutes. Test for doneness (juices run white). Serve with sauce below.

SAUCE:

    3 tablespoons oil
    ¼ pound fresh, whole button mushrooms
    1 small onion, chopped
    1 slice ginger root, minced
    4 cups chicken broth
    1 tablespoon sherry wine
    3 tablespoons soy sauce (white preferably)
    1 teaspoon sugar
    dash of fresh pepper
    ½ of 5 oz. can water chestnuts, drained, rinsed and sliced
    3 tablespoons cornstarch mixed with ¼ cup water

In a large skillet, heat oil and sauté mushrooms, onion and ginger root until onion is golden. Add chicken broth, sherry, soy sauce, sugar and pepper. Bring to a boil and then simmer for 5 minutes. Add water chestnuts and combine. Mix cornstarch with water and add gradually to sauce, mixing until thickened. Turn off heat and let sit 2 minutes. Remove chicken parts from oven and pour sauce over them. Serve with rice. This chicken dish can be used with other sauces (see index). Additional vegetables may be added to sauce (snow peas, bokchoy, celery, bamboo shoots). Serves 6.

Liu Liu:

The first part of recipe can be prepared 1 to 2 days in advance and refrigerated or frozen. The sauce can be made one or two days in advance, but don't add the water chestnuts and cornstarch until you are ready to serve it. Reheat chicken in oven without defrosting. Cover with foil to prevent browning too quickly.

Orange Chicken

1 broiling-frying chicken (about 3 lbs.), cut in serving pieces
3 tablespoons soy sauce
3 tablespoons cornstarch
3 tablespoons oil
2 cups orange juice
2 tablespoons brown sugar
½ teaspoon cinnamon
1 slice fresh ginger root, minced
½ cup white raisins
1 teaspoon salt
hot cooked rice
toasted coconut (see index)

Sprinkle chicken pieces with soy sauce and then cornstarch. Toss to coat well. Let sit for 1 hour. Drain (reserve soy sauce); heat oil in a large skillet and brown chicken pieces. Remove to a platter. Add orange juice to pan juices with leftover soy sauce. Stir and scrape bottom of skillet. Add brown sugar, cinnamon, ginger root, raisins and salt. Return chicken to skillet and simmer for 40 minutes, covered. When ready to serve, place chicken parts on a bed of hot rice. Pour sauce over chicken and sprinkle with toasted coconut. Serves 3-4.

Honeyed Chicken (Mali Mali Moa Keiki)

1 roasting chicken, 5 pounds

STUFFING:

2 tablespoons oil
¾ pound ground pork
¼ pound mushrooms, coarsely cut
2 scallions, chopped fine
2 garlic cloves, minced
1 slice fresh ginger root, minced
½ cup corn flake crumbs
½ can (5 oz.) water chestnuts, drained, rinsed and diced
2 tablespoons soy sauce
1 egg, beaten with 1 tablespoon sherry wine
3 cups chicken broth

1. Wash and dry chicken. Season with salt inside and out.
2. Heat oil in a large skillet and sauté ground pork, mushrooms, scallions, garlic, and ginger only until meat becomes white. With fork break meat into bits.
3. Remove from flame. Add corn flake crumbs, water chestnuts, soy sauce and egg. Mix well.
4. Add only enough chicken broth to make the mixture soft and pliable. Reserve remainder of broth.
5. Stuff chicken with this mixture.
6. Close opening with skewers and tie, shoe-lace fashion, with white cord. Tie legs together. Bend wings back and skewer.

SAUCE FOR THE PAN:

3 tablespoons soy sauce
5 tablespoons honey
2 tablespoons brown sugar
2 garlic cloves, minced
remainder of chicken broth from stuffing
sesame seeds

1. In a roasting pan combine soy sauce, honey, brown sugar, garlic, and chicken broth.
2. Place chicken in roasting pan and brush sauce over the chicken.
3. Preheat oven to 350° F.; place chicken, breast down, and bake for 1 hour. Turn breast up and baste.

4. Raise heat in oven to 375° F. and bake for another 30 minutes.

5. If sauce has not thickened by now, brush chicken with additional honey. When chicken looks glazed, sprinkle with sesame seeds and brown for 10 minutes.

6. If more gravy is needed, remove chicken and keep hot. Remove all but 1 tablespoon fat from pan drippings and add 2 cups hot chicken broth to pan. Stir and scrape pan drippings, and adjust seasoning. Optional: thicken with 2 tablespoons cornstarch that has been diluted with 4 tablespoons water. Serves 6.

Kamailio:

Chicken may be cut up and prepared as per recipe without stuffing. Bake, skin down, for 1 hour, turn and follow recipe.

Leftover chicken, pork or veal can be cubed or sliced and simmered in "sauce for the pan" for a few minutes. Makes a nice hors d'oeuvre.

A slice of fresh minced ginger can be added to sauce if desired.

Liu Liu:

Chicken may be prepared in advance through step 3 and refrigerated 1 day or frozen. When ready to serve, heat oven and continue with step 4. Frozen chicken need not be defrosted. Heat covered, for 30 minutes; uncover and bake until heated throughout.

Filipino Chicken and Rice (Arroz De Valenciana)

3 tablespoons oil
1 small chicken (2 to 3 pounds), cut up into 8 small pieces
1 pound pork, cubed
2 garlic cloves, minced
1 large onion, sliced fine
1 green pepper, cut in strips, 1 inch by 2 inches
1 can (16 oz.) tomatoes or 2 fresh, ripe tomatoes cut up
salt and pepper to taste
½ cup chicken broth
2 canned pimentoes, sliced
4 cups cooked rice
1 can (8 oz.) peas or ½ pound fresh

Heat oil in a large skillet and sauté chicken pieces and pork until golden. Remove from skillet and reserve. Sauté garlic, onion and green pepper until wilted. Add tomatoes and cook for 5 minutes. Return chicken and pork to skillet; add salt, pepper, chicken broth, pimentoes and rice. Mix well; cover and simmer slowly until thoroughly heated and liquid has evaporated. Add the peas and mix well. Serve hot on a large platter garnished with sliced hard-boiled eggs, stuffed black olives and parsley sprigs. Serves 4-6.

Hibachi Chicken

½ cup soy sauce
3 tablespoons oil
1 fryer cut into 8 pieces

Combine soy sauce and oil and brush or sprinkle over chicken pieces. Marinate for at least one hour. Broil chicken over the hot coals of a hibachi, basting with leftover marinade. Turn from time to time until tender. Serve the chicken with the sauce below, hot rice and sambals (see index). Serves 4.

HIBACHI SAUCE

1 onion, chopped fine
2 celery stalks, chopped fine
3 tablespoons oil
1 tomato, peeled and chopped
1 tart apple, peeled and chopped fine
2 cups chicken broth
1 tablespoon curry powder
salt and pepper to taste

Sauté onion and celery in oil until golden. Add chopped tomato and apple and sauté for 3 minutes, stirring to combine ingredients. Add remaining ingredients and simmer for 30 minutes.

Korean Chicken (Takh Pok-kum)

4 pound chicken, boned and cut into 1-inch squares
⅓ cup soy sauce
2 tablespoons sugar
freshly ground pepper
2 tablespoons oil
2 garlic cloves, minced
2 scallions, chopped
¼ pound mushrooms, sliced
3 tablespoons pulverized sesame seeds (see index)

Place chicken in a covered saucepan with just enough water to cover. Add soy sauce, sugar, dash of pepper and simmer until almost done. Heat oil in a skillet and sauté garlic, scallions and mushrooms until wilted. Remove and add to the saucepan in which the chicken has been cooked. Add sesame seeds and continue cooking until chicken is tender and half the liquid cooked away. Serve over hot rice. Serves 6.

Baked Coconut Chicken

1 roasting chicken, cut into 8 pieces
1 small can frozen orange juice, thawed
½ teaspoon salt
2 slices fresh ginger, minced (optional)
2 eggs
1 tablespoon soy sauce
½ teaspoon garlic powder
½ cup corn flake crumbs
1 package shredded coconut
2 cups chicken broth
1 teaspoon lemon juice
salt and pepper
2 tablespoons cornstarch mixed with 4 tablespoons water

Wash and dry chicken. Marinate in orange juice, salt and ginger for two hours at room temperature or overnight in refrigerator. Turn occasionally. Drain and reserve juice.

On a sheet of wax paper mix corn flake crumbs with coconut flakes. In a shallow bowl beat eggs with half the orange juice mixture, soy sauce and garlic powder. With tongs dip chicken pieces first into egg mixture and then into coconut and corn flake crumbs. Coat thoroughly by pressing coconut flakes and crumbs onto chicken with fingers. Place on a greased baking pan, skin side up. Bake at 350° F. for 1 to 1½ hours. If chicken browns too quickly, cover with foil. Remove to serving platter and keep hot. To pan juices add reserved orange juice mixture, chicken broth, lemon juice, salt and pepper to taste. Mix and add cornstarch paste slowly, stirring until sauce has thickened. Serve separately in gravy dish. Place chicken on a large platter; garnish with parsley and thin orange slices. Serve extra orange sauce on cooked rice. Delicious! Serves 6.

Liu Liu:

The entire recipe can be made in advance and refrigerated or frozen but don't add the cornstarch thickener to the sauce until ready to serve. Reheat the chicken, wrapped completely in foil, in a hot oven.

Cornish Hens Miko Moko

A whole plump Rock Cornish hen, filled with a delicious meat stuffing, browned to a delicate hue in a wine ginger sauce is served on half a pineapple.

    6 Cornish hens (1 pound each)
    ½ cup soy sauce
    2 tablespoons sugar
    ¼ teaspoon Five Spices (see index)
    2 slices fresh ginger root, minced
    2 tablespoons sherry wine
    2 garlic cloves, minced
    3 pineapples

1. Wash hens with cold water and dry inside and out with paper toweling.

2. Combine soy sauce, sugar, Five Spices, ginger, sherry, and garlic. Place hens in a shallow baking pan and brush inside and out with the mixture (use pastry brush). Pour leftover mixture over hens and marinate 2 to 3 hours at room temperature or overnight in refrigerator. Turn occasionally.

3. Stuff birds loosely with meat stuffing below. Close opening with a skewer and tie legs together.

4. Leave marinade in pan. Roast in oven, breast down, at 400° F. for 45 minutes. Turn birds; reduce heat to 325° F. and roast for another 30 to 35 minutes.

5. Baste with drippings that have combined with marinade. If needed, add a little chicken broth or water.

6. Remove birds from pan, untie legs and place each one on half a pineapple. (Split pineapple in half horizontally from base to crown with the leaves left intact. The fruit in the pineapple is cored and cubed but left inside to be eaten with the Hens Miko Moko). Spoon some of the pan juices over each hen and serve with fried rice.

MIKO MOKO STUFFING

2 tablespoons sesame oil
2 garlic cloves, minced
3 scallions, chopped fine
1½ pounds ground pork
¼ cup soy sauce, light preferably
3 tablespoons sherry wine
1 teaspoon sugar
½ teaspoon salt
dash of freshly ground pepper
2 tablespoons cornstarch mixed with 4 tablespoons water

Heat oil in a large skillet and add garlic and scallion. Sauté until garlic is golden. Add pork and sauté until pork loses all trace of pinkness. With a fork break up bits of meat while cooking. Remove from flame and add soy sauce, sherry, sugar, salt and pepper. Stir together cornstarch and water and add to mixture. Mix well, taste and adjust seasoning. When cool, stuff birds. Serves 6.

Kamailio:

Although the Hens Miko Moko are served *on* a halved pineapple at the Hawaii Kai, you might wish to remove fruit and place Cornish hens *in* pineapple. Core and remove fruit carefully; leaving a 1-inch-thick shell. Fruit can be cubed and put into roasting pan during the last 15 minutes. Baste with pan drippings and serve alongside of the hens. Or use in Hawaiian Fruit Salad.

If you like, ¼ pound chopped mushrooms can be added to the stuffing after the pork has been sautéed.

Liu Liu:

The recipe can be completed in advance through the first part of step 4 and refrigerated up to 2 days or frozen (cool birds quickly to freeze). Pan drippings and marinade can be put in a plastic container and refrigerated or frozen. When ready to serve, preheat oven to 325° F. and continue with recipe. If hens are refrigerated, roast for about 50 minutes. If frozen, bake until piping hot throughout. Cover with foil to prevent browning too rapidly.

Kona Cornish Hens, Island-Style

6 Cornish hens (1 pound each)
salt and fresh pepper

GLAZE:

1 cup honey
½ cup soy sauce
½ teaspoon cinnamon
¼ cup guava jelly
3 tablespoons light rum (optional)
dash of garlic powder
syrup from 1 can (30 oz.) pineapple tidbits
1½ cups chicken broth (for the pan)

Wash and dry hens inside and out. Season with salt and pepper. Stuff birds with stuffing below. Close opening with a skewer and tie legs together. Combine all glaze ingredients. Brush or rub birds thoroughly with glaze. Roast (breast down) in a baking pan at 400° F. for 40 to 50 minutes, brushing and basting birds with glaze and pan juices frequently. Turn birds to brown evenly. Add 1½ cups chicken broth to pan juices. Scrape pan well. Add leftover glaze and mix well. Baste hens with this mixture and lower oven to 325°. Roast for approximately 30 minutes more.

STUFFING:

½ cup chopped macadamia nuts, roasted peanuts or walnuts
1 can (30 oz.) pineapple tidbits, drained
½ cup seedless white raisins
2 mangoes or peaches, fresh or canned, cut in small chunks
2 tablespoons vinegar
½ scallion, chopped fine
1 tablespoon brown sugar
2 tablespoons Plum Brandy Sauce (see index)
1 tablespoon soy sauce
dash of garlic powder

Combine all ingredients in a large bowl and stuff birds. Serves 6.

Kamailio:

1. Individual Cornish hens are excellent for barbecuing outdoors. Prepare birds and wrap well in foil. Remove foil and baste with glaze during last 30 minutes.

CARVE and BONE a Cooked Duck

① use cleaver or
sharp knife to remove backbone

do not cut through the
breast bone ... it would
split the duck in half

②

③

give bone a
push in
before loosening

④

Carefully pull rib cage
bones away from duck

⑤

deboned duck breast

2. Other fruits such as apricots, cherries or apples can be substituted in the recipe. *Hoopihoihoi* (sensational)!

For a Luau:

1. Make a stuffing of wild or fried rice and nuts.
2. Stuff birds with parboiled yams, apples and jam.

Everything can be prepared in advance. Roast hens for 40 minutes and refrigerate. Prior to serving, preheat oven to 325° F. and roast until browned and heated throughout.

DUCK

No Polynesian menu is complete unless it offers at least one duck entrée. This versatile and tasty bird reaches the height of its culinary glory in the hands of the incomparable Chinese cooks. But the Hawaiians have gone one step further and have given the popular duck dish a special flavor and treatment not found in other national cuisines.

To Carve and Bone Cooked Duck

(It's much easier than it sounds)

1. Chop off lower part of wings and discard.
2. On a chopping board, place duck on breast and with a cleaver or sharp knife, make an incision from top to bottom of duck half an inch to the left of backbone. Do the same on the right side of backbone (do not go through breast). This will leave you with a long 1-inch strip of spine. Discard. Bend legs back and forth at thigh joint until they loosen. Slip out bones. Do the same with wings. Don't worry if they break off. Use them to nibble on. Open bird on its breast and chop through. You now have two halves. Hold one half firmly with left hand and with the right hand pull carefully and separate rib cage from the duck. Do likewise with the other half. Remove remaining thigh bones carefully. Turn skin side up and cut up duck as recipe calls for. *Pau*—Hawaiian for "it's finished."

Duck Manchu

　　5- to 6-pound duck
　　2 celery stalks, cut in 2-inch pieces
　　4 scallions, cut in 2-inch pieces
　　¼ cup soy sauce
　　1 tablespoon sugar
　　2 tablespoons honey
　　2 cups water
　　2 tablespoons sherry wine

Rinse duck in lukewarm water and discard fat. Place half the celery and scallions in duck cavity. Combine remaining ingredients in a large covered Dutch oven with the duck. If possible, place duck on a trivet or rack. Bring to a boil and then simmer for about 1½ hours. Duck should be done, but still firm. Drain and reserve liquid for sauce, removing all but 2 tablespoons fat. Let duck cool and then bone it (see above). Chop boned bird into 4 equal portions. Sections will resemble squares. Serves 4.

STUFFING FOR PRESSED DUCK

　　1 pound cooked pork
　　2 tablespoons oyster sauce
　　1 teaspoon sugar
　　1 teaspoon sherry wine
　　¼ cup soy sauce (light preferably)
　　2 tablespoons cornstarch

Cut pork into julienne strips, ¼ inch by 2 inches long. In a bowl make a mixture of remaining ingredients and pour over pork strips. Toss and turn to coat well. Place duck quarters, skin side down, on a flat surface. Divide pork mixture into 4 parts. Press mixture into duck, flattening it down as hard as you can (using the palm of your hand is good). When each quarter is stuffed and pressed (to about 1 or 1½ inches thick), sprinkle stuffing generously with additional cornstarch and press into duck. Place duck quarters into a heatproof bowl which will fit into a large pot. Fill pot with 2 to 3 inches of boiling water. Put bowl into pot. Cover and steam duck for 45 minutes. Remove and cool. Refrigerate overnight. When ready to serve, heat oil for deep frying (very hot) and add duck quarters, one at a time. Deep fry until golden brown. Keep hot in preheated oven until four quarters are done.

SERVE WITH THE FOLLOWING SAUCE:

2 cups duck broth (fat removed)
1 cup chicken broth
¼ cup soy sauce
1 tablespoon sugar
1 teaspoon oyster sauce
2 tablespoons cornstarch

Combine all ingredients and heat in a saucepan until mixture thickens.

Kamailio:

At the Hawaii Kai, water chestnut flour is used in the pressing of the duck. However, cornstarch is an adequate substitute.

Liu Liu:

Since there are several steps to the recipe, you can prepare duck in advance and stop at any point. Duck can be refrigerated for 2 to 3 days or frozen. Reheat (defrosting is not necessary) until piping hot. Cover with foil if duck is browning too quickly.

Chestnut Duck

5- to 6-pound duck
2 celery stalks, cut in 2-inch pieces
4 scallions, cut in 2-inch pieces
2 slices fresh ginger root, minced
1 tablespoon sugar
2 tablespoons sherry wine
3 cups water
¼ cup soy sauce

1. Rinse duck in lukewarm water and discard all fat. Place half the celery, scallions and ginger root in duck cavity. Put remaining ingredients in covered pot with the duck (giblets can be added). Bring to

Chestnut Duck

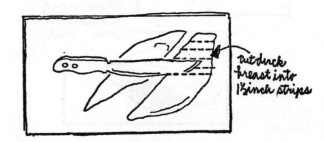

cut duck
breast into
1½-inch strips

a boil and then simmer, covered, for 1¼ hours. Turn duck occasionally. Remove duck and drain. Reserve liquid (remove all but 2 tablespoons fat). Cool.

2. Preheat oven to 450° F. and place duck, breast side down, on a rack or trivet over a drip pan containing several inches of water. Roast for 20 minutes. Turn over and roast until crisp and brown.

3. Cool, bone duck, and cut into strips 1½ by 3 inches. Thirty minutes before serving, preheat oven to 400° F. and heat duck until piping hot. Serve with sauce below. Makes 2 to 4 portions.

SAUCE:

3 cups duck broth (add chicken broth if needed to make 3 cups)
juice of 1 lemon
1 navel orange, grated with rind and juice
1 cup orange juice
1 slice ginger root, minced
½ teaspoon hoisin sauce (see index)
2 tablespoons sherry wine
3 tablespoons sugar
1 can (5 oz.) chestnuts, drained
1 can (15 oz.) pineapple slices, drained and halved
1 can (16 oz.) mandarin oranges, drained
3 tablespoons cornstarch mixed with 4 tablespoons water

In a saucepan, heat all ingredients except the last 3. Simmer for 5 minutes. Add halved pineapple slices and mandarin oranges and heat thoroughly. Taste for additional seasoning. When ready to serve, mix cornstarch and water and add to sauce slowly, stirring all the time. When sauce has reached the desired thickness, turn off heat and cover.

TO SERVE:

On a large platter or tray overlap slices of duck (skin side up), alternating each slice with ½ slice of pineapple. Pineapple half should be visible between duck slices. Pour sauce over duck and arrange mandarin oranges attractively around the platter. Sprinkle with toasted almonds and garnish with parsley sprigs. Serve with hot fried rice.

Kamailio:

1. Do not be fooled by size of duck, since there is a great loss of weight after cooking and boning. At the Hawaii Kai, a 5-pound duck

is used for 2 large portions. In a family, a larger duck can be stretched to serve 3 or 4 people.

2. You could have your butcher bone the duck and then follow recipe.

3. The Chestnut Duck can be roasted on a rotisserie or outdoor barbecue (see index) and does not have to be boned, if you wish. Chop into small sections and use with sauce which has been prepared in advance.

4. At the Hawaii Kai Restaurant, the chefs use dried chestnut meats which are soaked overnight and then simmered until soft. They can be bought in Italian and Oriental food stores. However, the canned chestnuts are an adequate substitute and can be readily purchased in any supermarket. Fresh chestnuts (see Sources) can also be used.

Liu Liu:

There are 4 steps in this recipe—boiling, roasting, boning and lastly, making the sauce. You can prepare the duck in advance and stop at any point. The duck can be refrigerated up to 3 days or frozen until ready to use. Duck can then be reheated in oven while making the sauce.

King Kaulooloo Duck

Fit for the king in your house.

5- to 6-pound duck, boned, with wings left on
    (cut through backbone only)

MARINADE:

2 garlic cloves, minced
1 tablespoon brown bean sauce (sold in cans; see Sources)
2 tablespoons hoisin sauce
2 tablespoons soy sauce
2 tablespoons sesame oil
3 tablespoons chicken broth

Rinse duck in lukewarm water; remove and discard any fat. Combine all ingredients in a bowl and with a pastry brush, coat duck, inside and out, with mixture. Let duck sit in bowl for 1 to 2 hours at room temperature or overnight in refrigerator.

King Kauloobo Duck

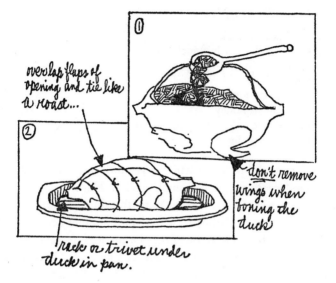

overlap flaps of opening and tie like a roast...

don't remove wings when boning the duck

rack or trivet under duck in pan.

STUFFING:

10 slices stale white bread, crusts removed
water
1 can almond paste
3 eggs, beaten
⅛ teaspoon salt

Soak bread in cold water for ½ minute. Put into colander and squeeze out most of the water. Place in a large mixing bowl; add almond paste, eggs and salt. With a large or wooden spoon mix until all ingredients are combined and smooth. Lay duck on flat surface with skin down. Heap the stuffing down the center of duck. Close the duck by bringing one side over the other, overlapping. Skewer or tie around with white cord in 3 or 4 places. Bend wings to back and skewer. Preheat oven to 350° F. Place duck on a rack or trivet over a drip pan or roasting pan containing 2 inches of water. Roast 20 minutes to the pound. If browning too quickly, cover with foil. Remove foil the last 15 minutes. Serve with Chestnut Duck Sauce or Plum Brandy

Sauce (see index for both sauces). (Duck that has not been boned can be used also.) Serves up to 4.

Kaka Waikiki Duck

Tender slices of pressed duck

5- to 6-pound duck
2 celery stalks, cut in 2-inch pieces
4 scallions, cut in 2-inch pieces
¼ cup soy sauce
1 tablespoon sugar
2 tablespoons honey
2 cups water
2 tablespoons sherry wine

Rinse duck in lukewarm water and discard fat. Place half the celery and scallions in the duck cavity. Place remaining ingredients in a large covered Dutch oven with the duck. If possible, place duck on a trivet or rack. Bring to a boil and simmer for about 1½ hours. Duck should be cooked but firm. Drain and reserve liquid. Remove all but 2 tablespoons fat. Let duck cool and then bone it. Bird should be cut in half only. (See How to Carve and Bone Cooked Duck.)

STUFFING:

1 pound cooked pork
2 tablespoons oyster sauce
1 teaspoon sugar
1 teaspoon sherry wine
¼ cup soy sauce (light preferably)
2 tablespoons cornstarch

Cut pork into julienne strips ¼ inch by 2 inches long. In a bowl, make a mixture of remaining ingredients and pour over pork strips. Toss and turn to coat well. Place duck halves, skin side down, on a flat surface. Divide pork mixture in half and press it into the duck, flattening it down as hard as you can. When each half is stuffed and pressed (to about 1 or 1½ inches thick), sprinkle stuffing generously with additional cornstarch and press again into duck. Place duck halves into a heatproof bowl which will fit into a large pot. Fill pot with

2 to 3 inches of boiling water. Put bowl into pot. Cover and steam duck for 45 minutes. Remove and cool. Refrigerate overnight. When ready to serve, chop halves into strips 1½ inches wide. Heat oil for deep frying and add duck strips, one at a time. Deep fry until golden brown. Keep hot in preheated oven until all the strips are done. Serve on a bed of fried rice with the following sauce:

SAUCE:

3 tablespoons oil
1 garlic clove, minced
1 slice ginger root, minced
¼ pound mushrooms, sliced lengthwise
¼ pound snow peas or ½ package frozen
½ of 5-oz. can water chestnuts
½ of 5-oz. can bamboo shoots
2 cups duck broth
1 cup chicken broth
¼ cup soy sauce
1 tablespoon sugar
salt and pepper to taste
2 tablespoons cornstarch mixed with 4 tablespoons water

Heat oil in a skillet and sauté garlic and ginger for 2 minutes. Add mushrooms and sauté until wilted. Add snow peas, water chestnuts and bamboo shoots. Stir and cook only until heated throughout. Add duck broth, chicken broth, soy sauce, sugar, salt and pepper. Heat to boiling. Turn down flame, mix cornstarch mixture and add it gradually, stirring all the time. When sauce has thickened, turn off heat and cover. Serves about 4.

Kamailio:

For preparing in advance and amounts to serve per person, see Chestnut Duck.

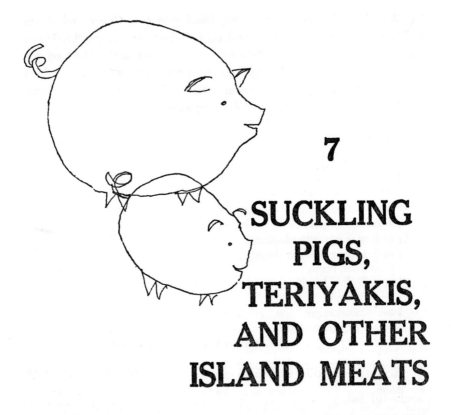

7

SUCKLING PIGS, TERIYAKIS, AND OTHER ISLAND MEATS

On a quiet summer day in the year 1792, an English merchant schooner under the command of Captain George Vancouver dropped anchor off the palm-lined shores of Hawaii. Deep in the hold of his ship, he carried strange cargo—three American Hereford cows and one bull. Raunchy and seasick as they undoubtedly were, this tiny bovine herd was destined to add a new chapter to the economic and social history of the Hawaiian Islands.

During his many previous trips to these lovely Polynesian Islands the good captain had acquired a genuine affection for its people and their culture. As a token of his friendship, he presented his live cargo as a personal gift to the great tribal chief—Kamehameha. The clever chief was not one to look a gift cow in the mouth so he graciously accepted the strange beasts. However, at first sight, the king was terribly concerned that the "great hogs" would bite him.

In a remarkably short time, those four historic cows became 500 and the 500 became 5,000 and these in turn multiplied and flourished into one of the largest and finest cattle herds in the world—a herd so big and splendid that it soon formed the nucleus of the famous Parker Ranch, second only to the mighty King Ranch.

Had the popular poet Kipling been witness to this agricultural phenomenon he might never have penned his famous words "East is East and West is West and never the twain shall meet." Because that is exactly what did happen—right smack in the middle of the Pacific Ocean! Eager to develop their growing livestocks the natives embarked on a progressive plan of emulation. They imported fast riding, cattle-wise Vaquéros from Mexico, sturdy, long horn breeding stock from Texas and ranch-trained quarter horses from California. Now the mighty stage was set for a western epic that would surpass the greatest of Cecil B. DeMille's western productions.

Aloha Pahdner! Hawaiian-style Cowboys called Paniolas, took to the saddle as expertly as they did to their surfboards. Adapting ranch-style techniques to suit their own particular needs, they took the best from the West and left the rest—no six shooters, no cattle rustlers, no hired guns, . . . just plenty of good beef. What the Japanese achieved with beer and massage, the Paniolas achieved with their special cattle diet of natural molasses, coconut palms and a touch of pineapple. Though pork and fish still remained prominent in their cooking the resourceful natives varied and enhanced their colorful cuisine with many new and exciting beef dishes.

In their own inimitable style they roasted it, boiled it, barbecued it, fried it and even came up with a new recipe for Singapura Steak. Not to mention Teriyaki! And if by chance this savory Japanese-style beef dish doesn't suit your fancy then we suggest that you try a Steak Bora Bora or a Polynesian Meat Loaf, or a Pork Lelani or one of the popular specialties from the famous Hawaii Kai restaurant—Beef Mai Kai. If none of these succulent dishes appeal to your taste, then you can't really think of yourself as a meat lover.

When it comes to meat dishes, the imaginative Hawaiians have really dug down deep into their international grab bag. The results are an endless variety of meat cuts, sauces and recipes. Even the most demanding meat connoisseur is sure to find one or more dishes to his liking from the many exciting pork and beef recipes native to our 50th state.

Whatever recipe you choose, pork or beef, or even a combination of both, if you make it like the Hawaiians do—you'll certainly have nothing to beef about!

Roast Suckling Pig (Puaa Keiki)

It's not an authentic luau unless you have one. Polynesians consider the skin and fat a great delicacy, and cut them into strips for serving before the pig is carved.

        1 suckling pig, 10-12 pounds (boned and dressed by butcher)
        2 tablespoons sesame oil
        ½ cup hoisin sauce
        ½ cup soy sauce
        ¼ cup honey
        ⅛ cup brown sugar
        4 garlic cloves, minced fine
        2 tablespoons sherry wine
        pinch of 5 Spices (see index)
        2-3 teaspoons tomato shade
        ½ cup brown bean sauce
        vinegar

1. Wash pig well, inside and outside with cold water and dry well. Pierce skin all over with skewer or point of sharp knife.

2. In a bowl, combine all ingredients except vinegar and mix well. You will have a thick paste which you can dilute if you wish with some chicken broth, to facilitate brushing.

3. Place pig flat on its back and with pastry brush, coat inside thickly with mixture. Refrigerate overnight or for at least 3 hours at room temperature.

4. Preheat oven to 450° F. Skewer the opening of pig with poultry picks or metal skewers and lace with string.

5. With metal skewers, pin front legs and pull forward; pin hind legs and pull backward. Open mouth and place a potato into it (for the apple that will be inserted later). Cover the ears with thick silver foil.

6. Brush outside skin of pig with vinegar and place pig on a rack over a pan which has 2 inches of water in it (to catch drippings and prevent smoking).

7. Bake for 40 minutes; turn heat down to 325° F. and roast for about 3 hours, until meat is tender and thoroughly cooked. If the pig browns too rapidly, cover with brown paper or silver foil.

8. When ready to serve, place pig on large platter and plump out sides. Place an apple in its mouth, deck the neck with a lei, or a cranberry necklace and put a big bow on the tail. Surround with greens (leaves, ferns, parsley, etc.), fruits, coconuts, etc. You could decorate the pig further by skewering the skin with bamboo sticks of pineapple, cherries, lichees and kumquats. Serves 6-8 as entrée. If served with other foods, will be enough for twice as many servings.

Kamailio:

At the Hawaii Kai, the suckling pig is brought out to show (and it is indeed a sight to see), then returned to the kitchen for carving. In the restaurant kitchens the pig is hung by a hook piercing the neck, and roasted in a simulated *imu* or smoke oven. You too can roast the pig in this fashion very simply if your oven is large enough. Place a shallow roasting pan filled with water on the lowest rack of your oven to catch drippings. Buy rustproof S-shaped hooks, such as curtain hooks sold at hardware and dime stores. Insert one or two of these hooks through the chin and hang the pig from the highest rack of oven, above the pan of water. Or you could suspend pig with 2 or 3 hooks as if hanging a hammock (see drawing p. 57).

If you have a large outdoor barbecue oven, with an electric spit, you could insert the rod through the center of the pig, from front to back, and roast in that fashion. Don't forget to use a pan with water to catch the drippings.

Ham Alii (Royalty)

 1 ham, whole or half (precooked)
 1 can (15 oz.) crushed pineapple
 2 slices fresh ginger root, minced (see index)

Bake ham in a 350° F. oven for one hour. Thirty minutes before ham is finished baking, score fat with diagonal slashes ½-inch deep and 1-inch apart. Fill grooves with crushed pineapple combined with ginger root. Bake for 30 minutes more until pineapple is golden brown.

Spareribs with Black Bean Sauce

 3 pounds spareribs, small and lean
 3 tablespoons oil
 2 tablespoons fermented black beans, soaked and mashed (see index)
 2 garlic cloves, minced
 2 slices fresh ginger root, minced (optional)
 1 scallion, chopped
 2 tablespoons soy sauce
 1 tablespoon sugar
 ¾ cup chicken broth (or water)
 1 teaspoon sherry wine
 2 tablespoons cornstarch mixed with 4 tablespoons water

Cut ribs apart, remove any fat and, with a cleaver, chop into 1-inch sections (through bone and all). Heat oil in a large skillet and add mashed black beans, garlic, ginger root and scallions. Stir and sauté for a few minutes. Add spareribs and brown. Drain oil from skillet. Add soy sauce, sugar, chicken broth and sherry. Bring to a boil; stir and simmer covered for 45 minutes. Shake skillet occasionally. Add additional broth or water if necessary. Stir cornstarch and water and add gradually to skillet, mixing until sauce has thickened. Serve over rice or noodles. The black bean sauce is delicious and if you would like more of it for the rice or noodles, double the amount of the ingredients. The entire recipe can be prepared in advance, if cornstarch mixture is not added. Refrigerate or freeze. Reheat slowly in covered skillet or oven and add cornstarch mixture as described in recipe. Serves 3 to 4.

Teriyaki Spareribs

(*Japanese*)

2 racks spareribs (small and lean)

MARINADE

1 cup soy sauce
⅓ cup brown sugar
2 tablespoons sake or sherry wine
1 slice fresh ginger root, minced
2 cloves garlic, minced

Marinate ribs overnight in marinade made by mixing the five ingredients. Preheat oven to 375° F. Place ribs in large roasting pan and pour marinade over them. Bake for 1 hour, turning and basting occasionally. Take ribs out of oven and remove all fat from sauce. Baste and place under broiler 3 inches from flame until brown and crisp. Baste and broil on other side. Watch for charring. Sauce will become glazed. Serves 4.

Kamailio:

Care must be taken not to char broiled foods that have been marinated. One-half cup pineapple juice can be added to marinade.

Liu Liu:

Entire recipe can be completed except for broiling. Refrigerate or freeze in sauce. Reheat by broiling slowly. Ribs can be cut through to make individual ribs or cut into small chunks.

Spareribs and Pineapple (Poh Loh Poi Kwut)

    3 pounds spareribs, lean and small
    3 tablespoons oil
    1 garlic clove, minced
    2 slices ginger root, minced
    ½ cup soy sauce
    1 can pineapple chunks (16 ounces)
    ⅓ cup sugar
    ⅓ cup vinegar
    ⅔ cup water
    ½ teaspoon paprika
    salt to taste
    2 tablespoons cornstarch mixed with 4 tablespoons water

Cut ribs apart and chop with a cleaver into 1-inch pieces. Heat oil in a large skillet. Add garlic, ginger root and ribs. Brown ribs and drain fat from skillet. Add soy sauce, pineapple juice (from can of pineapple chunks), sugar, vinegar, water and paprika. Heat to boiling and then simmer for 45 minutes, covered. Add salt to taste, pineapple chunks and cook until thoroughly heated. Stir cornstarch and water and add gradually to skillet, stirring until sauce is thickened. Serve over rice. Serves 4.

Kamailio:

For a more pungent taste, add chopped sweet mixed pickles (half of an 8-ounce jar) to sauce while cooking. Leftover meats and poultry can be cubed and heated in the sauce. *Ono loa* (delicious)! The entire recipe can be prepared in advance, but don't add the cornstarch. Refrigerate or freeze. Reheat slowly in covered skillet and when hot add cornstarch mixture as described in recipe.

Korean Pork (Ton Yuk Kui)

The pork butt, when trimmed, will have a lot of waste. Therefore, a pork tenderloin, which is lean, might be a better buy.

5 pounds fresh pork butt, fat removed and cut into thin slices 2 inches long
¾ cup soy sauce
3 tablespoons sugar
2 scallions, chopped fine
2 garlic cloves, minced
fresh ground pepper
½ teaspoon fresh ginger root, minced
1 tablespoon toasted sesame seeds, pulverized (see below) with 1 tablespoon oil (sesame preferred)

Combine all ingredients in a large shallow broiling pan and place meat in this marinade. Toss and turn to coat well. Marinate for at least 2 hours at room temperature (or overnight in refrigerator), turning occasionally. When ready to serve, broil in same pan for 5 minutes on each side. Serve with rice and use the heated marinade as a sauce. Serves 4 to 6.

TO TOAST AND PULVERIZE SESAME SEEDS

Koreans in the Islands use sesame seeds in many types of food preparation. The seeds are toasted until golden brown, a little salt is added and then the seeds are pulverized with a mortar and pestle or wooden potato masher. You can do the same or use the blunt end of a large knife to mash the seeds.

Pork Pango Pango

3 pound boned loin of pork
1 cup soy sauce (light preferably)
2 tablespoons honey
2 tablespoons sherry wine
2 garlic cloves, minced
1 tablespoon tomato coloring (see index)
¼ cup sugar
¼ cup chicken broth
1 tablespoon oyster sauce
dash of fresh ground pepper

Put loin of pork in a shallow pan. Combine all other ingredients and use to marinate pork loin for 2 to 3 hours at room temperature or overnight in refrigerator. Turn occasionally. Drain, but reserve marinade. Preheat oven to 425° F. and place meat on a grill, rack or trivet over a shallow baking pan containing an inch or two of water; or suspend "imu fashion" (see index) from hooks. Roast for 20 minutes and reduce heat to 375° F. Turn meat (if not suspended) and brush with marinade. Roast for 30 minutes longer or until meat is done, basting occasionally. Cut into thick slices and skewer 5-6 slices per person on a metal skewer. Place on a bed of fried rice and pour the following sauce over the sliced pork. Garnish platter with spiced crab apple and Hawaiian Fritters (see index). Serves 6.

SAUCE

1 cup Plum Brandy Sauce (see index)
2 tablespoons lemon juice
2 tablespoons orange juice
1 teaspoon grated orange rind
3 tablespoons soy sauce
1 teaspoon sugar
leftover marinade
2 tablespoons cornstarch mixed with 3 tablespoons water

Combine all ingredients except cornstarch mixture in a saucepan and heat. Simmer for 5 minutes. Add cornstarch mixture gradually, stirring constantly until sauce thickens. Pour over pork slices.

Pork Chops Hawaiian Style

6 lean center-cut pork chops
1 can (13 oz.) pineapple chunks
2 tablespoons soy sauce
1 tablespoon brown sugar
pinch of 5 Spices (see index)
1 tablespoon cornstarch mixed with 2 tablespoons water

Buy large, thick pork chops and slice a few slivers of fat off the edges. Heat skillet and rub with fat slivers. Brown chops slowly on both sides and when done, drain any excess fat from skillet. Drain juice from pineapple cubes into skillet; add soy sauce, brown sugar and 5 spices. Combine and simmer for 20 minutes. Add pineapple cubes, stir cornstarch mixture and add gradually to the skillet. Stir until thickened. For more sauce, add an 8-ounce can of pineapple juice. When you are using fresh pineapple, you'll need additional juice. Serves 6.

Crown Roast of Pork, Island Style

    1 crown roast of pork (see below)
    3 tablespoons soy sauce
    1 teaspoon garlic powder
    3 cups chicken broth
¼ cup soy sauce
    3 tablespoons sugar
    1 garlic clove, minced

STUFFING:

    2 cups celery, sliced fine
    1 large onion, minced
¼ pound mushrooms, sliced
    4 tablespoons oil
    1 can (5 oz.) water chestnuts, drained, rinsed and diced
½ cup roasted peanuts, chopped
    3-4 cups cooked wild rice (hot)
⅓ cup parsley, chopped
    salt and fresh pepper to taste

GARNISH:

    1 can or jar kumquats (16 ounces), drained
    parsley sprigs

Have butcher prepare a crown roast or try doing it yourself. Buy two rib ends of pork loin with the backbone removed. Cut away meat from tips of bones and mince; reserve. Make a small cut at the base between each rib. Bend each loin into a half circle. Join the ends together and sew or skewer them with white cord.

Heat oven to 425° F. and rub meat with some of the soy sauce mixed with garlic powder. In a large roasting pan, *invert* roast over a small pyrex cup to help keep the shape. Add only 1 cup chicken broth, ¼ cup soy sauce, 3 tablespoons sugar and minced garlic to bottom of pan. After 1 hour reduce heat to 350° F. and baste with pan juices. Bake for 1½ hours. If roast browns too quickly, cover with foil.

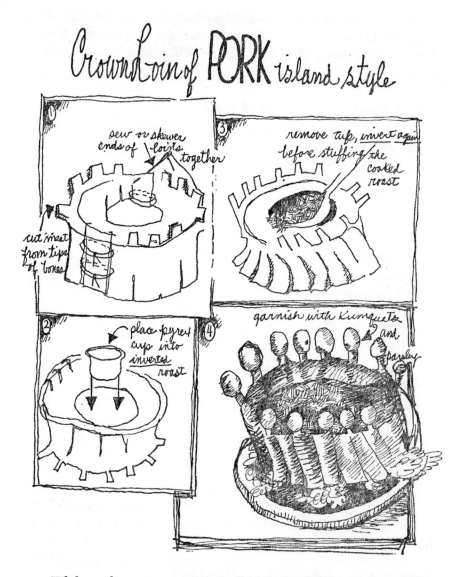

Crown Loin of PORK island style

1. cut meat from tips of bones — sew or skewer ends of loins together

2. place pyrex cup into inverted roast

3. remove cup, invert again before stuffing the cooked roast

4. garnish with kumquats and parsley

While pork roasts, prepare stuffing. Sauté celery, onion, mushrooms and reserved minced pork until tender. Add diced water chestnuts and peanuts and cook only until heated. Add cooked hot wild rice, parsley, salt and fresh pepper to taste. Cover and keep hot.

Put the finished roast on a serving platter (without the cup).

Heap the center with stuffing and keep hot. To make gravy, pour off all but 1 tablespoon fat. Add remaining 2 cups chicken broth and scrape pan. Bring to a boil and simmer for a few minutes. Correct seasonings. Thicken with 2 tablespoons cornstarch mixed with ¼ cup water if desired.

Put a kumquat on the end of each rib bone and brush with gravy. Decorate platter with parsley sprigs. Carving is very simple. All you have to do is carve between the rib bones. Serves 6 to 8.

Liu Liu:

The roast crown of pork can be prepared in advance. Bake it for about ¾ hour, then refrigerate or freeze it. Bake for ¾ hour before serving (defrost it first if it has been frozen). The stuffing can be made ahead also and refrigerated or frozen separately. Reheat by adding a few tablespoons of hot chicken broth. You can make the gravy ahead, too, but don't thicken it until you are ready to serve it (if you do want it thickened).

Molokai Roast Pork with Peanut Butter Crust

Strangely enough, peanut butter is a favorite of the Islanders and is used constantly.

    6 pound boneless pork roast (loin)
    ½ cup peanut butter
    ½ cup orange juice
    ¼ cup soy sauce
    1 slice fresh ginger root, minced

1. Roast pork for 2 to 2½ hours on a trivet set over a pan that has 2 inches of water in it.

2. About 30 minutes before roast is done and every trace of pink is gone, combine remaining ingredients and brush over roast. Continue cooking and basting until roast is crisp looking, brown and coated with peanut butter. Garnish with slices of oranges, limes, or kumquats. The roast can be barbecued outdoors on a spit over medium coals. Spit must be raised far above the coals with no coals directly under the roast. Serves 6 to 8.

Filipino Pork en Adobo (Adobong Baboy)

This, the Filipino national dish, is one of those versatile recipes that can be done as well with chicken or beef, or with a combination of chicken and pork. Green pepper strips or fresh spinach can be added five minutes before the meat is done. You can cook everything ahead and reheat it just before serving.

1½ pounds lean pork or 6 large trimmed pork chops cut into cubes
    (or left whole)
1 small onion, chopped fine
2 garlic cloves, minced
1 teaspoon paprika
½ cup soy sauce
¼ cup vinegar
3 bay leaves
1 slice fresh ginger root, minced
salt and fresh ground pepper to taste

Place pork in a large skillet or saucepan; combine remaining ingredients and pour over pork. Let stand for 30 minutes, turning occasionally. Add just enough boiling water to cover the meat and simmer, covered, until most of the juices have cooked away and the sauce is thick and brown. Turn the cubes to brown all sides. It may be necessary to add a little water. Let that cook down also. Serve hot with rice. Yield: 4 to 6 servings.

Noodles with Pork—Filipino Style (Pansit)

3 tablespoons oil
2 garlic cloves, minced
1 slice ginger root, minced
1 onion, sliced thin
2 celery stalks, sliced thin
1 pound pork, cut in thin strips, 1 inch by 2 inches
½ pound chicken, cut in thin strips, 1 inch by 2 inches
3 tablespoons soy sauce
3 tomatoes, sliced
1 tablespoon sugar
½ pound fine egg noodles, cooked and drained

Heat oil in a large skillet and sauté garlic, ginger root, onion and celery until onion is golden. Remove from pan and reserve. Add pork and chicken strips and brown (additional oil may be needed). Add soy sauce, tomatoes and sugar. Return garlic, ginger root, onion and celery to skillet. Combine well and simmer, covered, for 45 minutes. A little water can be added if needed. Put noodles in a colander and pour hot water over them. Drain and combine with meat and vegetables in skillet. Cook until noodles are piping hot. Serve on a large platter garnished with finely chopped peanuts, egg threads (see index), lemon slices and chopped scallions or sliced hard-boiled eggs. Serves 6.

Kamailio:

1. Shrimp can be added to recipe with pork and chicken or substituted for chicken.

2. Cooked chicken or pork can be substituted for uncooked (omit browning).

3. Thinly-sliced cabbage can be added instead of, or combined with, tomatoes.

Portuguese Pork with Clams (Carne de Porco)

1½ pounds boneless pork, cut into small cubes
Pickling Sauce (below)
olive oil for frying (or substitute corn or peanut oil)
18 Little Neck clams or steamers, cleaned
6 slices day-old white bread

Marinate pork in pickling sauce for 2-3 days. Turn daily to marinate thoroughly. Drain and heat oil in a large skillet. Sauté the pork until brown and well done. Add a few tablespoons of the pickling sauce and simmer until sauce is reduced (about 10 minutes). Add clams and simmer until they open. Meanwhile, in another skillet, heat additional olive oil, dip white bread into pickling sauce and fry until brown. Serve pork and clams on a platter over the fried bread. Serves 6.

PICKLING SAUCE

1 cup vinegar
2 cups water
2 garlic cloves, minced
3 tablespoons pickling spices
3 teaspoons sugar
1 teaspoon salt

Combine all ingredients, pour over pork and marinate for 2 to 3 days, turning several times. The Portuguese pickle much of their pork and beef, which they then fry with potatoes and bread.

Kamailio:

1. Clams may be omitted and potatoes substituted. Sauté potatoes in oil with pork and continue with recipe.
2. Fish, whole or sliced, can be pickled in this sauce and fried.
3. The recipe may be prepared in advance up until the clams are added. The fried bread too, can be prepared ahead and refrigerated. Before serving sprinkle bread with a few drops of pickling sauce and heat in oven.

Polynesian Butterflied Pork Chops

6 double pork chops (loin)
2 tablespoons oil
1 slice fresh ginger root, minced
4 tablespoons soy sauce
4 tablespoons honey
½ cup Plum Brandy Sauce (see index)
1 tablespoon sherry wine
2 cups chicken stock
¼ teaspoon salt
dash of fresh pepper

Slice through the meat of each pork chop, almost to the bone; open out like a book and flatten to resemble the wings of a butterfly.

Heat oil in large skillet and brown each chop with the ginger root. Arrange them in a large baking pan or casserole.

Combine remaining ingredients and pour over chops, ascertaining that each chop is coated.

Preheat oven to 350° F. and bake for 1 hour, covered, basting occasionally.

Uncover chops for 10 minutes to brown. Sauce should be thick and glazed. Serve with pineapple slices that have been baked in a small amount of the sauce and with fried rice or noodles (see index).

Kamailio:

Leftover chicken, veal, breaded fried pork chops and other meats are delicious done this way; just bake them in casserole, covered with sauce, until thoroughly heated and glazed.

About Flambées

There is nothing more imposing and dramatic in the dining room than a tray of food brought in flaming, or flambéed right at the table. Flickering blue flames, particularly in a candlelit room, attract every eye, and the rich aroma of the sizzling food assails the nostrils and sets the taste buds tingling in anticipation. You can bring distinction to the simplest of dishes just by adding a can of Sterno to the table equipment.

Rum, brandy, vodka and kirsch are the best flaming agents. Liqueurs containing a high alcoholic content combined with rum or brandy can be flambéed successfully. The Hawaii Kai now uses a foolproof and economical product for flambéeing called *Flambé Fanfare*. It is derived from pure ingredients, flames instantly with no preheating, and is long lasting. It comes in four flavors: brandy, fruit, rum, and herb. Since only ½ ounce or less is needed per portion, it costs only pennies per serving. See "Sources" for where it can be obtained.

HOW TO FLAMBE:

The art of flambéeing is simple if you remember that the liquor must always be warmed before using.

1. You will need 4 ounces of brandy, rum or vodka, of a high alcoholic content.

2. Warm the liquor slowly in a long-handled utensil (like a butter melter). Or, more safely, warm in a double boiler.

3. Bring the food and warm liquor to the table on a heat-resistant platter or in a chafing dish.

4. Pour the warmed liquor around the edge of the food and ignite with a long match. Or, you can warm a tablespoon of brandy with the lighted match; when brandy ignites, use it to flame the brandy around the food.

When a dish is prepared with a sauce, it is usually best to pour the warm liquor into a ladle, ignite it, and when the flame is burning brightly, pour it over the food.

Flaming Pork Ipo (He hana i pookela)

A masterpiece!

2 eggs
1 cup cold water
2 tablespoons soy sauce (light preferably)
2 tablespoons sherry wine
1 cup flour
¼ cup cornstarch
1 teaspoon sugar
½ teaspoon salt
dash of fresh pepper
oil for deep frying
1½ pounds lean boneless pork, cut into 1-inch cubes

In a deep bowl, beat eggs with water and add soy sauce and sherry. Mix well. Gradually add flour, cornstarch, sugar, salt and pepper, beating well until smooth and batter has consistency of heavy cream. Heat the oil in a large skillet; using tongs, dip pork cubes into batter, coating well. Add the pork cubes, a few at a time, to the heated oil. Deep fry until golden brown (about 6-8 minutes). If a large amount of oil is used, the pork cubes will rise to the top and float when done. You can also check for doneness by cutting open one cube to see that it is no longer pink. Remove and drain on absorbent paper. You can do all this in advance, and refrigerate it for 2 days or freeze it and defrost before using.

When ready to serve, put on foil-lined pan and place in 325° F. oven, to keep hot while making sauce.

SAUCE:

2 tablespoons oil
2 garlic cloves, minced
1 onion, medium size, chopped
1 green pepper, cut into 1 inch squares
2 carrots, cut at an angle into thin slices
1 teaspoon fresh ginger root, minced
1½ cups chicken broth
1 jar sweet pickles (sliced) or sweet mix (8 ounces)
2 tablespoons soy sauce
1 can (13 oz.) pineapple chunks with juice
½ cup vinegar
2 tablespoons brown sugar
2 tablespoons honey
pinch of freshly ground pepper
2 tablespoons ketchup
1 can bamboo shoots (5 ounces) drained
2 tablespoons cornstarch mixed with ¼ cup water

Heat oil in large skillet (10-inch) and add garlic and onion. Sauté quickly for about 2 to 3 minutes. Add green pepper and carrots and sauté for about 3 minutes; add minced ginger. Add the chicken broth and all ingredients except bamboo shoots and cornstarch paste. Mix well and simmer for 8 to 10 minutes, covered; do not permit vegetables to become too soft. (You can do this part ahead and store it for 1 or 2 days.) Add bamboo shoots, stir well to combine all ingredients and slowly pour in cornstarch paste, stirring constantly until thickened. Turn off heat and cover. Remove pork from oven, place on heat-resistant glass or stainless steel platter. Pour sauce over pork. Serve with fried rice (see index). To flame, use 151-proof rum and see above under Flambé for procedure. Serves 4-6.

Kamailio:

Gene buys fresh pork butts for the cubes. These can weigh from 3 to 6 pounds and are boned and cut into 3 or 4 rectangular strips (2 inches wide, 2 inches thick). Most of the fat is then removed and the scraps and bone are used later for soup stock (see index). Pork shoulder, loin or thick chops may be used in the same fashion. If you can't use all of the butt or shoulder, freeze it.

Leftover roast pork can be cubed and used in the recipe in place of raw pork. Shrimp, veal, beef cubes or chicken livers can also be used, cooked or uncooked.

You may add or substitute the following vegetables: snow peas, water chestnuts, mushrooms, small whole onions, serrated cucumber slices, turnip slices, squash, apple, tomato wedges or cherry tomatoes. Just remember—keep them crisp!

Pork Lelani

1 pound barbecued roast pork (see recipe)
4 scallions
4 stalks bokchoy or celery
1 can (5 oz.) bamboo shoots, drained and rinsed
3 tablespoons oil
2 garlic cloves, minced
¼ teaspoon salt
½ pound bean sprouts (fresh preferably) or
    1 can (16 oz.) bean sprouts, drained and rinsed well
3 tablespoons soy sauce
1 teaspoon sugar
1 cup chicken broth
1 tablespoon sherry
salt and fresh pepper to taste
¾ pound cooked Long Life Noodles (see below)

1. Slice barbecued roast pork into thin 3-inch long strips, julienne style, ⅛-inch thick.

2. Cut scallions, bokchoy and bamboo shoots into thin 1-inch long strips.

3. Heat oil in large skillet and add scallions, bokchoy or celery, garlic and salt. Sauté only until vegetables are translucent, not soft.

4. Add bamboo shoots and bean sprouts (if using fresh bean sprouts, they must be blanched; see index). Combine well with other vegetables and cook quickly for 2 to 3 minutes.

5. Add pork strips and the remaining ingredients. Combine, cover skillet and cook for 3 minutes.

6. Add cooked Long Life Noodles and mix well. Taste for additional salt and pepper. Reheat on low flame only until noodles are hot and all the liquid absorbed. Serves 4 to 6.

LONG LIFE NOODLES

These are extremely long (about 3 feet), fresh egg noodles which can be purchased in oriental food stores. In texture they resemble thin spaghetti; when cooked, they remain firm but spongy. (You can substitute #8 spaghetti or fine egg noodles.)

For ¾ pound of noodles, bring 10 cups of water to a boil. Add salt and gradually add small amounts of noodles to keep water constantly boiling. Stir noodles from the bottom and cover. Cook 4-5 minutes and test for doneness. They should be firm, not soft and mushy. Drain in a colander and rinse first with cold water and then with hot. Stir and separate them with a fork, adding a few drops of sesame oil. Cover and set aside until needed. When ready to use you can first reheat by running them under very hot water and draining; or combine them with the pork and vegetables and heat.

Kamailio:

If it is not convenient for you to use barbecued roast pork, as at the Hawaii Kai Restaurant, you can substitute 1 pound uncooked lean pork (any cut) sliced into strips as per recipe. After step 2, heat 2 tablespoons oil in a skillet and sauté pork strips until all trace of pinkness is gone. Remove to a platter and continue with recipe.

You can make a number of new and interesting combinations by substituting or adding leftover chicken, meat, shrimp, crabmeat, ham, lobster, mushrooms and chopped spinach.

If you want a slightly different taste, you can add 2 tablespoons oyster sauce in step 5 instead of the soy sauce. The entire recipe can be made in advance and when needed reheated quickly. If too dry add ½ cup chicken broth, 2 tablespoons of soy sauce and 1 teaspoon sugar.

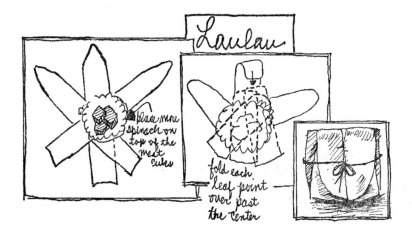

Laulau

One of the main dishes used for a luau, it consists of beef, pork, salted (not smoked) salmon, and taro tops wrapped in ti leaves and steamed in the imu. Since ti leaves and taro tops are difficult to obtain on the Mainland, we are substituting husks from ears of corn for the ti leaves, and spinach, Swiss chard or bokchoy for the taro tops. One ear of corn will yield about 14 husks; you can wrap them in foil and refrigerate the husks for about a week.

1½ pounds of beef
1½ pounds of pork
1½ pounds salted salmon, or fresh salmon steaks coated and rubbed with
    coarse salt and let stand 2-3 hours; rinse off excess salt before using
30 ti leaves or corn husks
1 pound fresh spinach, washed and drained
3 scallions, chopped fine
salt

Cut beef, pork and salmon into ten cubes each. If using ti leaves, remove the fibrous rib with a sharp knife. Cross 2 ti leaves or corn husks on flat surface making an X. If needed put a third ti leaf or corn husk through the center making a sort of six-pointed star. Place a little spinach in center of star; top with one cube each of beef, pork and fish. On these put one tablespoon of chopped scallion. Salt. Put a little more spinach on top and wrap by bringing each of the four or six points past the center, overlapping them as shown, page 145. Tie with string and place laulaus on a rack over a large covered pot in which there is 1 inch of boiling water. Steam for 3-4 hours. Remove string and serve hot with Poi (see index). Serves 10. You can steam the laulaus a day before the luau, and refrigerate them overnight. Reheat by steaming thoroughly.

Kamailio:

1. If you find 3 ti leaves or corn husks are too small to handle well, cross 4 or 5 in similar fashion. Or you can back the leaves with large squares of foil and fold and seal the laulaus with string.

2. Using a pressure cooker for steaming will cut your time considerably.

Korean Broiled Beef (Pul Koki or Kui)

1½ pounds steak (lean and tender)
¼ cup soy sauce
3 tablespoons oil (sesame preferably)
4 tablespoons pulverized sesame seeds (see index)
2 tablespoons sugar
1 small onion, chopped fine
1 scallion, chopped fine
1 garlic clove, minced
dash of fresh ground pepper
1 slice fresh ginger, minced (optional)

Cut steak into thin slices 3 inches long or into 3-inch squares. Combine remaining ingredients in a bowl and marinate steak slices for at least 1 hour at room temperature. Broil quickly 3-4 inches from flame, turning once. Serves 4 to 6.

Kamailio:

The Koreans also fry or panbroil meat using the same marinade. A little marinade is added during the frying process.

Short Ribs (*Kalbi Kui*) can also be broiled as above. However it is best to first score the short ribs in a checkerboard fashion. Cut each rib first across, almost down to the bone, and then do the same on the opposite side. The cuts should be ⅛-inch apart. Marinate overnight.

Korean Broiled Short Ribs: KALBI-KUI

1½" lengths

Cut meat before marinating

Pork (*Ton Yuk Kui*) and Chicken (*Tak Kui*) slices are delicious prepared like the steak.

Stuffed Meat Rolls, Filipino Style (Morcon)

A Holiday Treat

1 pound round steak, sliced thin
1 teaspoon salt
1 cup olive oil
¼ cup vinegar
1 garlic clove, minced
dash of fresh ground pepper
¼ pound thinly-sliced ham, cut in strips
2 hard-boiled eggs, sliced
½ pound ground pork
3 tablespoons sweet pickles, chopped
1 onion, chopped
2 tomatoes, chopped
2 celery stalks, chopped
salt and pepper to taste
stuffed olives and parsley for garnish

Cut round steak into 6 long, thin strips. Marinate in salt, olive oil, vinegar, garlic and pepper for 30 to 45 minutes. Remove steak from marinade, drain, and spread each slice with ham strips, egg slices, and a tablespoon of ground pork. Roll and tie with cord or skewer. Combine remaining ingredients and place in a covered pot. Put steak rolls on top. Cover and simmer for 1½ to 2 hours, until meat is tender. Shake pot occasionally to turn the meat. If needed, add a little water to pot. Remove strings before serving. Serve with pan sauces. Garnish with stuffed olives and parsley. Serves 6.

Kamailio:

Ham strips, egg slices and ground pork should be divided into six equal portions. You can cook meat rolls in advance and reheat when needed.

Flaming Tahitian Beef Brochette

Watch their eyes light up when you serve this dish!

MARINADE

2 tablespoons sesame seed oil
1 garlic clove, minced
2 tablespoons sherry
¾ cup soy sauce
¼ cup brown sugar
2 tablespoons wine vinegar
1 tablespoon ketchup
pinch of Five Spices, optional

3 pounds prime fillet of beef (cut into 1-1½ inch cubes)
2-3 sweet green peppers, cut in squares
2-3 sweet red peppers, cut in squares
18 medium size mushrooms, caps
12 cherry tomatoes
1 can (15-oz.) pineapple chunks, drained
skewers, 10-12 inches long

In a deep bowl, combine all marinade ingredients and mix well. Place beef cubes in marinade, tossing them several times so that meat is well coated. Marinate 2-3 hours at room temperature or overnight in refrigerator. Turn them, whenever you remember to.

Drain and arrange meat cubes on a 10-inch metal skewer, alternately with green pepper squares, red pepper squares, mushrooms, cherry tomatoes and pineapple. There should be about 3 to 4 meat cubes and 2 of each vegetable and pineapple on each skewer. Brush brochettes with marinade and broil 3 to 4 inches from flame; turn several times and brush with marinade. Watch that vegetables do not char. Plan on about 10 to 15 minutes. Remove to a large serving tray and flambée (see index) at the table.

At the Hawaii Kai Restaurant, the brochette is presented to you with a flair. It is flambéed on a small stand near your tables by the service captain and then removed from the skewers to your plate, which has meanwhile been colorfully enhanced with a mound of fried rice, a slice of spiced apple ring, in the center of which is placed an orange kumquat. Serves 6.

Kamailio:

1. Although the Hawaii Kai uses only prime fillet of beef, you may substitute any cut you prefer—skirt steak, sirloin, cross rib, round (tenderized) or even lamb.

2. The Islanders broil their brochettes on bamboo sticks which have been soaked in cold water for 1 hour.

3. Onion wedges or small boiled onions may be substituted or added to skewers.

4. You can thread strips of steak (cut thinly) alternately with vegetables accordion style.

5. Brochettes may be charcoal broiled outdoors—but must be watched so that vegetables do not char.

6. Plan on ½ pound meat per person, 3 mushrooms per person and 3 squares of each vegetable.

7. You might find it more convenient when broiling to suspend the brochettes across the edge of a low baking pan, filled with 1 inch of water. (This prevents spattering.)

8. Marinade can be heated and used as a sauce. Thicken with 2 tablespoons cornstarch mixed with ¼ cup of water and let cook until cornstarch loses its raw flavor and sauce becomes glazed—about 5 minutes.

Liu Liu:

All of the recipe, except for the actual broiling or charcoaling, may be prepared well in advance. To save time, after marinating the meat, place prepared brochettes (on the skewers) into a large flat pan and pour marinade over them. Let them remain thus until ready to broil.

Or, follow all recipe instructions but broil meat very rare. Reserve marinade. Refrigerate for 1-2 days covered with Saran wrap. Before serving, remove from refrigerator, baste with marinade and broil as per recipe.

Steak Singapura

A sizzling sliced, thick steak garnished with exotic Island vegetables makes a sure-to-win-compliments dinner.

> 1 steak per person, prime sirloin (12 to 16 ounces)
> 3 tablespoons oil
> 2 garlic cloves
> 3 stalks bokchoy or celery sliced into 1-inch diagonal sections, with some greens
> ½ pound fresh mushrooms, sliced lengthwise
> 3 scallions, cut into 1-inch sections
> 3-4 cups chicken broth
> 3 tablespoons soy sauce
> 1 teaspoon sugar
> dash of fresh ground pepper
> 2 teaspoons sherry wine
> 3 tablespoons cornstarch mixed with ¼ cup water
> 1 can (5 oz.) bamboo shoots, drained and rinsed
> 1 can (5 oz.) water chestnuts, drained, rinsed and sliced
> ½ pound fresh snow peas, or ½ package frozen

If you prepare all your items in advance, you can cook your vegetables and sauce as the steak is broiling and probably be finished before the steak is done. If you're afraid to try this, prepare sauce in advance, or cook part of it and finish while steak is broiling.

TO BROIL STEAK:

Place in broiler on rack 3 inches from flame; the right "doneness" for you is the way you like it. Cut near bone to see if it's right.

VEGETABLES AND SAUCE

Heat oil in a large skillet and add garlic and bokchoy or celery. Sauté and stir to coat vegetables. Cook for about 3 to 5 minutes on medium flame. Add mushrooms and cook quickly, tossing and turning, until they lose their resiliency. Add scallions; stir and cook for 2 minutes. Add chicken broth, soy sauce, sugar, pepper and sherry. Stir and bring to boiling point. Turn down heat and simmer for 5 minutes. Mix the cornstarch and water together and add slowly, stirring all the time. When sauce has thickened and is glazed, turn off heat. Add bamboo shoots, water chestnuts and snow peas. Mix well and cover skillet tightly. Let sit for 2 minutes or until steak is ready. Remove steak from broiler, cut into thick diagonal slices and place on individual sizzling steak platters (which have been heated in oven while steak was cooking). Pour sauce and vegetables over each steak and serve with fried rice (see index). Serves 6.

Liu Liu:

For a barbecue, sauce may be made earlier in the day, but omit thickening with cornstarch. While steak is broiling on the barbecue, the sauce and vegetables can be heated and completed.

Beef Mai Kai

Mai Kai means the "very best".

1½ pounds filet mignon, cut into slices ⅛ inch thick
4 tablespoons oil
2 garlic cloves, minced
¼ pound fresh mushrooms, sliced lengthwise
2 green peppers, cut into square pieces
3 cups chicken broth
2 tablespoons soy sauce
1 teaspoon sugar
dash of pepper, freshly ground
¼ teaspoon thick soy sauce (or brown gravy sauce, bead molasses type)
1 tablespoon sherry wine
2 tomatoes, peeled (see *Kamailio*), cut into wedges
2 tablespoons cornstarch mixed with 4 tablespoons water
2 scallions, minced
1 can (5 oz.) water chestnuts, drained, rinsed and sliced

1. Heat oil in a large skillet and add garlic. Sauté until golden, then add as much of the sliced steak as you can without crowding. Sauté quickly, just until steak loses its redness. Remove from pan to a platter. Repeat until all the steak has been sautéed.

2. If necessary, add additional oil to skillet and sauté mushrooms for 3 minutes, stirring to coat evenly.

3. Add green pepper and sauté only until wilted.

4. Add chicken broth, soy sauce, sugar, pepper and thick soy sauce. Stir well and heat until boiling point. Turn down heat and simmer.

5. Add sherry and tomatoes and stir.

6. Return steak slices to skillet and combine until heated throughout.

7. When piping hot, mix cornstarch mixture and add gradually to skillet. Stir until thickened and glazed.

8. Turn off flame; add scallions and water chestnuts. Cover tightly and let sit for 2 minutes. Served with fried rice at the Hawaii Kai. Makes 4 to 6 servings.

Kamailio:

1. If all the ingredients are prepared in advance, the entire recipe should take a little over 10 minutes. All that is needed to make it a complete meal is the "starch". Beef Mai Kai can also be served with white rice or Noodles Ono Loa (recipe given elsewhere; see index).

2. Filet mignon is used at the Hawaii Kai, but at home the most economical steak for this type of recipe is flank. Its flat, slab-like appearance, with a long grain running throughout in one direction, makes it easy to slice against the grain. If bought whole, it can be cut lengthwise, with the grain, into 3 or 4 strips, 2 inches wide. Use as much as you need for this recipe and freeze remaining strips. Incidentally, partially frozen meat slices much more easily than fresh meat.

3. Leftover roast beef or pot roast may be substituted for steak. It can be sliced or cubed. Merely omit sautéeing.

4. We like to use tiny whole cherry tomatoes in place of quartered ones. Tomatoes can be peeled easily by putting a fork through center and plunging them into boiling water for 1-2 minutes.

5. For company, we transfer the Mai Kai to an elegant silver tray and decorate with parsley, kumquats and drained, spiced apple rings or crabapples.

Liu Liu:

You can prepare the Beef Mai Kai in advance and refrigerate up to 2 days if you omit the water chestnuts and the cornstarch. Add them after reheating, since cornstarch thins out if reheated and the water chestnuts should be crisp.

Freeze the Beef Mai Kai in the same fashion.

Steak Bora Bora

filet mignon (8 ounces per person), cut into 1 to 1½-inch cubes

MARINADE

1 cup soy sauce
2 teaspoons sugar
2 tablespoons sesame oil (see index)
2 garlic cloves, minced

Combine marinade ingredients. Put steak cubes in a large bowl and sprinkle with marinade. Toss and turn to coat well. Marinate for at least 1 hour. You can cook the vegetables and sauce while steak is being marinated.

SAUCE AND VEGETABLES

3 tablespoons oil
2 garlic cloves, minced
2 slices fresh ginger root, minced (see index)
2 stalks bokchoy or celery cut in 1 inch-wide strips
½ pound fresh mushrooms, sliced lengthwise
3 scallions, cut into 1-inch sections
2 tablespoons oyster sauce
3-4 cups chicken broth
3 tablespoons soy sauce
1 teaspoon sugar
dash of fresh ground pepper
2 teaspoons sherry wine
3 tablespoons cornstarch mixed with ¼ cup water
1 can (5 oz.) bamboo shoots, drained and rinsed
1 can (5 oz.) water chestnuts, drained, rinsed and sliced
½ pound fresh snow peas or ½ box frozen

Heat oil in large skillet and add garlic and ginger root. Sauté until golden. Add bokchoy or celery. Cook for 3 minutes and add mushrooms; cook only until they begin to wilt. Add the scallions and mix well. Add oyster sauce, chicken broth, soy sauce, sugar, pepper and sherry. Bring to a boil and then simmer for 3 to 5 minutes. Stir and taste for further seasoning. Stir together the cornstarch and water and add slowly, mixing all the time. When sauce has thickened and is glazed, turn off heat. Add bamboo shoots, water chestnuts, and snow peas. Combine well and cover skillet. Let sit 2 minutes or until steak is **ready. Serves 6.**

TO COOK THE STEAK CUBES:

Remove from marinade and drain on absorbent paper. Heat a large skillet with 3 tablespoons oil and sauté steak quickly. Do not crowd. If the skillet is too small for all the steak, remove cubes to a heated platter as they are finished and cover. Place about six steak cubes on a sizzling steak platter (heated in oven) and pour the hot vegetables and sauce over them. Serve with fried rice (see index).

Kamailio:

At the Hawaii Kai Restaurant, only filet mignon is used. Needless to say, filet mignon is expensive for the average housewife, so you can substitute any good cut of steak. The thick chicken or minute steaks are good to use.

Liu Liu:

Vegetables and sauce can be made in advance up until thickened with cornstarch. Cornstarch must be added only prior to serving since it thins out during reheating. Steak tastes best when cooked just before eating.

Sukiyaki or Hekka

The Japanese custom is to cook Sukiyaki in a frying pan over a charcoal brazier or a hibachi at the table. However, it can also be cooked in an electric skillet, on the stove, over butane gas or on an open charcoal grill. It is most important that the food to be used is arranged attractively on a platter and in the order it is to be cooked.

    2 pounds steak (sirloin, flank or round), sliced thin against the grain
      into strips about 2 inches long
    3 tablespoons oil
    2 onions, sliced thin
    ½ pound mushrooms, thinly-sliced lengthwise
    3 stalks celery, sliced diagonally in 1-inch pieces
    ¼ cup sugar
    1 cup soy sauce
    1 cup chicken broth
    ¼ cup sake or sherry wine (optional)
    1 can bamboo shoots, sliced thin
    4 pieces tofu (bean curd, see index) cut into 1-inch cubes (optional)
    ½ pound watercress, spinach or bean sprouts
    4 scallions, cut into 2-inch lengths

Arrange meat and vegetables attractively in sections on a platter or tray, or divide them equally on 2 platters to make 2 separate batches of Sukiyaki. Heat oil in a large skillet and add steak, onions, mushrooms and celery. Sauté quickly until meat loses pinkness. Add sugar, soy sauce, chicken broth and sake or sherry. Cook for a few minutes and add bamboo shoots. Add tofu cubes, watercress (bean sprouts or spinach) and scallions. Stir well and cook only until watercress or spinach is wilted. Cover and serve. Guests are given individual bowls into which they break a raw egg. The hot Sukiyaki is placed on top and the egg becomes coddled due to the heat of the food. Serve with rice. Makes 4 to 6 servings.

Kamailio:

1. We mentioned above that meat and vegetables could be divided onto 2 platters to make two batches of the Sukiyaki. This is necessary because the skillet cannot hold all the meat and vegetables at the same time. Therefore, spices and other ingredients should also be divided equally for the two batches.

2. Chinese long rice, or vermicelli (see index) is sometimes added to this recipe. If used, it should be soaked in warm water for 30 minutes and then cut into 3-inch lengths. It is added with the bamboo shoots.

3. Chicken or pork can be substituted for steak. Cut into 1 to 1½-inch pieces.

4. Peeled tomatoes can be added with the vegetables.

5. Canned mushrooms can be substituted for fresh but are not as tasty.

6. Guests can cook their own Sukiyaki at the table if they wish.

Liu Liu:

Clean, cut and arrange vegetables on platters. Cover and refrigerate in advance. Slice meat (best done when partially frozen). Have ready on a separate tray the measured amounts of remaining ingredients.

Polynesian Beef, Chicken or Shrimp Fondue

Poi oh Poi . . . Hawaiian Fondue!

The Swiss are famous for their Yodeling.
The Hawaiians are famous for their Hula Dancing.
The Swiss are good on Skis.
The Hawaiians are great on Surfboards.
The Swiss make wonderful watches.
The Hawaiians make the finest flower garlands.
The Swiss make Fondue.
The Hawaiians make Fondue too!

The Hawaiians make Fondue?
That's right! And what's more—they make an exotic tangy Fondue that can be eaten with one-, two- or three-finger poi. So if you're fond of Fondue, and who isn't, why not try this pleasing, palatable, Polynesian potpourri . . . it's finger-licking good!

3 pounds sirloin steak, chicken or shrimp

MARINADE:

1 cup soy sauce
⅓ cup brown sugar
2 tablespoons sherry
2 cloves garlic, minced
2 slices fresh ginger root, minced
1 scallion, chopped fine
dash of fresh pepper
3 cups oil for fondue pot

Cut steak or chicken into one-inch cubes. Shrimp should be left whole, cleaned and deveined.

Combine marinade ingredients and pour over cubes of beef, chicken or whole shrimp. Toss and turn to coat well. Marinate overnight in refrigerator, or 3-4 hours at room temperature. Drain and arrange attractively on a large serving tray with salad greens, parsley or watercress.

Fill the fondue pot ½ full of oil. Heat to about 375° F. (you can test oil with a small cube of bread; if it cooks brown and crisp in half

a minute, the oil is hot enough for fonduing). Adjust burner so that oil will remain at the boiling point throughout the meal.

Each guest spears a cube of meat, chicken or whole shrimp with the fondue fork or a skewer and dunks it into the hot oil, cooking it to his taste—10 to 12 seconds for rare and almost a minute for well done.

Malama pono! (be careful). Guests must transfer meat to a dinner fork as the fondue fork or skewer will be very hot.

Serve with hot rice and a green salad. 6-10 servings.

Kamailio:

A combination of beef, chicken and shrimp can be used for the fondue.

Another style of fonduing, particularly good with pork: marinate 3 pounds of boned pork (tenderloin, butt or shoulder) in above marinade as per recipe. Drain and slice thinly (2 inches by 3). Roll pork slices and arrange them attractively on a large platter or tray which has been covered with salad greens, parsley or watercress. Substitute 3 cups of chicken broth for the oil and continue with above recipe.

Butterfly Steak

    1 filet mignon per person
    ½ cup soy sauce
    1 teaspoon garlic powder
    1 teaspoon fresh ginger root, minced (optional)
    dash of fresh pepper

Slice the filet mignon through center to ½ inch from the end and open it out gently into the shape of a butterfly wing. Place in a large shallow pan. Make a mixture of the remaining ingredients and pour over the steaks, tossing to coat. Marinate 3-4 hours or overnight, turning occasionally. Broil in pan (not on rack) 3 inches from flame, about 3 to 4 minutes on each side. Baste steaks with sauce when turning. Remove to sizzling steak platters and spoon the pan juices over steaks.

Beef with Peanut Sauce

1 large onion, chopped
3 tablespoons oil
2 pounds beef, cut into 1-inch cubes (any tender cut)
2 tablespoons soy sauce
1 teaspoon sugar
½ teaspoon brown bean sauce (see index)
4 cups chicken broth
½ cup peanut butter (crunchy style)
salt and pepper to taste
12 cherry tomatoes, peeled (see index)

Sauté onions in oil in a large skillet until soft. Add beef cubes and brown on all sides. Stir in soy sauce, sugar, brown bean sauce and chicken broth. Mix well and simmer for 45 minutes. Add peanut butter, salt, and pepper. Stir and cook for 30 minutes or until beef is tender. Add cherry tomatoes and cook for 5 more minutes. Serve over rice. Makes 6 servings.

Liu Liu:

The recipe (up until cherry tomatoes are added) can be cooked in advance and refrigerated or frozen.

Hawaiian Hamburgers

2 pounds ground beef
½ cup soy sauce
1 tablespoon sugar
1 teaspoon salt
dash of fresh ground pepper
1 teaspoon fresh ginger root, minced
1 garlic clove, minced
¼ can bean sprouts, rinsed and drained
1 can (5 oz.) water chestnuts, drained, rinsed and chopped
3 scallions, chopped fine

Combine meat with ¼ cup of soy sauce, sugar, salt, pepper, ginger root and garlic. Mix until well blended. Shape into 12 large thin patties. Combine bean sprouts, water chestnuts and scallions. Spread 2 or 3 tablespoons of this mixture over 6 patties. Cover with the other 6. Pinch edges together. Brush with remaining soy sauce. Broil 3 to 4 minutes on each side, 4 inches from flame, basting with soy sauce during cooking. Serve—but not in buns please! Makes 6 servings.

Polynesian Meatloaf

The lowly meatloaf becomes a conversation piece when presented in Island fashion. Not only is it lovely to look at, but also delightful to eat.

> 2 pounds ground beef, pork or combination of the two
> ½ teaspoon salt
> ⅛ teaspoon fresh pepper
> ½ cup coarse bread crumbs
> 2 cloves garlic, minced
> 1 teaspoon paprika
> 1 small onion, grated
> 2 tablespoons oyster sauce
> 1 tablespoon brown sugar
> 2 eggs, beaten with ¼ cup soy sauce

Combine all ingredients well. Mixture should not be too soft. Line a 5 x 9 x 3-inch meat loaf pan with oiled silver foil, extending the foil over the edge for 2 inches to aid you in lifting out the loaf. Wet hands and, on wax paper, shape the meat mixture with your hands to make an oval loaf. Put in pan; smooth it to an even and well-shaped appearance. Bake for 1 hour in preheated oven, 375° F. Cool.

MEANWHILE MAKE THE SAUCE

> ¼ cup honey
> 1 can (20 oz.) pineapple slices drained, and slices reserved
> 1 teaspoon hoisin sauce, (see index)
> 2 cups of chicken broth
> ¼ cup soy sauce
> 1 tablespoon brown sugar
> salt and pepper to taste
> 2 tablespoons cornstarch mixed with 4 tablespoons water

Polynesian Meat Loaf

① tinfoil liner

②

don't forget that the pineapple slices expand the meat loaf...use a properly sized platter

FOR GARNISH

parsley or watercress, 1 can (16 oz.) spiced crab apples, drained
    well, 1 jar (3 oz.) maraschino cherries, drained

In a saucepan combine all ingredients except cornstarch paste, and
heat to boiling point. Turn down heat; stir cornstarch paste and add
slowly to pan until thickened. Remove from heat and cover. When meat
loaf is cool enough to handle, loosen sides of the loaf and lift onto a
flat surface. Loosen bottom carefully and cut into 1-inch slices. With a
spatula, gently remove to a very large heatproof baking pan or tray,
retaining the shape. Place a pineapple slice in between each slice,
raising it 1 inch above the meat loaf so that it is visible (your meat
loaf will become twice as long as previously). You can use two bamboo
or metal skewers to hold the ends together. Pour a little of the sauce
over it and return to oven to heat thoroughly. When ready to serve,
heat sauce and put into a server. Take meat loaf out of oven. Using a
fancy pick, secure a maraschino cherry to pineapple. Decorate with
spiced crab apple and parsley or watercress. Serves 6.

Kamailio:

To achieve an attractive presentation of this dish, it is necessary to have the proper size and shaped ovenproof or heat-resistant platter to reassemble the meat loaf on and serve. The meat loaf can be baked in advance and refrigerated or frozen. It can be reassembled early in the day and then reheated later. The sauce can be made in advance (without cornstarch mixture) and reheated when needed. (Add cornstarch mixture just before reheating.)

Meatballs Bali Bali

2 pounds chopped beef, pork or half and half
1 teaspoon salt
¼ teaspoon fresh pepper
½ cup coarse bread crumbs
2 garlic cloves, minced
1 teaspoon paprika
1 small onion, grated
2 eggs, beaten with ¼ cup water

Combine all ingredients well. Mixture should be soft and pliable. Wet hands and form into small balls.

SAUCE

½ cup cornstarch
3 tablespoons oil
1 garlic clove, minced
1 slice fresh ginger, minced
1 small onion, chopped fine
1 green pepper, cut in strips
1 red pepper, cut in strips
1 can pineapple chunks, (13 ounces)
2 cups chicken broth
3 tablespoons soy sauce
¼ cup vinegar
3 tablespoons brown sugar
2 tablespoons honey
½ teaspoon Five Spices or cinnamon
salt and pepper to taste

FOR GARNISH

toasted almonds, chopped chives or shredded coconut

Spread cornstarch on large sheet of wax paper or foil. Roll meatballs in this, coating well. Heat oil in large skillet and brown meatballs.

Add more oil if necessary. Remove to a platter covered with absorbent paper. Drain all but 2 tablespoons oil from skillet. Sauté garlic, ginger and onion just for a minute. Add green and red pepper strips and sauté until translucent only. Remove from skillet. Drain juice from pineapple chunks and add juice to skillet along with remaining ingredients. Add meatballs, stir and simmer for 10 minutes. Return red and green pepper strips to skillet and add pineapple chunks. Combine and cook for 3 to 5 minutes. If a thicker sauce is desired make a thin paste of 2 tablespoons cornstarch diluted with water and add slowly until desired consistency is reached. Place on large platter or tray and sprinkle with toasted almonds, chopped chives or shredded coconut. Serves 6 as a main dish.

Kamailio:

1. Maraschino cherries or green grapes add a touch of color to this dish and can be added just after thickening the sauce.

2. Crunchy, sliced water chestnuts can be added also at that time.

3. Used as a hot hors d'oeuvre, these meatballs look elegant in a chafing dish.

4. When preparing a large number of meatballs, you'll find it easier to brown them on a greased shallow baking pan in a 375° F. oven. Turn and shake them to brown evenly. This can be done in advance and meatballs refrigerated 1 to 3 days, or frozen (wrap, label and seal). Or, the entire recipe can be completed and refrigerated or frozen. Do not thicken with cornstarch until ready to serve. Heat meatballs on top of, or in stove.

Beef in Lettuce Leaves

Hawaiian version of the Mexican taco

3 tablespoons oil
2 garlic cloves, minced
1½ pounds chopped beef
8 large mushrooms, chopped or cut coarsely
½ pound fresh peas or ½ package frozen
4 tablespoons oyster sauce
2 tablespoons sherry wine
3 tablespoons soy sauce
1 teaspoon salt
fresh ground pepper
2 tablespoons cornstarch mixed with 3 tablespoons water
½ can water chestnuts, drained, rinsed, and diced
2 scallions, chopped
1 head Iceberg or Bibb lettuce

Heat oil in a large skillet and add garlic and ground beef. Sauté until meat is no longer red. Remove to a platter. If need be, add additional oil, heat, and add mushrooms and peas. Sauté until soft. Add oyster sauce, sherry, soy sauce, salt and pepper. Stir well to combine. Return meat to skillet and reheat. Mix cornstarch and water and add gradually to skillet, stirring until thickened. Add water chestnuts, stir and cover. The entire mixture can now be placed in a heated casserole or chafing dish and garnished with chopped scallions or toasted, slivered almonds. Keep hot. Core the lettuce and separate leaves to a serving platter. To serve, place a heaping tablespoon of meat mixture a little below center of each leaf; turn bottom part of leaf up over the filling. Bring the right and left side over to the center and roll up. Serve as an hors d'oeuvre, appetizer or entrée.

Korean Fried Liver (Kahn Juhn)

All Korean fried foods are prepared in the following manner. You can substitute meat, seafood and most vegetables for the liver and serve with a vinegar-soy sauce (or shoyu as they say it), or Korean Hot Sauce. See below.

1 pound beef liver
2 eggs, beaten with 2 tablespoons water
½ cup flour combined with 1 teaspoon salt and ⅛ teaspoon fresh ground pepper
3 tablespoons oil (sesame preferably)

Boil liver in water to cover. Drain and cut away gristle and skin. Cut into ⅛-inch thin slices. Dip into egg. Dredge with flour and dip back into egg. Fry quickly and then cut into small strips, 2 inches by 1 inch. Serve with Vinegar-Shoyu Sauce or Korean Hot Sauce. Serves 4.

In place of liver, the following foods can be fried in the same manner; however eliminate the parboiling: Shrimp (*Sao-o*), oysters (*Kool*), fish (*Sang-Suhn*), lobster (*Ke*); eggplant (*Kah-ri*), onion (*Ok-chong*), potatoes (*Kam-ja*), sweet potatoes (*Ko-koo-mah*), squash (*Ho-pahk*), spinach (*Sikimch'i*), and string beans (*Cheng t'ai kongla*) are all cut into slices or strips, *juhn*—fried as above, and served with Vinegar-Soy Sauce or Hot Sauce.

VINEGAR-SHOYU SAUCE

Combine equal amounts of soy sauce and vinegar (6 tablespoons soy sauce, 6 tablespoons vinegar). Add 3 tablespoons sugar and mix well. To serve: put 2 tablespoons of the sauce into individual dishes. Sprinkle each dish with chopped pine nuts which have been toasted. Individual dishes are used because all foods are dipped into them before eating.

KOREAN HOT SAUCE

1 teaspoon oil (sesame preferably)
1 teaspoon sugar
1 teaspoon sesame seeds, pulverized (see index)
1 scallion, minced
1 garlic clove, minced
1 slice fresh ginger root, minced
3 tablespoons soy sauce
¼ cup water
Tabasco sauce to taste
pine nuts, toasted and chopped

Combine all ingredients except pine nuts. Simmer until heated. Serve hot in individual dishes; sprinkle with toasted pine nuts.

Curry

Curry is controversial. Everyone has some favorite spice that he or she thinks is *the* one to use in making the sauce. You can make your own curry by combining turmeric, coriander, cinnamon, cardamon, ginger, cumin, pepper, chilies, cayenne, etc., or you can buy a good prepared curry and add a touch of this or that. Vegetables, such as carrots, green string beans, peppers, cucumbers, tomatoes, mushrooms, lemons and limes can be added. Coconut milk (see index), yogurt or fresh milk will vary the flavor. Some people prefer to simmer the sauce for several hours until thickened. Others will thicken it with cornstarch. The important thing is how *you* like it.

Basic Curry for Meat and Chicken

—and shrimp and lobster too

¼ pound sweet butter
2 cloves garlic, minced
1 onion, chopped fine
3 stalks celery, chopped
1 green pepper, chopped
1 apple, peeled and chopped
2 tablespoons curry powder
3 cups chicken broth
2 tablespoons sherry
2 tablespoons soy sauce
1 teaspoon sugar
½ teaspoon salt
dash of fresh pepper
2 tablespoons cornstarch mixed with 4 tablespoons water
hot boiled rice
1 scallion, chopped

In a large skillet, melt butter and add garlic, onion, celery and green pepper. Sauté until translucent. Add apple and curry powder. Stir and cook for about 3 minutes until apple is soft. Add chicken broth, sherry, soy sauce, sugar, salt and pepper. Combine well and add your *cooked* shrimp, lobster meat or chicken. Heat thoroughly; stir cornstarch paste and add gradually until thickened. Pour over hot boiled rice and sprinkle with chopped scallion.

At the Hawaii Kai Restaurant, curries are accompanied by a monkey-pod wood Lazy Susan filled with sambals. These are shredded coconut, plump raisins, slivered almonds and chutney.

Kamailio:

1. I have not stated amounts for the shrimp, lobster, chicken and meat. If two pounds of cooked shrimp are enough for your family, use that amount. The same holds true for beef, chicken and lobster.

2. Curry is a wonderful way to use up leftover meat and chicken. Just cut into cubes. Gravy can be substituted for chicken broth.

3. Curry is exciting and showy when used on a buffet table. The center of the table could hold a large, beautiful chafing dish filled with hot rice and curry, and around it an assortment of sambals in individual handsome bowls.

4. Another attractive way to serve the curry is in individual coconut shells. (See index under Chicken Keo Keo for cutting coconut shells).

5. Don't stick to the commonplace sambals only, vary them with crumbled, crisp bacon, chopped cashew nuts, fresh or crystallized ginger root, mandarin orange segments, cucumber cubes, tomato wedges or mini-tomatoes, pine nuts, coconut chips, sliced bananas (sprinkled with lemon juice), peanuts, chopped egg yolk, diced pineapple, button mushrooms (canned), sour cream or yogurt.

6. Pappadum (a thin, spiced wafer type of bread) is a novelty (can be purchased in gourmet food shops). These are fried in deep fat and puff up beautifully. Serve cold.

All of the recipe can be prepared, cooked and refrigerated ahead of time. However, the cornstarch paste must be added just before serving (but it too must be cooked until the sauce glazes).

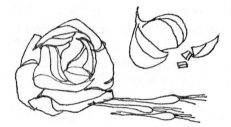

SALADS AND SAUCES
THAT YOU CAN RELISH

Getting tired of those routine lettuce-bed salads? Is your condiment and garnish tray lacking in relish? Is your salad dressing sinking to the bottom of the bowl unnoticed? Are you in a pickle when it comes to perking up a leftover? Don't despair—there's a whole, wide, wonderful world of Hawaiian salads and relishes just waiting to go to work for you.

First—there's the ever-popular Kim Chee (pickled cabbage). It may not sound like much but it's a perennial favorite in the Islands. Then there's pickled mushrooms, pickled cucumbers, and naturally pickled pineapple. Used individually as a garnish or as part of the meal they can be a zestful departure from the ordinary.

When it comes to creative salad making, Hawaiians are totally uninhibited. With equal ease they will use fruit, fish, chicken, pork, vegetables and even rice (often mixed) to make a surprisingly varied and tasty salad.

The sauces are best described by that jack-of-all phrases that means anything and everything, thingamajigs and whatdoyoucallits. In short, they're *da kine* you use for dipping, or to heat leftovers in, or for marinating or—you know, *da kine*.

Island Shrimp Salad

Don't be awed by the list of ingredients. They're all tossed together with a minimum of trouble . . . no pilikia, as the Hawaiians say. There are two versions. We prefer the one using a bit of gelatin, which is just enough to mold the salad perfectly but does not make it gooky. Try it and see.

WITHOUT GELATIN:

1½ pounds cooked shrimp (any size)
5 celery stalks, finely chopped
1 medium onion, grated
4 slices white bread, crusts removed and diced
3 tablespoons lemon juice
4 tablespoons ketchup
2 tablespoons white prepared horseradish
1 tablespoon vinegar
1 teaspoon Worcestershire sauce
1 tablespoon soy sauce
½ teaspoon sugar
salt and pepper to taste
mayonnaise

FOR GARNISH:

1 can (5 oz.) water chestnuts, drained, rinsed and sliced thin
1 red pepper cut into match thin strips
1 olive
lemon rosettes (see page 170) or wedges dipped into chopped parsley
    or sprinkled with paprika
cherry tomatoes
avocado chunks
pickled mushrooms (see index)
cucumber canoes (see page 171)
jade trees (see page 172)
greens (parsley, watercress, lettuce etc.)

1. Cut cooked shrimp in half or thirds, reserving 2 whole ones for garnish.

2. In a large bowl, combine all ingredients thoroughly. Add only enough mayonnaise to bind ingredients together. Do not use too much since mixture will run. Taste for additional seasonings. You might like a bit more horseradish.

3. Spoon into a 1-quart fish mold. Pack down well with back of spoon. If any salad is left over, reserve. Refrigerate 2 hours or overnight and then drain excess liquid from mold. Refill with reserved salad and refrigerate until 1 hour before serving.

4. To unmold, run blade of knife around edges. Place the platter

you will use over the top of mold and invert. If necessary, restore shape.

5. Use strips of pepper for tail and fins. Sliced water chestnuts for scales. Circle the two shrimp for the eye. Put the olive in center.

6. Surround fish with greens and decorate with lemon rosettes, cherry tomatoes etc.

WITH GELATIN:

1 envelope unflavored gelatin
¼ cup cold water

Soften gelatin in cold water. Heat in top of double boiler until liquified and clear. Cool and add after step 2. Mix thoroughly into shrimp salad and continue with recipe.

LEMON ROSETTES

Draw a pencil line around center of lemon (a large oval shape is best). With the point of a sharp knife, make a deep V through the center of the line. Continue making V's, connecting each one to the next (VVV) until you reach the first one. Pull apart and dip halves into chopped parsley or dust with paprika.

Island Shrimp Salad

cut from scallions

Shrimp and Pineapple Salad with Mauna Lau Dressing

1 pineapple, peeled and cored (see index)
1 pound cooked small shrimp
1 can (5 oz.) water chestnuts, drained, rinsed and sliced
1 head Boston or Bibb lettuce
dressing (recipe below)
toasted sesame seeds for garnish (see below)

Cut pineapple fruit into small tidbits. Combine with shrimp and water chestnuts. Line a salad bowl with lettuce leaves and arrange salad mixture on them. When ready to serve, pour dressing over the salad and garnish with toasted sesame seeds.

MAUNA LAU DRESSING:

½ cup cider vinegar
¼ cup pineapple juice
¾ teaspoon salt
1 tablespoon sugar
dash of fresh pepper
½ cup salad oil
½ cup sesame oil (see index)
1 teaspoon lemon juice

Combine all ingredients in a jar and shake well. Will keep 2 to 3 weeks refrigerated.

Kamailio:

Canned pineapple tidbits (13 ounces) can be used in place of fresh. Use juices in dressing.

To toast sesame seeds, brown lightly in a dry pan, tossing and turning constantly over a low flame.

Oahu Cucumber Canoes and Outriggers

2 large cucumbers, 8"-10" long
1 teaspoon salt
¼ cup vinegar
½ cup water
4 tablespoons sugar
dash of fresh pepper
3 water chestnuts, diced
2 scallions, chopped fine

Slice cucumbers in half from end to end. With a spoon, scoop out cucumber meat, leaving a ¼-inch shell. Dice cucumber meat. Combine with remaining ingredients and marinate for at least 2 hours or overnight. When ready, fill cucumber boats with drained vinaigrette and salt to taste. Thread one 4-inch square of colored paper through an 8-inch bamboo skewer, one for each cucumber canoe, and insert upright in center of boat.

An outrigger canoe effect can be easily made by inserting bamboo skewers through the cucumber 1 inch from each end. Cross each skewer with another one at right angles and tie with colored thread or cord.

JADE TREES AND SCALLION BRUSHES

Cut off the leafy green tops and the root end of a thick scallion, leaving about 4 to 5 inches of firm stalk (reserve leafy tops in a plastic container for garnish in other dishes). Make at least 4 parallel cuts 1 inch deep at one end. Then make at least 4 more cuts horizontally across the first ones as if forming a checkerboard. If you score the scallion at the leaf end only, you will have a jade tree. If scored at both ends you have a scallion brush. Soak scallions for 1 hour in ice water so that ends will open and curl. Drain and use in salads or as a relish with hoisin sauce.

Lanai Chicken Salad

      4 cups cooked chicken meat, diced
      1½ cups chopped celery
      ½ small onion, grated fine
      1 can green grapes, drained well or 1 cup fresh
      1 can (13 oz.) pineapple tidbits, drained well
      1 cup mayonnaise
      salt and pepper to taste
      3 small coconuts, halved

Combine the first seven ingredients and refrigerate. Using a large scoop, heap salad into a halved coconut (see below). Decorate center of salad with a sprig of watercress. Serve cold.

About Coconuts

The coconuts can be cut in half with a saw. If they do not sit well, saw a sliver off bottom. Drain coconut milk as soon as saw has cut through. Sandpaper edges if need be. Rinse. Or, coax your butcher to cut them through with his bandsaw. It's worth the trouble of cutting the coconuts since they can be reused—just rinse them and store in the freezer between parties.

Kapaa Curried Chicken Salad

3 cups diced cooked chicken
¾ cup chopped celery
1 green pepper, chopped
1 apple, peeled and chopped
¼ cup chopped nuts (cashews, peanuts, etc.)
¼ cup white raisins
2 teaspoons salt
1 teaspoon curry powder
dash of fresh pepper
1 cup mayonnaise
½ pint commercial sour cream
6 large lettuce leaves

Combine all ingredients, except lettuce, in a large bowl. Chill well and then, with a large scoop, make a mound on each lettuce cup. Garnish with additional chopped nuts or raisins. *Ono* (delicious)!

Pahoa Crabmeat and Cucumber Salad

2 cucumbers
2 cups crabmeat
4 tablespoons soy sauce
3 tablespoons vinegar
1 teaspoon sugar
2 tablespoons sesame oil
6 lettuce leaves

Wash and split cucumbers in half lengthwise. Remove seeds and shred cucumbers on a coarse grater. Combine with crabmeat. Mix remaining ingredients except lettuce and pour over crabmeat and cucumbers. Toss and serve in lettuce cups.

Pickled Radishes

    1 bunch red radishes with fresh leaves
    1 teaspoon coarse salt
    2 teaspoons soy sauce
    2 tablespoons white vinegar
    3 tablespoons sugar
    2 teaspoons sesame oil

Wash radishes and trim leaves. Reserve. With the flat of a broad-bladed knife, crush radishes gently (do not break). Wash leaves and cut into small sections (½ inch). Mix salt with radishes and leaves and let stand 30 minutes. Drain. Mix remaining ingredients and pour over radishes and leaves. Marinate for at least 3 hours. Serve cold as a relish. Accordion and rosed radishes may be substituted.

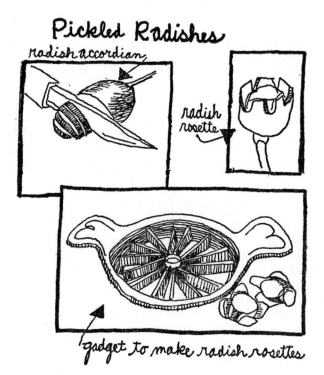

Pickled Radishes

radish accordian

radish rosette

gadget to make radish rosettes

Pickled Mushrooms Hilo

24 to 30 small button mushrooms
3 tablespoons soy sauce
4 tablespoons vinegar
2 teaspoons sugar
2 tablespoons sesame oil
2 garlic cloves, crushed
1 teaspoon onion powder

Rinse mushrooms in a colander and dry. Combine remaining ingredients in a saucepan and bring to a boil. Pour over mushrooms and cool. Marinate overnight. To serve, drain mushrooms but reserve marinade for the mushrooms you do not use. Will keep for two weeks in refrigerator.

Orange and Spinach Salad Molokai

1 pound raw spinach, washed, drained, and stemmed
¼ pound fresh mushrooms, sliced lengthwise or 1 can (4 oz.) sliced and drained
1 can (5 oz.) water chestnuts, rinsed, drained and diced
4 navel oranges, peeled and diced
¼ cup salad oil
2 tablespoons vinegar
2 tablespoons orange juice
1 tablespoon soy sauce
¼ teaspoon dry mustard
¼ teaspoon salt
dash of fresh pepper

Tear spinach coarsely into a large salad bowl. Add mushrooms, water chestnuts, and oranges. In a jar, combine oil, vinegar, orange juice, soy, mustard, salt and pepper. Shake and pour over salad. Toss well to coat solids with liquid.

Samoan Salad

DRESSING

1 package (8 oz.) cream cheese, softened
¾ cup mayonnaise
2 tablespoons vinegar
pinch of Five Spices
½ teaspoon sugar
½ teaspoon salt
1 tablespoon grated onion

Combine all ingredients well and refrigerate.

SALAD

lettuce leaves
2 cups fresh or canned drained pineapple cubes
2 cups tomato cubes, peeled (see index)
1 cup red and green pepper, chopped
1 cup cucumber, cubed

Line salad bowl with crisp lettuce leaves (or hearts of palm). Add remaining ingredients. Toss with Samoan dressing.

Kapaa Sesame Salad

1 head lettuce
1 bunch watercress, stems removed
2 cucumbers, pared and sliced thinly
1 can mandarin oranges (16 ounces), drained

Break washed and dried lettuce and watercress into bite-size pieces in a large salad bowl (reserve some whole watercress leaves for garnish). Arrange cucumber slices in a circle in center of bowl. Fill center with mandarin oranges. Circle edge of bowl with alternate slices of cucumber and mandarin oranges. Garnish with watercress. Just before serving, drizzle Sesame Seed Dressing over salad and toss lightly.

SESAME SEED DRESSING

Combine ½ cup salad oil with 4 tablespoons vinegar, 2 tablespoons sugar, 2 tablespoons juice from mandarin oranges, 2 teaspoons soy sauce and 2 teaspoons toasted sesame seeds in a jar. Cover and shake to mix.

Kamailio:

Other fruits (peaches, pineapple chunks, pears, etc.) can be substituted for the mandarin oranges.

Cucumbers look pretty when left unpeeled, scored deeply from top to bottom with the tines of a fork, and then sliced thin.

Chinese Salad with Sesame Dressing

> 1 can (5 oz.) water chestnuts, drained, rinsed and sliced
> 1 red sweet pepper, chopped very coarse
> 2 scallions, minced
> 2 celery stalks, sliced thin, diagonally
> ½ pound fresh blanched bean sprouts (see index), or 8 oz. canned, rinsed and drained on paper towels
> 2 stalks celery cabbage, shredded
> ¼ cup toasted slivered almonds, for garnish

Arrange the vegetables in a large salad bowl. Toss the salad with the dressing below and let it stand for 30 minutes before serving to absorb the flavors. When ready to serve, garnish with almonds.

SESAME OIL DRESSING

> ½ cup sesame oil
> 3 tablespoons soy sauce
> ½ teaspoon sugar
> 1 tablespoon lemon juice
> fresh pepper to taste

Combine all ingredients in a jar and shake well.

Papaya Salad

> 1 head Romaine lettuce, torn into bite-size pieces
> 1 bunch watercress, stems removed
> 1 pound cooked shrimp, lobster or crabmeat
> 1 papaya, peeled, halved, and seeds scooped out
> 1 can (4 oz.) hearts of palm, drained

Using a large salad bowl, place lettuce in center and watercress leaves on top. Mound cooked seafood in the center. Slice papaya and arrange slices pinwheel fashion around the seafood. Divide hearts of palm and surround papaya slices evenly. Decorate center with a few watercress leaves.

DRESSING

¼ cup salad oil
¼ cup pineapple juice
2 tablespoons white vinegar
2 tablespoons ketchup
salt and fresh ground pepper to taste

Mix above ingredients together in a jar and just before serving, pour dressing over salad. Mix lightly until well coated and serve.

Filipino Stuffed Tomatoes (Insaladang Camatis)

6 large tomatoes
1½ cups fresh pineapple, chopped or 1 can (8 oz.) crushed
1 slice minced fresh ginger
1 teaspoon lemon or lime juice
¼ cup chopped roasted peanuts
tangy French dressing
salt
6 parsley sprigs
6 lettuce leaves

Filipino STUFFED tomatoes

don't cut through bottom

stem end down

Cut a slice off stem end of tomatoes and with a sharp knife or spoon end, *akahele* (carefully), hollow them out. Chop pulp fine and combine with pineapple, ginger, lemon juice and peanuts. Mix with French dressing and season to taste with salt. Fill cavities of tomatoes with mixture and heap above tomato edges. Round off nicely. Chill. Garnish with parsley sprigs and place on a lettuce leaf when ready to serve. Serves 6.

Kamailio:

Instead of hollowing out the tomatoes, cut each tomato (stem end down) into six wedges, cutting *to* but not *through* the base of the tomato. To cut into six equal wedges, cut tomato in half and divide each half into three segments, like flower petals. Spread wedges apart gently and sprinkle with salt. Place on lettuce leaves and fill centers with stuffing.

Frozen Island Fruit Salad

    1 quart commercial sour cream
    3 tablespoons lemon juice
    dash of salt
    ½ cup maraschino cherries, chopped
    1 can (13 oz.) crushed pineapple, drained
    ½ cup sugar
    salad greens (lettuce, chicory, endive for garnish)
    6 kumquats (for garnish)

Mix all ingredients together lightly except the salad greens and kumquats. Put into 6 small individual molds and freeze only until firm. Unmold and arrange on salad greens. Garnish with kumquats.

Spring Kim Chee (A Korean Side Dish)

Kim chee is a relish made from raw vegetables and served at almost every meal as one would serve sauerkraut or cole slaw.

    1 celery cabbage, washed
    3 tablespoons salt combined with 3 cups water
    2 scallions, chopped
    1 garlic clove, minced
    1 teaspoon chopped, red chili pepper (optional)
    1 tablespoon sugar
    1 slice fresh ginger root, minced
    1 small onion, sliced thin

Cut celery cabbage into ½-inch squares. Cover with salted water and let stand. After cabbage has stood for 2 hours, squeeze tightly to remove water. Place cabbage in a large jar or plastic container. Add remaining ingredients and combine well. Leave out for one day to marinate at room temperature and then refrigerate. Can be kept for several weeks in refrigerator.

Kamailio:

Cucumbers (*o-i kim chee*) can be prepared in the same fashion. Use 3 large cucumbers in place of celery cabbage. Or, combine with celery cabbage.

Pickled Cucumbers, Japanese Style (Kyuri Namasu)

A "must" at Japanese weddings and all big occasions.

2 cucumbers
½ cup white vinegar
½ cup water
1 slice fresh ginger root, minced
3 tablespoons sugar
2 tablespoons soy sauce

Peel cucumbers and, with the tines of a fork, dig deeply into meat of cucumbers from top to bottom. Continue this all the way around. Slice cucumbers thinly. Slices will resemble a flower. Mix remaining ingredients and pour over cucumber slices. Refrigerate and serve in individual small dishes.

Kamailio:

In Hawaii, a bit of whitefish, dried shrimp or seaweed (*wakame*) is sometimes added to sauce. Carrots and lotus root (see index) may be added to the cucumbers. Prepare carrots in same fashion as cucumbers.

Bean Sprout Vinaigrette

> 1 can (16 oz.) bean sprouts or ½ pound fresh bean sprouts, blanched
>   (see index)
> 1 cup water
> ½ cup white vinegar
> 3 to 4 tablespoons sugar
> 1 garlic clove, minced
> 3 scallions, chopped
> ½ teaspoon salt
> dash of fresh pepper

Rinse bean sprouts thoroughly with cold water and drain well. Combine all ingredients in a bowl or jar and marinate for several hours or overnight (or even several days) in refrigerator. Turn occasionally. Drain before serving; serve with meat or chicken dishes.

Native Vinaigrette

> 1 large cucumber
> 1 fresh pineapple
> 1 cup water
> ½ cup white vinegar
> ¼ cup sugar
> dash of salt

Cut cucumber and pineapple fruit into 2-inch fingers (see index). Combine remaining ingredients and marinate cucumber and pineapple for several hours or overnight in refrigerator. Turn occasionally. When ready to serve, drain and garnish with a few sprigs of watercress or parsley. Recipe can be made and kept refrigerated for one week.

Native Mustard

> 2 cups water
> ½ cup dry mustard

Heat water to boiling point and add very gradually to the mustard, stirring all the time, until the mixture becomes smooth and paste-like. Allow the flavor to develop for 10 minutes. May be kept indefinitely in refrigerator in a well-covered receptacle. No harm is done if mustard separates. Just stir well. Some people like a teaspoon of wine vinegar added to mixture. We don't bother.

Plum Brandy Sauce

¼ cup chutney, chopped fine
¼ cup chili sauce
¼ cup plum preserves
½ cup apricot preserves
 pinch of Five Spices
 1 teaspoon brandy (optional)
¼ teaspoon salt
 2 tablespoons honey
½ cup brown sugar
½ cup cider vinegar
½ cup applesauce (see below)

In a saucepan, combine all ingredients. Blend well and heat slowly, stirring steadily. Simmer 5-10 minutes (if you like the sauce thinner add a little water). Cool and pour into a container and seal well. May be kept indefinitely if applesauce is omitted in cooking. Applesauce can be added to sauce when served.

Kamailio:

1. There are many ways of preparing this sauce. You can omit any one of the preserves or the chutney and still have an excellent sauce, but this is the way it's done at the Hawaii Kai.

2. Bottled or canned Duck Sauce may be substituted, if you add a pinch of Five Spices, ½ teaspoon of brandy and applesauce (1 part applesauce to 2 parts Duck Sauce).

3. At the Hawaii Kai, the Plum Brandy Sauce is mixed for you at the table with a dash of Native Mustard.

Mali Mali Sauce

(*For pork, chicken and seafood*)

½ cup soy sauce
 2 tablespoons honey
 1 teaspoon sugar
 2 tablespoons sherry
 dash of pepper
 1 garlic clove, minced
½ cup chicken stock or consommé

Combine all ingredients and heat thoroughly. Serve hot (leftovers can be heated in sauce).

Mauai Tangy Sauce

For seafood, chicken, duck, beef.

¼ cup water
½ cup sugar
½ cup vinegar
1 tablespoon ketchup
2 teaspoons soy sauce
salt and pepper to taste
1 tablespoon cornstarch mixed with 2 tablespoons water

Combine all ingredients and bring to a boil. Simmer until sauce thickens. Serve in individual small bowls as a dipping sauce.

SAUCES

Sweet and Sour Sauce

For pork, chicken, beef or fish

3 tablespoons oil
2 onions, chopped coarse
2 green and red peppers, chopped coarse
2 cups chicken broth
1 jar sweet pickle mix (8 ounces), chopped
1 teaspoon honey
1 teaspoon thick soy sauce or brown gravy sauce (bead molasses type)
2 slices fresh ginger root, minced (see index)
1 tablespoon lemon juice
salt and fresh pepper to taste

In a large skillet sauté onions in oil until golden. Add green pepper and sauté until wilted. Add remaining ingredients and simmer for 15 minutes. Taste for additional seasonings. Serve hot over pork, chicken, beef or fish (your family won't recognize yesterday's pork or chicken).

Aloha Dipping Sauce

For poultry or pork

1 cup soy sauce
2 tablespoons molasses
2 tablespoons honey
1 garlic clove, minced
dash of fresh pepper

Combine all ingredients and simmer for 10 minutes. Serve in individual small sauce dishes as a dipping sauce.

Oahu Spicy Sauce

For seafood, chicken, duck and beef.

Mix together ¼ cup vinegar, 4 teaspoons sugar, ½ cup water, ¼ cup soy sauce and 2 tablespoons red horseradish. Simmer for 10 minutes. Serve in individual small bowls as a dipping sauce. (Can be thickened with 2 tablespoons cornstarch mixed with ¼ cup water.)

Peanut Sauce

For meat, chicken or duck.

½ cup crunchy peanut butter
1 cup boiling water
2 tablespoons molasses
2 tablespoons soy sauce
1 garlic clove, minced
dash of lemon juice

Combine all ingredients in a saucepan. Blend well and simmer slowly for 15 minutes, or until somewhat thickened. Serve hot.

Almond Sauce

For chicken, pork and fish.

8 ounces almonds, blanched (see below)
3 tablespoons oil
2 celery stalks, chopped
1 onion, diced
¼ pound mushrooms, diced
1 can water chestnuts (5 ounces) drained, rinsed and diced
3 tablespoons soy sauce
salt and fresh pepper to taste
½ cup chicken broth or water

In a large skillet, sauté blanched almonds in oil until golden and remove from pan. Add celery and onion and sauté until golden. Add mushrooms and cook for 3 minutes. Return almonds to skillet and add water chestnuts, soy sauce, salt, pepper; and chicken broth; cook only until hot. Serve over chicken, pork and fish (revitalizes leftovers).

TO BLANCH AND REMOVE SKINS:

Almonds can be purchased blanched or you can soak them in boiling water for 5 minutes and slip off skins. Dry on absorbent paper.

Lychee Sauce

For pork, chicken or duck.

1 can (16 oz.) lychee fruit
1 cup chicken broth
1 tablespoon soy sauce
1 tablespoon honey
2 tablespoons Plum Brandy Sauce
1 tablespoon cornstarch mixed with 2 tablespoons water

Drain juice into a saucepan and reserve lychees. Add remaining ingredients except cornstarch mixture. Simmer for 5 minutes. Stir cornstarch mixture and add to saucepan slowly, stirring until thickened. Add lychee fruit and stir gently. Heat thoroughly and serve over pork, duck or chicken (can be heated together with sauce).

Kumquat Dipping Sauce

1 cup Plum Brandy Sauce
1 tablespoon dry mustard
1 tablespoon sherry
6 kumquats, chopped fine, with 3 tablespoons kumquat syrup
3 tablespoons soy sauce
1 teaspoon garlic powder

Combine all ingredients and simmer for 5 minutes. Use hot or cold with pork, beef, veal, chicken and duck. Serve in individual sauce bowls for dipping. *Hoomalimali* (tempting)!

Hawaiian Barbecue Sauces

WAIKIKI SAUCE

In a saucepan, combine 2 tablespoons sesame seed oil with ½ cup ketchup, ½ cup orange juice, ½ cup honey, ¼ cup lemon juice, 2 tablespoons soy sauce and 1 slice minced fresh ginger root. Heat and stir until smooth. Use to baste poultry, ham, pork, on grill. Makes 2 cups.

PINEAPPLE SAUCE

Combine in a bowl, ½ cup ketchup, 1 cup pineapple juice, 3 chopped scallions and ½ teaspoon chili powder. Makes 1½ cups. Use to marinate and baste poultry, spareribs, steak bits and pork.

PIQUANT SAUCE

In a bowl, combine 1 cup ketchup, ¼ cup water, 3 tablespoons vinegar, 2 tablespoons sugar, 1 teaspoon salt, 1 teaspoon chili powder, 1 teaspoon garlic powder and a dash of Worcestershire sauce. Use to marinate or baste spareribs, beef, lamb, pork or chicken.

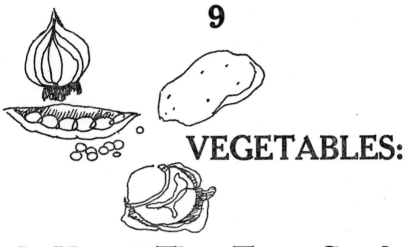

9

VEGETABLES:

In Hawaii They Taste Good

Pity the poor vegetable—it has never held a position of high esteem on the American bill of fare. Frozen, canned and even garden fresh, the lowly vegetable remains the stepchild of every meal. It's an entirely different story on the typical Hawaiian menu. Here, the vegetable enjoys a special status and shares equal billing with their cousins the tubers, yams and fruits.

The Hawaiians have a talent for taking a variety of vegetables and incorporating them into the main dish. Surprisingly, the result is never a mish-mash like stew but a delightful blend of enriched flavors.

If you prefer to serve your vegetables separate from the main dish, as do most families, you can still select from a wide variety of popular greens and leafs. Broccoli, spinach, tomatoes, corn, cauliflower and eggplant all rate high on Hawaiian dishes. Whatever your choice, stewed, boiled, baked or pickled . . . do it the Hawaiian way—they know their onions!

Bean Sprouts and Peppers

3 green or red sweet peppers
1 pound fresh bean sprouts, blanched or 1 can, drained and rinsed
  (1 pound)
3 tablespoons oil
1 tablespoon sherry wine
1 teaspoon soy sauce
salt and fresh pepper to taste
1 teaspoon onion powder (optional)

Remove seeds from peppers. Cut into thin, long strips (¼ inch by 3 inches). Sauté peppers and bean sprouts in oil until wilted (about 3 minutes). Add remaining ingredients, stir and cook for another minute. Serve hot. Serves 4 to 6.

Stuffed Bitter Melon

½ pound lean pork
1 tablespoon fermented black beans (soaked and mashed)
1 garlic clove, minced
1 scallion, chopped
1 tablespoon soy sauce
1 teaspoon sugar
1 tablespoon sherry wine
1 tablespoon cornstarch
2 tablespoons water
3 bitter melons, medium size (see index)

Mince pork and combine with remainder of ingredients. Mix well. Cut bitter melon in half, scoop out and discard seeds and white pulp in center, parboil for 3 minutes and drain. Heap meat mixture into each melon half. Arrange melon on a trivet in a heatproof baking dish which has 2 inches of boiling water at bottom. Cover tightly and bake for 30-45 minutes. Serves 6.

Portuguese Fried Broccoli (Brocolos Fritos)

1 bunch broccoli (fresh) or 2 packages frozen
5 tablespoons olive oil
2 garlic cloves, minced
1 small onion, chopped
salt and fresh pepper to taste

Discard tough portion of the stems and cut broccoli into 1-inch-long pieces. Parboil in salted water for just 1 minute. Remove and drain well. You can do this ahead, or use leftover cooked broccoli. Heat olive oil and sauté garlic and onions until golden brown. Add the broccoli, stir and sauté until heated throughout. Add salt and pepper to taste. Serve hot. Serves 6.

Cauliflower with Water Chestnuts and Mushrooms, Chinese Style

½ pound fresh mushrooms, sliced lengthwise
3 tablespoons oil
1 large cauliflower, washed and cut into flowerlets
1 cup chicken broth
1 teaspoon sherry
2 tablespoons soy sauce mixed with 1 tablespoon cornstarch
½ can water chestnuts (5 ounces), drained, rinsed and sliced
½ teaspoon salt
1 scallion, chopped fine

Parboil cauliflower for 5 minutes in salted water. Drain. Heat oil in large skillet and sauté mushrooms until wilted. Add chicken broth, sherry wine, soy sauce and cornstarch. Stir until thickened. Put cauliflower in skillet and simmer until soft. Add water chestnuts, stir and simmer only until heated through. Taste for additional salt. Place on a platter and garnish with chopped scallions. Serves 6-8.

Corn from the Islands

2 cups milk or light cream
2 cups water
1 tablespoon butter
2 teaspoons sugar
6 ears corn, cleaned and rinsed

In a large saucepan, combine milk or cream and water. Add butter and sugar. Stir. Bring just up to a boil, add corn and return to almost a boil (milk and cream should cover corn). Cover tightly and let corn simmer for 3 to 5 minutes. Serve with salt and additional butter. You've never tasted anything so *mikioi* (tasty).

Leftover corn cooked in this fashion can be reheated as above and you'll never know the difference.

Eggplant in Coconut Cream

    2 large onions, chopped
    3 tablespoons butter
    1 large eggplant, peeled and sliced thin
    1 teaspoon dried red chili pepper (optional)
    salt and fresh pepper
    2 cups coconut cream (see index)

Sauté onions in butter until golden. Arrange sliced eggplant in a large buttered casserole dish. Cover with sautéed onions. Sprinkle with chili pepper (optional), salt and fresh pepper to taste. Pour 2 cups coconut cream over this. Cover and bake at 375° F. for 40 minutes. Uncover and bake 15 minutes longer. Serves 6.

Filipino Pinacbet

Eggplants with tomatoes, string beans and cucumber

    3 tablespoons oil
    ½ pound ground pork
    1 clove garlic, minced
    1 large onion, chopped
    2 tomatoes, sliced
    1 can (2 oz.) anchovy fillets, cut in 1-inch pieces
    ¼ pound green beans, cut in 1-inch pieces
    3 long eggplants, cut in 2-inch pieces
    1 large cucumber, sliced
    salt and fresh pepper to taste

Heat oil in a large skillet and sauté pork, garlic and onion until golden. Add tomatoes, anchovies, string beans and eggplant. Stir well to combine; cover tightly and cook until eggplant is tender (a little water can be added during cooking if ingredients look dry). Add the cucumber and cook only until wilted. Season with salt and pepper. Serve hot with rice. Serves 6-8.

Kamailio:

This recipe has been modified since some of the ingredients are unattainable on the mainland. In the Islands, bitter melon, patolas and patis are also used in this dish.

Baked Papaya

The unripe papaya doubles as a vegetable.

1 medium, unripe papaya
1 onion, chopped fine
1 green pepper, chopped
3 tablespoons butter
2 tomatoes, peeled and chopped (see index)
salt and fresh pepper
bread crumbs
butter

Cut the papaya in half and scoop out the seeds. Cook in boiling water for 15 minutes. Drain. Scoop out flesh carefully and mash. Leave a ½-inch wall in the papaya. Reserve shells. Sauté onions and green pepper in butter until golden. Add tomatoes, salt, pepper and the mashed papaya. Combine well. Stuff shells with this mixture and sprinkle with bread crumbs. Dot with butter and bake in 375° F. oven until top is brown. Serves 6.

Poi

Poi is a fermented paste derived from the taro plant. Its consistency varies and the terms "one-finger, two-finger" etc. designate how many fingers are needed to get it from the serving dish to the mouth without having it dribble on the chin. A thick poi is a one-finger poi.

Many mainlanders say that poi smells like sour wallpaper paste, and resembles it in color and taste. But poi is *the* native dish, and a Hawaiian cookbook without some reference to it would be unthinkable. The following adaptation will be more palatable to *malihini* (greenhorn or newcomer) tastes than the authentic version.

Poi Malihini

Poi is available canned or frozen in specialty shops (see Sources) and is easily reconstituted by steaming as per directions. To make Poi Malihini add an equal amount of milk to poi and mix in a blender. Add ¼ cup sugar and taste for additional sweetening. Serve in *umeke* (bowl).

Sweet Potato Mock Poi

6 sweet potatoes, boiled, or 1 can (40 oz.)
salt and fresh pepper to taste
coconut milk (see index)

Mash sweet potatoes and season with salt and pepper to taste. Beat in gradually enough coconut milk to make the desired consistency: one-finger, two-finger, etc. Serve in individual small bowls or coconut shells.

Samoan Baked Spinach

2 pounds spinach or 2 packages frozen
1 teaspoon salt
2 cups coconut cream (see index)

Wash fresh spinach and remove fibrous stems. Place in baking pan, add salt and coconut cream and bake in oven 300° F. until spinach is tender. Low heat is a *must* as coconut cream will separate if boiled. Serves 6.

Korean Spinach and Pork

2 pounds fresh spinach or 2 packages frozen
2 tablespoons sesame oil
1 garlic clove, minced
1 pork chop, ground (6 ounces)
salt and pepper to taste
2 tablespoons sesame seeds, toasted and pulverized (see index)
1 egg, beaten well

Wash fresh spinach and discard fibrous stems. Cut into small pieces. Heat oil in a large skillet and sauté garlic and ground pork until brown. Break up pork particles with a fork. Add spinach, salt and pepper, cover and cook until spinach is tender. Turn off heat. Add scallion, sesame seeds and egg. Stir well. Cover and let sit 3 minutes. Serve hot. Serves 6.

Tomato Flowers

6 large firm but ripe tomatoes
3 tablespoons butter sautéed with garlic clove, minced
salt and pepper
sesame seeds

Using a sharp knife, cut a connected series of deep V's through diameter of the tomato (see Lemon Rosettes). Do this completely around until you meet the first V. Separate and you will have two flower halves. Drizzle tomatoes with garlic butter, salt and pepper. Sprinkle with sesame seeds. Bake for 15 minutes at 350° F. in a greased pan. Serves 6.

Candied Tomatoes

3 large tomatoes, peeled (see index)
1 onion, chopped fine
4 tablespoons butter
½ cup brown sugar
1 tablespoon honey
¾ teaspoon salt
melted butter

Slice each tomato in half. Sauté onion in butter until golden. Add brown sugar, honey and salt; stir until sugar is melted. Add 1 cup of bread crumbs and mix well. Place tomatoes in a buttered shallow baking pan, flat side up, and with a small scoop or spoon, place a mound of mixture over each half. Drizzle a little melted butter over tops and bake for 25 minutes in preheated 375° F. oven. Serves 6.

Portuguese Tomatoes and Scrambled Eggs (Ovos Batidos)

2 tablespoons olive oil
2 garlic cloves, minced
3 tomatoes, cut in small pieces
1 tablespoon sugar
dash of fresh pepper
1 teaspoon salt
3 tablespoons chopped parsley
6 large eggs, beaten

In a large skillet, heat the oil and sauté the garlic until golden. Add tomatoes and remaining ingredients except eggs. Cook on a high flame until tomatoes are soft and all the liquid has evaporated. Add beaten eggs, stir and cook slowly only until eggs are creamy. Serve hot. (A small chopped onion can be added when sautéeing the garlic.) Serves 6.

Sesame Tomatoes

1 pound tomatoes, green
2 eggs
2 tablespoons soy sauce
⅛ teaspoon salt
dash of pepper
sesame seeds
oil for frying

Slice green tomatoes thickly (¼ inch). Beat eggs with soy sauce and add salt and pepper. Spread sesame seeds thinly on foil. Heat oil in large skillet. With tongs, dip tomato slices first in egg and soy mixture and then coat thinly with sesame seeds. Fry on both sides until sesame seeds are golden. Drain on absorbent paper. Serves 6.

Tomatoes Island Style

3 tablespoons butter
1 red pepper, chopped coarse
1 green pepper, chopped coarse
1 small onion, minced
1 garlic clove, minced (optional)
1 teaspoon salt
freshly ground pepper
6 firm but ripe tomatoes
4 water chestnuts, chopped

In a large skillet, heat butter and add red and green pepper, onion and garlic. Sauté until soft. Add salt and pepper. Cool.

Meanwhile cut off a slice of tomato at stem end. With a sharp knife, cut around sides of tomato, working towards the bottom. Leave a ¼ inch shell. Remove tomato pulp; chop and combine with pepper mixture and water chestnuts. Sprinkle cavity of tomato with additional salt and pepper. Fill tomatoes with mixture and dot with butter. Bake for 20 minutes at 350° F. in a greased pan. You can substitute a jar of fried peppers for the fresh in recipe. Serves 6.

Korean Vegetables in Batter (Chasoh-Juhn)

An interesting way of cooking vegetables (Korean style) such as potatoes, scallions and carrots is by shredding or chopping finely two of each vegetable and combining with a batter made of 2 eggs, ¾ cup flour, ¼ cup water, 1 teaspoon salt, dash of pepper, 1 tablespoon pulverized sesame seeds (see index) and 1 teaspoon baking powder. This is then dropped by spoonfuls into hot oil in a skillet and browned well. Serve with Vinegar Shoyu Sauce (see index). Serves 6-8.

Vegetables Japanese Fashion with Sesame Vinegar Sauce

Cooked vegetables, such as bean sprouts, carrots, spinach, string beans, celery, cabbage, watercress, etc. are served mixed with a Sesame Vinegar Sauce. Raw cucumbers, daikon (white radish) and turnips are sliced thinly or grated, then mixed with this sauce also.

SESAME VINEGAR SAUCE

2 tablespoons sesame seeds
2 tablespoons sugar
2 tablespoons soy sauce
2 tablespoons white vinegar

Toast sesame seeds in oven or in a pan over a low flame until golden brown. Crush with a mortar and pestle or wooden potato masher. In a bowl combine sesame seeds, sugar, soy sauce and vinegar. Mix sauce with cooked or raw vegetables.

Pickled Turnips

4 small white turnips
3 tablespoons coarse salt
1 cup white vinegar
¾ cup sugar
½ teaspoon paprika

Peel turnips and slice thinly crosswise (⅛-inch thick). Sprinkle coarse salt over slices and let stand for 1 hour. Drain. Heat remaining ingredients, add turnip slices and bring to a boil. Simmer for 3 minutes. Cool, place in a bowl and refrigerate. Serve cold. Serves 6-8 (small portions).

10

NATIVE RICE, NOODLES, AND YAMS

"All that meat and no potatoes?" Don't be misled—when it comes to potatoes and yams the Hawaiians have no equal. As for their basic staple, rice, they're in a class by themselves. With equal skill and savvy they know how to boil it, fry it, bake it and even pickle it! And what's more they can serve all these types of rices in Japanese, Chinese, or Korean style. Their favorite however is good old-fashioned native style.

To add variety and flavor to their starches, the Islanders frequently mix their noodles and rice with fruit, nuts, eggs and spices.

If someone in your family has a yen for yams—try one of the Island yam and sweet potato recipes such as Yams and Apples or Orange Sweet Potato Rosettes. They're exciting, different and not at all difficult to prepare. If noodles are your thing, then try the "Noodles Ono Loa", a subtle nut-flavored treat that is sure to have your guests begging for more.

RICE (*HUA LAIKI*)

In the Islands, rice is valued not only for its nutritional but also for its aesthetic quality. Its texture and whiteness provide an excellent background for other foods and their colors, and its blandness enhances the flavor of the food it accompanies.

When properly cooked, rice should be dry and white; the grains firm and separate. It should never be lumpy or sticky. Hardness or softness can vary according to one's taste, but it must never be *too* hard or *too* soft, and always dry. A drop of sesame oil, soy sauce or butter can be added to cooked rice for flavor.

Gene buys only #103 old crop, long-grain rice for the restaurant. This can be purchased at all oriental shops (see Sources of Supply). A good substitute is Carolina or converted rice. The latter does not need to be rinsed. Cook it according to directions on package.

The secret of fluffy rice is in thorough washing to remove the excess starch. Rinse the rice under cold running water in a fine sieve or colander, set in a large pan, and stir and rub the grains between the palms of your hands until the water runs clear. Don't shortcut this procedure.

The quantity of water you use affects the texture of the rice. For firm and more separated grains, use a little less water; for softer grains, use more water.

If you are cooking rice in hard water, 1 teaspoon lemon juice (or vinegar) added to water will keep the rice white.

One cup raw rice cooked in 1½ cups water will yield 3 cups cooked rice. Depending on the rest of the menu, this will serve 3 good-sized to 5 or 6 small portions.

Basic Boiled Rice

BOILING-WATER START:

Wash rice thoroughly. In a large saucepan heat necessary amount of water and bring to a boil (remember that 1 cup raw rice will yield 3 cups cooked). Add rice and bring back to a boil. Cover tightly and cook over very low heat for about 7 to 10 minutes until most of the water is absorbed. Stir the rice very gently from the bottom up and scrape off the rice stuck to the sides. This permits even cooking and there's less chance of burning the bottom. Cover and cook for about 15 minutes longer and when the rice is done, lift the lid and stir the rice just once with a lifting motion. With a fork, quickly fluff rice to separate grains. Replace lid, turn off flame and let steam for at least 5 minutes. Your rice will be soft, fluffy and ready to serve.

COLD-WATER START:

Or wash rice (see above), then cover it in a saucepan with enough cold water to rise ½ inch above the rice. Cook uncovered over high heat until small holes begin to form on the surface of the rice and most of the water has been absorbed (about 3 minutes). Cover saucepan, lower heat to simmer and cook for 15 to 20 minutes. Remove pan from heat and let "relax" for 5 to 10 minutes. During this period any remaining water is absorbed and cooking is completed. Rice will remain hot, if kept covered, for half an hour. Allow ½ to 1 cup per serving.

Kamailio:

1. For a change of taste, spread rice out on a shallow pan and brown (without fat) on top of stove or in a 375° F. oven. Stir or shake occasionally to brown rice evenly. Store in a covered container and use as you would white rice. You'll be pleasantly surprised at the nut-like flavor.

2. It may happen that, when the flame is too high, the water in cooking rice is absorbed too quickly. Don't be afraid to add a little more *hot* water and stir with a quick lifting motion.

3. If rice is still too sticky after it has been cooked, place in a colander and rinse under very hot water to separate the grains and remove the starch. Toss with a fork to fluff. Return to a heated saucepan, cover and let sit for 5 minutes.

4. Sometimes a crust will form at the bottom of the pan. If the heat is kept low it will not burn. To wash the pan, soak in cold water. The Chinese, however, refrigerate and save the crusts to make congee or rice gruel (a form of cooked cereal); or deep fry small pieces until golden, nut-like and crunchy, to garnish soup or as an hors d'oeuvre or side dish.

5. The Japanese prefer the oval or short-grained rice; they like its flavor and softer, stickier texture. This is a good choice for puddings and other creamy dishes.

6. Natural brown rice which has an outer covering of bran is high in nutritional value since nothing has been removed through processing. It can be substituted in all recipes.

7. Wild rice is not a true cereal, as rice is, but the seed of an aquatic grass found in many of the states East of the Rockies. Its

unusual flavor is considered quite a delicacy and because the demand is greater than the supply, it is expensive. It is harvested only by the Indians who paddle out to the swamps and freshwater lakes to bring it in.

8. Note that, like the Oriental, we do not use salt in cooking basic rice; we prefer the blandness that offsets accompanying flavor.

Liu Liu:

Leftover rice can be refrigerated for one week if cooled and placed in a covered container. To reheat cold rice, rinse quickly in a colander or sieve with very hot water. Separate grains with a fork. Heat in a covered saucepan over low flame (or oven) with 1 tablespoon water or broth for each cup of rice. Shake once or twice without removing cover.

To freeze rice, place in a plastic container or wrap in foil and when ready to use, thaw for 3 to 4 hours. Follow directions (above) for reheating.

Fried Rice

6 cups cold boiled rice
6 tablespoons oil
2 garlic cloves, minced
1 onion, cut in thin slices
3 stalks celery cut diagonally into ⅛ inch pieces
2 eggs beaten with 2 tablespoons water
3 tablespoons soy sauce
salt and fresh pepper to taste
1 teaspoon sugar
½ teaspoon thick soy sauce
    or brown gravy sauce (bead molasses type)

1. Break up the cold rice so that grains are separate and there are no lumps.

2. Heat 3 tablespoons oil in a large, deep skillet and sauté garlic, onions and celery just to soften slightly. Remove to a platter.

3. Heat remaining oil to very hot (almost smoking) and add rice, turning constantly so that it does not stick.

4. When rice is hot, slowly add beaten eggs and stir constantly until eggs are set. Turn down heat to medium and blend in soy sauce, salt, pepper and sugar.

5. Drizzle a little thick soy sauce or brown gravy sauce (bead molasses type) to brown the rice. Stir and mix well.

6. Turn off heat and cover.

7. Serve, garnished with chopped scallions. Serves 6 or more.

Kamailio:

This recipe is the basic one. To make the others on the Hawaii Kai menu, merely add one of the following: 1½ cups of roast pork or chicken cut in thin strips or cooked shrimp cut in half or thirds. For that special Hawaii Kai fried rice, add 4 sliced water chestnuts, ½ can of bamboo shoots and ½ can or 8 ounces bean sprouts. There is no limit to what can be added to fried rice: cooked roast beef, pork, lamb, chicken, ham, bacon and any cooked seafood. Cooked vegetables too: green peas, julienne carrot strips, mushrooms, green or red peppers, string beans, etc.; even nuts and raisins.

Japanese Sushi or Zushi (Rice in Vinegar Sauce)

½ cup vinegar (white)
4 tablespoons sugar
1 tablespoon salt
4 to 6 cups cooked rice (see index)

Combine vinegar, sugar, and salt to make Vinegar Sauce, cooking until dissolved. Cool. Place cooked rice in a bowl and pour Vinegar Sauce over it. Mix well until rice is coated. The Japanese eat it cold, but it may be served hot. Makes 4 to 6 large portions.

AUI ANA (A VARIATION):

The above is the basic Sushi. To it can be added the following:

2 dried black mushrooms
2 carrots, shredded
½ cup string beans, shredded or ¼ package frozen (French style)
1 cup water
3 tablespoons sugar
2 tablespoons soy sauce

Soak black mushrooms in cold water for 1 hour. Drain (reserve water), and cut into fine pieces. In a saucepan, combine all ingredients (using water from mushrooms also), cover and cook until tender.

Drain, cool, and combine with basic Sushi. Toss well to coat rice. This too the Japanese serve cold as a rule, but it may be served hot.

Portuguese Fried Rice (Arroz Frito)

5 tablespoons olive oil
2 garlic cloves, minced
6 cups cold boiled rice
salt and fresh pepper

Heat oil in large skillet and sauté garlic for a minute or two. Add cold rice and fry, stirring frequently until the rice becomes golden brown. Add salt and fresh pepper to taste. Serves 6.

Cinnamon-Nut Rice

6 cups hot boiled rice
3 tablespoons butter
3 tablespoons honey
pinch of cinnamon
1 teaspoon sugar
1 cup chopped peanuts, almonds or brazil nuts

Combine all ingredients and toss with rice. Serve hot. Serves at least 6.

Coconut Rice

Especially good with curry.

1 small onion, chopped
3 tablespoons butter
4 cups cooked rice
coconut milk (see index)

Sauté onion in butter until golden and reserve. Cook rice as per recipe for boiled rice, substituting coconut milk for water. Care must be taken to simmer the coconut milk; do not boil, or it will separate. When rice is done add sautéed onions. Serves 4-6.

Javanese Rice

Sauté 1 small onion, minced, in 3 tablespoons butter. Add 6 whole cloves and ½ teaspoon cinnamon. Sauté with onion for 5 minutes.

Remove cloves. Mix sauce with 4 to 6 cups cooked rice and toss well. Serve hot.

Orange Rice

2 cups wild rice (white or brown may be substituted)
2 tablespoons dehydrated onion soup
2 cups orange juice
dash of sugar
salt and pepper to taste

Cook wild rice, white or brown rice as per directions. When soft remove to a heatproof serving dish and add dehydrated onion soup, orange juice, sugar, salt and pepper. Mix well. Bake in oven until juice has evaporated. If you prefer, this can be done on top of the stove. You can also add a few tablespoons of chopped peanuts, walnuts or macadamia nuts. Serves 4-6.

Saffron Rice

Steep 1 teaspoon fine crumbled saffron in a little boiled water until diluted. Add to 4 to 6 cups hot cooked rice and mix well. Add plump raisins, slivered toasted almonds (see index), chopped peanuts or chopped macadamia nuts and toss to mix. Serves 6-8.

Rice with Ginger

Cook rice as per directions, and when done, add 2 tablespoons fresh, minced ginger root, 1 tablespoon chopped nuts (macadamia, peanuts, walnuts, toasted almonds) and 1 tablespoon white raisins. Mix well.

Korean Rice with Nuts (Yak Pahb)

¼ cup soy sauce
¼ cup brown sugar
2 tablespoons honey
1 tablespoon oil (sesame preferably)
4 to 6 cups hot cooked rice
½ cup toasted almonds, coarsely chopped
½ cup cooked chestnuts or 1 small (5 oz.) can, cut in small pieces
¼ teaspoon cinnamon
3 tablespoons toasted pine nuts

In a saucepan, combine soy sauce with brown sugar, honey and sesame oil and heat until sugar has dissolved. Lower heat, add rice and combine well. Add chopped almonds, chestnuts and toss to mix. Serve hot, garnished with cinnamon and toasted pine nuts (see below). Serves 6 or more.

TO TOAST NUTS:

Spread out in a shallow baking pan in a 325° F. oven and bake until lightly browned. Toss or turn for even browning.

NOODLES

Rice Flour Noodles

An unusual garnish for meats, poultry, etc.

½ cup rice flour noodles (sometimes called bean threads)
2 inches oil for deep frying

Break off about ½ cupful of rice noodles and separate the strands. Heat oil in a large skillet until very hot. Test for proper heat by tossing in one or two noodles. They should puff up very quickly and become snow white, if oil is properly hot. Add remainder of noodles a little at a time and follow directions as above. Drain on paper toweling and use as garnish. A little goes a long way since noodles puff up twice their original size. These noodles can be made early in the day, since they do not have to be hot when served. Serves about 6.

Noodles Ono Loa

Delicious! You will enjoy their nut-like flavor.

oil for frying
½ pound thin egg noodles
3 tablespoons soy sauce
2 cups chicken broth
1 garlic clove, minced (optional)
2 teaspoons sugar
1 teaspoon salt
dash of fresh pepper
2 scallions, chopped

Heat enough oil in a large skillet to cover 1 inch of bottom. Toss in raw noodles, a little at a time, lower heat and fry until golden brown on one side; turn and fry until golden brown throughout. Drain oil thoroughly from skillet. Add the remaining ingredients, except scallions, stirring well. Cover and simmer slowly until noodles are soft and most of the liquid absorbed (if needed, add more water or broth while cooking). Sprinkle with chopped green scallions and serve. Serves 6.

Kamailio:

You can use medium-thick noodles in lieu of the fine (incidentally, all the starch from the noodles accumulates at bottom of pan while frying and is removed when oil is drained). Noodles can be refrigerated 3-5 days or frozen. To reheat, add additional broth, soy sauce and adjust seasonings.

YAMS

Yams and Apples

5-6 large yams (2½ pounds), parboiled and peeled or 1 (40 oz.) can
3 tablespoons brown sugar
4 apples, peeled, cored and sliced into ¼-inch rings
3 tablespoons lemon juice
4 tablespoons cinnamon-sugar mixture
2 tablespoons honey

Slice yams ½-inch thick and place slices to form a layer on the bottom of a buttered casserole dish. Sprinkle with brown sugar. Make a layer of apple rings and sprinkle with lemon juice and cinnamon sugar. Continue making layers in the same fashion ending with apple rings. Drizzle top with honey and sprinkle with cinnamon sugar. Bake covered, for 30 minutes. Uncover and bake until top apple layer is browned and soft. Serves 6-8.

Liu Liu:

To prepare in advance, bake for 20 minutes. Refrigerate or freeze and when ready to serve, (defrost), heat covered in a 375° F. oven. Uncover to brown.

Hawaiian Sweet Potato Casserole (Uala Maoli)

6 large sweet potatoes (2½ pounds), parboiled and peeled
  or 1 (40 oz.) can
6 tablespoons margarine or butter
2 teaspoons salt
6 bananas, sliced
1 cup brown sugar mixed with 1 teaspoon cinnamon
1 can (16 oz.) crushed pineapple
1 cup pineapple juice mixed with 1 teaspoon lemon juice
2 tablespoons honey

Slice sweet potatoes ½-inch thick. Grease a heatproof casserole dish with a little of the margarine. Arrange in alternate layers starting with the sweet potatoes dotted with margarine and salt, then the bananas sprinkled with brown sugar, and then the crushed pineapple. End with the sweet potatoes or the crushed pineapple. Combine the pineapple, lemon juice and honey and pour over mixture. Bake in 350° F. preheated oven for 40 minutes, or until browned on top. Serves 6-8.

Kamailio:

If you like the refreshing taste of ginger root, mince and add it to the pineapple juice. Or use orange juice in place of pineapple juice. To make individual servings, use a pastry bag with a #6 star tip and

Hawaiian sweet potato casserole

press out large rosettes. The recipe can be prepared in advance and refrigerated for 2 days or frozen. Shorten baking time to 25 minutes. Reheat in oven at 300° F. until hot throughout.

Japanese Chestnut and Sweet Potato Cakes (Kuri To Satsuma Imo No Kinton)

1 pound chestnuts, shelled (see index)
1 pound sweet potatoes or 1 (16 oz.) can
1 cup sugar
1 tablespoon cornstarch
dash of salt
toasted sesame seeds or chopped toasted nuts

Cook the chestnuts in just enough water to cover, until soft. Drain, but reserve liquid. Pare and cook sweet potatoes until soft. Chop the chestnuts finely. Add sugar to the hot chestnut liquid and dissolve. Mash the sweet potatoes using sweetened chestnut water to soften. Combine with cornstarch, salt and chopped chestnuts; wet hands and shape into small balls with palms of hands. Roll in toasted sesame seeds or chopped nuts. Serve hot or cold. Serves 6.

Kamailio:

Although Japanese Islanders use the cakes as a dessert, we serve them as the starch part of a meal in lieu of rice or potatoes.

Canned chestnuts can be used, if desired. Two small cans (5½ ounces each) are needed. If canned chestnuts are packed in sweetened liquid, omit sugar from recipe. Everything can be prepared in advance and refrigerated or frozen. Reheat in preheated oven at 325° F. until piping hot.

Orange Sweet Potato Rosettes

3 large navel oranges
1 can (16 oz.) yams or sweet potatoes, mashed, or 3 large boiled yams
2 tablespoons honey
1 teaspoon fresh ginger root, minced (optional)
orange juice
brown sugar
flaked coconut

Follow instructions for cutting lemon rosettes (see index) and make orange rosettes. Scoop out contents of oranges leaving a ¼-inch

remove orange from shell with a grape-fruit knife

using a pastry bag... heap potato high above orange shell

ORANGE SWEET POTATO ROSETTES

shell. Remove fiber from orange pieces and dice. Combine well with mashed yams, honey and ginger root. Add enough orange juice to make a fluffy mixture. With a large scoop, heap mixture into orange rosettes. Dust with brown sugar and sprinkle with coconut. Bake in 350° F. oven until heated throughout. This looks particularly pretty if you use a pastry bag with a #7 star tip to fill the orange rosettes. Serves 6.

Sweet Potato Balls

    2 pounds sweet potatoes, yams or 1 large (40 oz.) can
    6 tablespoons sugar
    ½ cup flour
    ¼ teaspoon salt
    1 egg
    oil
    1 teaspoon powdered sugar or coconut

Cook sweet potatoes in boiling water until soft. Mash well, removing any stringy fibers. Mix with sugar, flour, salt and egg. With hands, roll about a tablespoon of mixture and form into small balls. Heat oil and deep fry over medium heat until slightly browned. **Drain, and roll in coconut or powdered sugar. Serves 6.**

11

SPECTACULAR DESSERTS

OK . . . you cautious, careful calorie counters . . . it's Hawaiian goodie time and contrary to what you've heard, not everything that's good is fattening. If you've been looking forward to the dessert section with mixed emotions, you can take comfort in knowing that most Hawaiian desserts call for fresh fruit and, therefore, tend to be a great deal less fattening than diet-destroying pies and cakes. So solaced, throw caution to the tropical winds and self-indulge.

If you happen to be one of the fortunate few who have had the unforgettable experience of eating a field-ripened Hawaiian pineapple or munched on fresh Island coconut, then you can readily understand why the natives call these two natural favorites the "King and Queen of Desserts". But just for good measure or to prove their omnipotence, it seems the Polynesian Gods further endowed the royal court of fruits and nuts with other delights such as: mangoes, bananas, kumquats, melons and those marvelous meaty macadamia nuts.

Because Hawaiian desserts tend to be very colorful, nourishing and relatively easy to make, they provide the overworked housewife with an excellent opportunity to add a festive touch to an otherwise so-so meal. They can also be the pièce-de-résistance that is sure to sweeten up a party. As for satisfying those off-hour sweettooth cravings, try the Samoan-style Bananas with Coconut sauce. They sound difficult and exotic but they're really a pussy-cat to make.

And here's more good news—once you've got the hang of it, you'll find that you can whip up more elaborate goodies like Pineapple

Froth, Drunken Bananas, Haupia Coconut Pudding and Pineapple Meringue in less time than it takes you to make a devilishly delicious devil's food cake.

If your dessert-loving family hasn't been asking for second helpings of your once-favorite apple pie . . . now's the time to go Hawaiian and give 'em their just desserts! *Aloha!*

(Samoan) Bananas with Coconut Sauce (Toifa'I)

    6 small bananas
    2 tablespoons butter
    1 cup grated fresh or packaged coconut
    1 cup light cream
    2 tablespoons sugar (omit for packaged coconut)

Sauté bananas whole in butter until soft and keep hot. Combine remaining ingredients in a saucepan and heat. Do not boil. Simmer for 15-20 minutes. Serve in a pretty fruit dish by pouring sauce over bananas and decorating with rosettes of whipped cream or maraschino cherries. Serves 6.

Flaming Bananas, Apples & Pineapple (Pele's Delight)

Pele is the Hawaiian Fire Goddess and only a spectacular dessert would be named in her honor.

    2 bananas
    2 apples
    1 can (13 oz.) pineapple chunks, drained,
       or fresh pineapple cut into chunks
    2 eggs, beaten
    1 cup flour
    oil for deep frying
    ½ cup brown sugar
    ¼ cup water
    1 tablespoon oil
    ½ cup brandy or rum for flambéeing (see index)

1. Peel bananas and slice diagonally into 1-inch pieces. Pare and core apples; cut into thin 1-inch pieces. Dip fruit into beaten eggs, dredge in the flour and deep fry until golden brown. Drain. In a large saucepan, heat brown sugar, water and oil and cook until mixture becomes syrupy and thick. With tongs dip each fruit into syrup, stirring

carefully to coat. Oil a heatproof serving platter and transfer fruits to it. Keep hot in oven (a chafing dish is good too).

2. Bring fruit platter to the table accompanied by a large bowl of ice water. At the table, flambé the fruit with warmed brandy or rum (see index for flambéeing). Each guest can pick up the flaming fruit with a fork, tongs or 2 spoons and plunge into the iced water for a second to extinguish the flame. The sugar will crystallize but the fruit remains warm inside. Serves 6.

INDIVIDUAL FLAMBEES

Individual dessert flambées for each person are sensational. Even ordinary fruits such as cherries, pears, and peaches, fresh or canned, covered with a syrup or kirsch liqueur, can be served in small heatproof dishes. Flambéed at the table, they become a conversation piece. See Flambé Technique.

Banana Cream Dessert

1 envelope gelatin
¼ cup cold water
1½ cups boiling water
3 ripe bananas
1 teaspoon lemon juice
¼ cup sugar
1 cup heavy cream, whipped stiffly
fruit for garnish (lichees, kumquats, papaya, mangoes,
    strawberries, peaches, etc.)

In a bowl, soak gelatin in cold water for 5 minutes. Add boiling water and stir until dissolved. Mash bananas by hand or in blender and add to gelatin mixture. Add lemon juice and sugar and mix well. Cool and fold in whipped cream. Place in a 1-quart mold or in individual fruit molds that have been rinsed with cold water to chill. Refrigerate until firm. Run point of knife around edges and unmold. Garnish with fruits. Serves 6.

Banana Fritters with Coconut Whipped Cream

    1 cup flour, sifted
    2 teaspoons baking powder
    1 teaspoon salt
    ¼ cup sugar
    1 egg, beaten
    ⅓ cup milk
    2 tablespoons melted butter
    3 firm bananas
    ¼ cup cornstarch
    2 inches oil for frying

In a large bowl, sift together flour, baking powder, salt and sugar Combine egg, milk and butter and add to bowl. Mix together until smooth (this is a stiff batter). Additional milk can be added to facilitate dipping.

Cut each banana into 4 pieces crosswise. Roll in cornstarch and with tongs, dip into fritter batter. Heat 2 inches oil in skillet and fry bananas until golden brown. Turn to brown evenly. Drain on absorbent paper. Serve with Coconut Whipped Cream. Makes 12 fritters.

COCONUT WHIPPED CREAM

    1 cup heavy cream
    2 tablespoons sugar
    1 cup shredded coconut
    dash of rum flavoring

Whip the cream, add sugar and fold in the coconut. Flavor with rum. Serve over fritters.

Liu Liu:

Banana fritters can be completely finished in advance and refrigerated for one day. Reheat in 375° F. oven until hot throughout. Coconut cream can be refrigerated and stored like regular whipped cream.

Banana (Maia) Pudding

    2 cups milk
    2 tablespoons sugar
    ¼ cup raisins
    1 tablespoon chopped almonds
    3 medium-size ripe bananas, mashed

Scald milk in the top of a double boiler and add sugar, raisins, nuts and bananas. Cook 10 minutes, stirring constantly until mixture thickens. Remove from heat and spoon into individual serving dishes, distributing fruit evenly. Cool and refrigerate. Serve with a dollop of red jam, jelly or whipped cream. Serves 6.

Filipino Banana Fritters (Baruya)

    4 ripe bananas
    1 cup cake flour
    ½ cup evaporated milk
    2 tablespoons sugar
    ¼ teaspoon vanilla extract
    oil for frying
    cinnamon sugar or powdered sugar

Slice bananas ½ inch thick. Make a batter of the flour, evaporated milk, sugar and vanilla. Heat 2 inches oil in a large skillet and with tongs dip bananas into the batter and fry (do not crowd). Turn until golden on all sides. Remove and drain on paper towel. Dust with cinnamon sugar or powdered sugar. Serve hot. Serves 8 to 10.

Liu Liu:

Fritters can be fried golden in advance and then reheated in 325° F. oven for 20-30 minutes before serving.

Hawaiian Banana Pie

    4 cups firm bananas, sliced
    1 small can crushed pineapple, drained
    ½ cup sugar
    1 teaspoon cinnamon
    1 teaspoon lemon juice
    pastry for two-crust pie
    2 tablespoons butter

Combine all ingredients except butter. Place in pastry-lined, 9-inch pie pan. Dot with butter. Cover with top pastry crust. Bake for 40 minutes at 375° F. (Chopped macadamia nuts or coconut flakes can be added to pie mixture.) Serves 6.

Bananas and Pineapple Kauai

4 ripe bananas
¼ cup lemon juice
¼ cup honey
¼ cup banana or rum liqueur
6 tablespoons fresh pineapple or canned crushed pineapple
flaked coconut (fresh or packaged)

Slice bananas into 6 dessert coupettes. Combine lemon juice, honey and liqueur and pour over bananas. Place a tablespoon of shredded fresh or canned crushed pineapple on top of bananas. Sprinkle with flaked coconut. Serves 6.

Drunken Bananas (Maia Ona)

6 small, firm bananas
½ cup rum mixed with 2 teaspoons lemon juice
1 egg, beaten
¾ cup flaked coconut or chopped nuts (almonds, macadamia, walnuts)
oil for frying

Soak whole bananas in rum and lemon juice for about 1 hour. Turn frequently. Dip bananas in egg and roll in coconut or chopped nuts.

Heat ½ inch of oil in skillet and fry bananas slowly until brown on all sides and tender. Drain on paper toweling and serve hot. Serves 6.

Kamailio:

You can do everything in advance and then reheat the bananas in a foil-lined pan, one layer deep, in oven set at 350° F.

Crystal Bananas

An exotic presentation of a crystallized banana.

6 bananas (small but not too ripe)
6 tablespoons oil
1 slice fresh ginger root, minced
½ teaspoon salt
2½ cups sugar
2 cups water
dash of cinnamon (optional)
½ tablespoon vinegar
large bowl of ice water

1. Peel bananas and sauté in heated oil with ginger root and salt until bananas are golden brown. Remove to a large greased platter.

2. Combine remaining ingredients in a saucepan; add any of the oil remaining from the bananas and bring to a boil. Simmer slowly just until mixture becomes syrupy. Place into a larger saucepan filled with 2 inches boiling water (to keep syrup from thickening too quickly) and keep hot. Test syrup by putting a small amount on edge of spoon and dipping it into cold water. Syrup should spin a thread when ready.

3. With tongs dip bananas into syrup, coating well and then immediately plunge into ice water. Banana split dishes are nice to use for serving. Serves 6.

AUI ANA (A VARIATION):

The chafing dish can be used very elegantly to make this exciting dessert.

In the blazer pan of the chafing dish, sauté bananas with a little oil until golden brown. Combine ¼ cup corn syrup or honey, ½ cup brown sugar, ¼ cup water mixed with 3 tablespoons cornstarch, 1 tablespoon oil, 1 slice minced, fresh ginger root, and a dash of salt and cinnamon. Pour mixture over bananas and simmer for 5 to 10 minutes, until mixture thickens and is good and hot. Place a crystal bowl filled with ice water next to the chafing dish. Have each guest pick up a banana with tongs and dip into the ice water. Place on a doily-covered dessert plate and *e ai* (eat)! *Hoopi hoi hoi* (Exciting).

Kamailio:

Fruit should be warm inside after crystallizing. Other fruits can be used in a similar fashion (fresh grapes, canned or fresh halved peaches, or pears). Large bananas should be halved. Bananas and syrup can be prepared in advance and combined in the chafing dish. Prior to serving, heat until syrup becomes thick. Proceed with crystallizing.

Bananas on the Half Shell

6 firm bananas
6 tablespoons rum
1 can (8 oz.) crushed pineapple, drained
2 tablespoons lemon juice
1 teaspoon fresh ginger root, minced
toasted almonds or grated coconut for garnish

Split the bananas in half lengthwise *malama pono* (carefully, in other words), and reserve the skins. Mash bananas and combine with remaining ingredients. Place combined purée in a pastry bag and use a #5 star tip to pipe banana decoratively into halved skins. Bake in 450° F. oven until the fruit is golden brown. Sprinkle with toasted almonds or grated coconut. Serve on leaves, ferns or leaf-covered narrow, long dessert plates (like a corn on the cob or banana split plate). Serves 6.

Burning Banana Sauce (Maia Wewela)

6 ripe bananas, thinly sliced
3 tablespoons butter
6 tablespoons brown sugar
dash of cinnamon
1 tablespoon lemon or lime juice
1 teaspoon orange rind, grated
½ cup rum or brandy
6 scoops pistachio ice cream

Sauté bananas in the blazer pan of your chafing dish or in a skillet with the butter and sugar until sugar begins to carmelize a little. Add cinnamon, lemon juice and orange rind. Mix well and cook until hot. Flambé sauce with heated rum or brandy (see How to Flambé) and spoon over scoops of pistachio ice cream served in a pretty crystal dish or in individual coconut shells (see index). Serves 6.

Another way of preparing this dessert without the ice cream is to use whole small bananas. Preheat oven to 400° F. Melt butter in a pretty fireproof baking dish. Mix remaining ingredients, except rum or brandy, in baking dish. Add bananas and toss and turn to coat well. Bake until sugar has melted and is carmelized. Remove from oven and flambé at table with heated rum or brandy (see How to Flambé).

KO WAHO (OUTDOOR):

Whole bananas can be put on foil, sprinkled with above mixture (omit rum or brandy), wrapped well in foil, and baked outdoors on grill for 10 to 15 minutes. Serve with a dollop of whipped cream.

Cherry-Pineapple Sauce

    1 can frozen pineapple juice concentrate
    2 tablespoons lemon juice
    1 can (8oz.) crushed pineapple
    ½ of 4-oz. bottle maraschino cherries,
        chopped coarsely with 2 tablespoons juice
    1 cup heavy cream, whipped

Stir the first four ingredients into the whipped cream and freeze in a refrigerator dish. Two hours before serving, defrost until mushy and whip up with a whisk. Spoon over fruit, ice cream, mangoes, papayas, fresh pineapple slices, or combine with kumquats and other fruits. Serves 6.

Coconuts

In Hawaii, coconut has as many uses as there are days in the year. The meat of a fresh young coconut is truly ambrosial. However, outside of their native lands, fresh young coconuts are difficult to obtain. Choose one that feels heavy to the hand and when shaken sounds full of liquid.

TO GRATE COCONUT:

Pierce eyes at one end of coconut with an ice pick. Drain and reserve liquid only if light colored. Using a hammer, bang the shell all over without breaking it. Crack it open and most of the meat should come away from the shell. Some people find that heating the coconut in a very hot oven for a few minutes makes it easier to crack. Remove remaining coconut with a knife and peel off dark skin. Coconut pieces can be eaten like any other nuts.

To shred coconut, use a hand grater or electric blender. With the latter you will have to add a little coconut liquid or water. Fresh grated or shredded coconut can be refrigerated in a plastic bag for one week or frozen for months.

Coconut Milk

> 2½ cups fresh coconut
> 1 cup water (use part coconut liquid *if light colored*; remainder water)
> 1 cup milk

Grate coconut as directed above. Boil water with milk and pour over coconut. Let stand for at least half an hour. Strain through a very fine sieve or double thickness of cheesecloth, pressing down hard to squeeze out all the liquid. Store in refrigerator like fresh milk. Never boil in recipes or milk will curdle.

Coconut Cream

Make as above using 1 cup heavy cream and 1 cup milk or 2 cups medium cream. To whip coconut cream, use 2 cups heavy cream and make as above. Chill before whipping.

Packaged Coconut

Comes in cans or bags, flaked, grated or shredded. Coconut milk or cream can be made from these also, but it is much sweeter than when made from the fresh. For coconut milk, add 2 cups hot milk for each cup of flaked coconut. Let stand 30 minutes and then strain as above. For coconut cream, use medium or heavy cream and no milk. Coconut cream made with heavy cream can also be whipped if chilled.

At the Hawaii Kai, a prepared coconut powder is used. This can be purchased at gourmet shops and at food departments in better stores.

There is also a new product just out—Durkee's Imitation Coconut Flavor. Three teaspoons to 1 cup of milk or heavy cream will give you an excellent substitute for coconut milk or cream. Your local grocer might have it in stock.

Toasted Coconut

Spread fresh grated, or packaged coconut out on a shallow baking pan. Heat oven to 325° F. and toast until lightly browned. Stir for even toasting.

Chili or Curry Coconut

Add 1 teaspoon chili or curry powder to 1 cup of grated or shredded coconut before toasting.

Colored Coconut

Put flaked or shredded coconut in a large jar and add 2 tablespoons colored fruit gelatin. Cover and shake until coconut is tinted evenly.

Coconut Chips

1 fresh coconut, shell removed (see above)

Break coconut into large pieces and grate it on the largest side of a cole slaw grater. Spread chips out on a shallow baking pan and bake in preheated oven 350° F. until golden brown. Stir occasionally to brown evenly.

Coconut Pudding (Haupia)

This island dessert is a "must" at every luau.

3 cups coconut milk (see above)
4 tablespoons sugar
dash of salt
dash of vanilla
3 tablespoons cornstarch

In a saucepan heat all but ¼ cup coconut milk over low heat (do not boil). Add sugar, salt and vanilla. Mix remaining coconut milk with cornstarch and add gradually to pan, stirring until mixture thickens. Pour into a square cake pan. Chill.

Traditionally, the pudding is cut into small cubes and placed on clean ti leaves. However, we sometimes use a mold for the pudding and serve it with globs of whipped coconut cream or we decorate the mold with tinted coconut (see above). Try serving it cubed in individual crystal coupettes decorated with crushed pineapple or kumquats and whipped cream. Try it also with other dessert sauces (see index). Serves 6.

Island Coconut Custard

A velvety smooth custard, chilled and served with a meringue topping.

> 2 cups milk
> 1 can (3½ oz.) flaked coconut or freshly grated coconut
> 4 egg yolks, beaten
> ⅛ teaspoon salt
> ¼ cup sugar
> 1 teaspoon rum flavoring
> 10 maraschino cherries, chopped
> 4 egg whites
> ½ cup sugar
> 6 whole maraschino cherries (for garnish)

In a saucepan, combine milk and coconut and cook over low heat for 5 minutes, stirring occasionally. In top of a double boiler, combine egg yolks, salt and ¼ cup sugar; mix well. Gradually add milk mixture to egg yolk mixture and cook over boiling water, stirring constantly, until spoon becomes coated. Remove from heat and add rum flavoring. Cool slightly. Turn into pretty crystal parfait dishes and chill. Top with chopped cherries. Beat egg whites until foamy (not too stiff). Gradually add ½ cup sugar, beating constantly until whites are stiff and glossy. Mound over coconut custard and top with a whole maraschino cherry. Serves 6.

Ko Ko Nut Ball

Island ice cream in a fresh coconut topped with chocolate sauce and whipped coconut cream.

Place a large scoop of coconut ice cream in half a coconut (see index) and drizzle chocolate syrup over it. Sprinkle grated coconut on this and top with whipped cream (use a pastry bag and star tip). Decorate with a maraschino cherry, fortune cookie and decorative paper fan (*Denguri*) placed into side of coconut.

Coconut Parfait

1⅓ cups water
⅔ cup sugar
1 tablespoon rum or orange flavoring
2 cups grated fresh coconut or 1½ cups packaged, grated coconut
1 cup heavy cream whipped and tinted deep pink
(use vegetable coloring)

Make a simple syrup of water and sugar by boiling together for 3 to 5 minutes. Pour into pyrex dish and cool. Stir in 1 tablespoon of rum or orange flavoring. Add grated fresh coconut or 1½ cups of grated, packaged coconut that has been soaked in 8 tablespoons of milk for 30 minutes and then drained. Add tinted whipped cream, mix well, and place in freezer. Freeze until mushy. Remove from freezer and beat with whisk until frothy. Fill parfait glasses with mixture and freeze until firm. Garnish with candied violets or slivered almonds. Serves 6.

Polynesian Fruit Cup

1 cup papaya (fresh or canned), diced
1 cup mangoes (fresh or canned), diced
1 cup fresh pineapple, diced
1 cup lychees
½ cup kumquats, diced
1 cup shredded fresh coconut
1 tablespoon fresh ginger root, minced
2 teaspoons grated orange peel

Combine above ingredients in a large bowl. Mix together 1 cup orange juice, 1 tablespoon lemon juice and ¼ cup light rum or brandy. Pour over fruits and chill thoroughly. Spoon into 6 coconut shells (see index) or halved and scooped-out pineapples (use fruit), and garnish with whipped cream. Serves 6.

Korean Candied Ginger (Sang Juhn Kiva)

Candied ginger is a very popular sweet with the Korean people in the Islands and is often used in their meat and poultry dishes in place of fresh ginger root.

1 cup fresh ginger root, peeled
¼ cup sugar
¼ cup light corn syrup
¼ cup water

Slice ginger into thin pieces. Place in a bowl and pour boiling water over them. Let sit for 5 minutes. Drain and dry on a paper towel. Boil sugar, corn syrup and water until a thin syrup forms. Add ginger and cook over a very low flame until there no longer is any syrup and the ginger is dry and crystallized. Place on a metal rack to dry completely. Serves 6.

Grapefruit Snow

1 grapefruit (large)
⅓ cup crème de menthe (green)
1 envelope gelatin (plain)
¾ cup water
½ cup sugar
chopped mint
juice of two grapefruits or 1½ cups canned grapefruit juice
1 tablespoon lemon juice
1 slice fresh ginger root, minced
2 egg whites

Cut grapefruit in half and scoop out sections. Remove seeds and membranes. Pour crème de menthe over sections and refrigerate. Soak gelatin in ¼ cup cold water until dissolved. Boil the remaining ½ cup water and add sugar. Cook until dissolved. Add the gelatin and water slowly and stir constantly. Add grapefruit juice, lemon juice and ginger root and combine. Place in 2 freezing trays until the edges are iced and the mixture is mushy (about 1 hour). Remove the mixture and place in a bowl. Beat egg whites until stiff and fold into the mushy sherbet. Beat with an electric mixer for 3 to 5 minutes. Place in a large, round, chilled 1½-quart mold or 8 individual molds and return to the freezer until stiff (about 2 to 3 hours).

When ready to serve, run a knife blade around the edge and turn out onto a pretty serving dish. Garnish with the green grapefruit sections and the chopped mint. Serves 8 to 10.

Kamailio:

You can substitute green vegetable coloring for crème de menthe. Simply dissolve ½ teaspoon coloring in ⅓ cup lightly salted water.

Island Mango Ice Cream (Waiu I Paa I Ka Hau)

2 soft, ripe mangoes or 1 can (16 oz.), drained
2 tablespoons lemon juice
1 slice fresh ginger root, minced
¾ cup sugar
2 eggs, separated
2 tablespoons sugar
1 cup heavy cream
½ teaspoon rum extract

Peel fresh mangoes and remove pulp. Mash fruit well. Add lemon juice, ginger root and sugar. Combine well and place in freezing compartment in a shallow tray for 1 hour. In a bowl, beat egg whites until stiff and add 2 tablespoons sugar. In another bowl beat egg yolks until light and fluffy and fold into the egg whites. Beat heavy cream until thick but not stiff and fold into egg mixture. Remove frozen mango mixture and add to egg and cream mixture. Add rum extract. Toss lightly and combine. Place mixture in a deeper freezing tray or individual sherbet glasses and freeze until stiff. Stir once or twice while freezing. Ice cream should be frozen in 3 hours. Garnish with chopped macadamia nuts, maraschino cherries or shredded coconut. Serves 6.

Mango Macadamia Delight

Tangy mango ice cream splashed with exotic crushed mangoes, macadamia nuts and whipped cream.

Place a large scoop of mango ice cream in half a coconut. Combine 2 ounces honey with 2 ounces chopped macadamia nuts and drizzle over ice cream. Top with whipped cream (use pastry bag for this). Top with additional chopped macadamia nuts. Garnish with a maraschino cherry. Place a Chinese paper fan into side of coconut and place a fortune cookie on side.

Mangoes in Honeyed Sauce

1 can (30 oz.) mangoes
1 cup honey
1 teaspoon fresh ginger root, minced
1 tablespoon lemon juice

Drain juice of mangoes into a large saucepan and heat with honey, ginger root and lemon juice. Simmer for 10 minutes. Put mangoes into large bowl and pour syrup over them. Cool and refrigerate overnight, turning occasionally. Serve in a crystal compote dish. Serves 10.

Kamailio:

Other fruits can be used in place of mangoes. Fresh fruit must be cored, peeled and cooked for 10 minutes in enough water to cover. Add sugar to taste. Rum, brandy or your favorite liqueur can be added.

Malihini Mélange of Fruits

Beautiful in fruit-shaped dessert dishes.

1 can (10 oz.) lychee fruits
1 cup fresh or canned papaya, drained
1 cup fresh or canned mangoes, drained
2 bananas, sliced
¼ cup orange juice (you can substitute syrup of canned fruits)
2 tablespoons lemon juice
12 maraschino cherries, halved, with juice
flaked coconut (fresh or packaged)

Combine all ingredients except maraschino cherries and coconut. Color with maraschino cherry juice. Stir and chill. Serve in a large crystal bowl or in individual dessert dishes. Garnish with halved cherries and sprinkle with coconut flakes. Serves 6.

Red Oranges (Alani Ulaula)

6 large navel oranges
1 cup water
1 cup sugar
½ cup corn syrup
3 tablespoons orange marmalade
1 cup water
1 can (13½ oz.) crushed pineapple, drained
2 tablespoons fresh ginger root, minced
3 tablespoons lemon juice
1 drop red vegetable coloring
3 tablespoons light rum or Curaçao

Peel 2 oranges with vegetable peeler. Cut peeled rind into 1-inch strips, ⅛-inch wide. Peel remaining oranges and discard rind. Put oranges in a large bowl and reserve. In a saucepan, combine orange rind and 1 cup water; cover and bring to a boil. Remove from fire, drain and rinse well in cold water. Reserve. Combine sugar, corn syrup, orange marmalade and 1 cup water in a large saucepan; bring to boiling point and stir to dissolve sugar. Simmer for 8 to 10 minutes. Add orange rind, crushed pineapple and minced ginger root. Cook uncovered until syrup becomes slightly thickened (about 30 to 45 minutes). Remove from heat; stir in lemon juice, red vegetable coloring and rum or curaçao. Pour hot syrup over oranges in bowl; toss and turn to coat. Cool and refrigerate overnight, turning occasionally.

When convenient, place each orange in a crystal stemmed coupette. Pour sauce over oranges. Garnish with shredded coconut, slivered almonds or chopped macadamia nuts.

If you're not dieting, put a bowl of whipped cream on the table. Serves 6.

Kamailio:

To make eating easier, oranges may be peeled and cut into six wedges; cut to, but not through, the base of the orange. Spread wedges apart slightly. To cut into wedges, cut each orange in half; then divide each half in three. (See index for Tomato Petals.)

Island Mandarin Oranges

½ cup honey
1 can (30 oz.) mandarin oranges
1 slice fresh ginger root, minced
½ cup white vinegar
3 tablespoons Kona Koffee liqueur
3 teaspoons soy sauce
3 tablespoons sugar

Boil honey, juice drained from oranges and ginger root for 2 minutes. Add vinegar, Kona Koffee liqueur, soy sauce and sugar. Simmer 3 minutes and pour over mandarin oranges. Marinate overnight in refrigerator. Drain and serve cold in individual footed coupettes. Garnish with maraschino cherries or shredded coconut. Serves 6.

Samoan Papaya Dessert

2 ripe papayas or 2 (16 oz.) cans, drained
1 teaspoon salt
1 slice fresh ginger root, minced
1 tablespoon lemon or lime juice
1 cup coconut cream (see index)

Purée peeled and seeded papaya fruit in a blender. Combine with remaining ingredients. Spoon into parfait glasses and chill. Garnish with maraschino cherries or tinted coconut. Serves 6.

Pineapple, the King of Fruits

Halikihiki is the Hawaiian word for it

Just as no one can date the arrival of the first settlers on the Islands, so little is known of when and how the King of Fruits first reached the Hawaiian shores.

Even today, using the most modern and efficient machinery available, and producing the world's largest crop, the human factor has not been eliminated. The human eye and hand are still the most reliable judges for selecting a "ripe" pineapple; picked right from the field this is the juiciest of all fruits. It contains 85% water and 15% sugar. But we on the Mainland rarely have access to a field-ripened pineapple. Unfortunately our pineapples ripen during the voyage from the Islands.

JUDGING RIPENESS

How can one determine if a pineapple is ripe? Color is not always indicative, since a pineapple shell may be green while the fruit inside is golden and juicy. Some people say that if you pluck a leaf from the crown and it pulls away easily, it's ready to eat. Others say if the pineapple's spikes are flattened rather than pointed, the pineapple is ripe.

Aroma can also be indicative of ripeness. However, if there is a very strong pineapple fragrance, check to be sure that the skin has not been pierced; if it has, the juices may have run out.

The best test is to thump the pineapple as one would a watermelon. A hollow sound means little juice. A dull thumping sound is good news. So when choosing a pineapple at the supermarket, we suggest you "play it by ear".

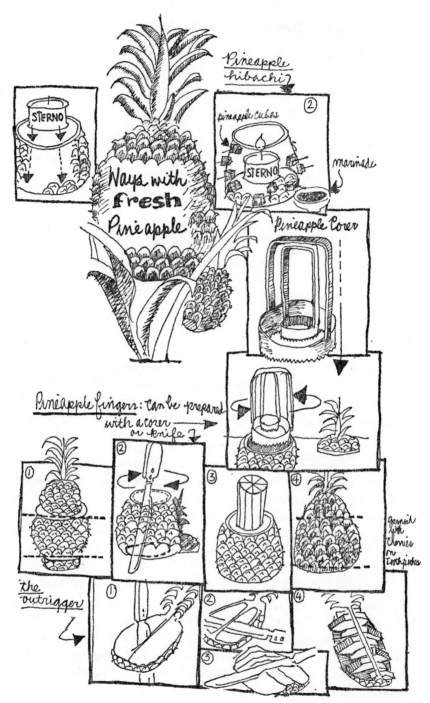

Ways with **fresh** Pineapple

STERNO

Pineapple hibachi

② pineapple cubes

STERNO

marinade

Pineapple Corer

Pineapple fingers: can be prepared with a corer or knife

① ② ③ ④

garnish with cherries on toothpicks

the outrigger

① ② ④ ⑤

If all your tests fail, you can improve the flavor of the pineapple by sugaring it lightly or pouring ½ cup of canned pineapple juice over it at least one hour before serving.

To Freeze Pineapple

Buy pineapples when in season and inexpensive. That's the time to freeze them.

CRUSHED PINEAPPLE:

Peel and core pineapples and cut into small pieces. Place a cupful at a time into blender container, sprinkle with ¼ cup sugar and blend for 8-10 seconds. Put the crushed pineapple into freezer bags or containers and freeze. When needed, defrost at room temperature and use as you would fresh crushed pineapple. In recipes calling for gelatin, fresh pineapple must be cooked for 5 to 7 minutes because it contains an enzyme which destroys gelatin and prevents solidifying.

PINEAPPLE CUBES, TIDBITS OR SLICES:

Peel and core pineapple and cut into cubes, tidbits or slices. Freeze separately in freezer bags. To use, defrost at room temperature for 1 hour.

PINEAPPLE FINGERS:

Peel and core pineapples; cut into 3-inch fingers and sprinkle with sugar. Freeze fingers *wickiwicki* (quickly) on a flat baking sheet and then store in freezer bags or containers. To use with drinks, put them frozen into drinking mugs.

TO CORE:

An ingenious and inexpensive device which can core and remove the fresh pineapple fruit, leaving the shell and bottom intact, is now available in all hardware and department stores.

Pineapple Ono Loa
Delicious!

1 large pineapple with top on
½ cup rum (light)
2 teaspoons lemon juice
3 tablespoons honey
¼ cup sugar
¼ cup pineapple juice

Use the new pineapple corer, or cut straight through pineapple 1-1½ inches from bottom. Do the same at the top. Reserve top and bottom slices. Using a long thin knife, remove contents from shell in one piece. Cut in half lengthwise, and make 8 wedges, as if cutting a pie; remove core. Marinate pineapple segments in remaining ingredients 2 to 3 hours or overnight. One hour before serving, replace bottom of pineapple and fasten with toothpicks. Replace drained pineapple spears in pineapple. Cover and refrigerate. Use bamboo skewers to spear pineapple. Serves 6.

Hibachi Pineapple

Another attractive way of serving the fresh pineapple is to use it as a centerpiece and hibachi. Follow directions above for cutting and coring pineapple. Place on a tray of greens (ferns, parsley, etc.) and insert a can of sterno into pineapple shell (to raise sterno, if necessary, use a small cup). Cut fruit into cubes, skewer with bamboo or fancy picks and insert all around the outside of the pineapple shell. Put rum marinade (above) in a small bowl on the tray. Light the sterno and have guests dip the skewered pineapple into the rum marinade and then warm it over the hibachi fire.

Banana chunks, first soaked in salted water to prevent discoloring, (1 teaspoon salt to a cup of cold water) can also be dipped into the rum marinade and heated in the same manner.

Beach Boys' Bash

2 cans (15 oz. each) pineapple tidbits, drained,
  or fresh coarsely grated pineapple
4 cups cooked rice, cold
2 cups miniature marshmallows
½ cup walnuts or macadamia nuts, coarsely chopped
½ cup sugar
1 jar (7 oz.) maraschino cherries, coarsely chopped
2 teaspoons lemon juice
½ teaspoon cinnamon
1 cup heavy cream, whipped

Combine all ingredients in a large bowl and toss lightly. Turn into a 1½-quart spring form mold and chill overnight. Individual molds are also nice for this. *Hauoli piha!* Delightful! Serves 10 to 12.

Roana and Gene's Pineapple Soufflé

Even the most experienced cook is in awe of the soufflé, cold or hot. We can't understand where this fear had its beginning because the most impressive soufflé can be achieved if you use a light touch to fold and combine the beaten egg white and yolks with other ingredients. Try this one, and go on fearlessly to other bigger and puffier soufflées. He pomaikai i ulia wale (translation: good luck)!

½ cup water
1 cup sugar
¼ teaspoon cream of tartar
5 eggs, separated
1½ cups sugar
1½ envelopes gelatin
½ cup pineapple juice
1 tablespoon lemon juice
2 cups crushed pineapple (cooked or canned), drained
1 cup commercial sour cream

1. Grease the bottom and sides of a 1-quart soufflé dish. Make a collar with a 26-inch length of wax paper that has been folded lengthwise in thirds. Grease one side of paper lightly and sprinkle with 2 tablespoons of sugar. With string or a large rubber band, tie collar (sugar-side in) around soufflé dish to form a 2-inch rim above the top edge.

2. In a saucepan, heat water and melt sugar with cream of tartar

over low heat. Boil rapidly over high heat until syrup forms. Beat egg whites in a heatproof mixing bowl until stiff and pour the syrup in a thin steady stream into the egg whites. Continue to beat mixture until it stands up in peaks. Place the bowl into a larger bowl filled with chopped ice and cool the meringue.

3. Beat egg yolks until light and fluffy and gradually add 1½ cups sugar. Soften gelatin in pineapple juice (use drained juice and add additional juice to make ½ cup) and lemon juice, then heat in top of double boiler until dissolved. Add gelatin mixture to crushed pineapple and stir in sour cream. Fold in beaten egg yolks. Combine and fold this mixture into the cooled meringue. Pour mixture into collared dish and chill overnight. Remove paper collar before serving. Serves 6 to 8.

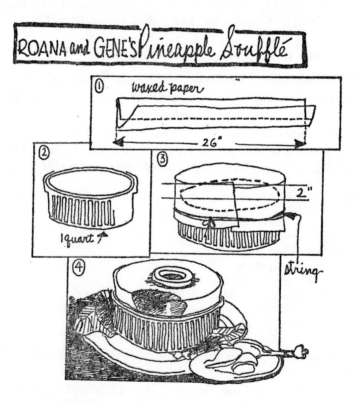

ROANA and GENE'S *Pineapple Soufflé*

Pineapple Oahu

    1 large pineapple
    ¾ cup strawberry jam
    6 macaroons, crumbled

Cut the top from a large ripe pineapple (reserve it) and scoop out fruit carefully so as not to pierce the shell (see index for procedure). Discard core and dice fruit. In a bowl combine strawberry jam and crumbled macaroons; toss with diced fruit. Fill pineapple shell with mixture and cover pineapple with foil. Place on a baking sheet and bake at 400° F. in a preheated oven for 30 minutes. Remove foil, put pineapple top on (it looks prettier when you bring it to the table this way), and bake for 15 minutes longer. Remove from oven, place on a bed of greens, and flambé (see index) at table with ¼ cup heated rum. Serves 6.

Liu Liu:

Pineapple can be prepared, covered with foil and refrigerated, unbaked, for a day or two. When ready to serve, bake as directed above. The filled, foil-wrapped pineapple (and the top too) can also be frozen. When ready to bake place in 400° F. oven (wrapped in foil) and bake for 45 minutes. Remove foil and bake additional 15 minutes. Then flambé as directed.

Fresh Hawaiian Sugar Loaf Pineapple Nuggets

Romanced with wild Kona honey.

Peel, core and cube a ripe pineapple. Place in a compote bowl and drizzle with Kona honey. Toss and turn to coat. Use fancy picks to serve. Serves 6.

Custard in a Pineapple

Hoopihoihoi! (*exciting!*)

3 small pineapples, cut in half lengthwise (leaves intact)
2 cups milk
½ cup sugar
4 egg yolks, beaten
¼ cup rum (optional)
½ teaspoon vanilla
24 maraschino cherries, halved
1 cup heavy cream, whipped and tinted pink with vegetable coloring
6 maraschino cherries

Scoop out the fruit from the halved pineapples. *Malama pono* (translation: carefully)! Leave a ½-inch wall of flesh attached to the shell. Remove core and cut fruit into small cubes. Reserve shells. In the top of a double boiler, over hot water, heat milk with sugar. Add the hot milk to the egg yolks, stirring occasionally. Return milk and egg yolks to double boiler and cook, stirring until the spoon becomes coated. Remove pan from heat and stir in rum and vanilla. Place pan over a bowl filled with ice cubes, stirring constantly. Chill well. Fold the pineapple cubes and maraschino cherries into the custard and fill shells with the mixture. Pipe edges of pineapple shell with whipped cream (use pastry bag and #5 star tip) and place a large whipped cream star in the center. Top with a maraschino cherry. Serves 6.

Kamailio:

If you're pressed for time, substitute 2 packages vanilla pudding for custard. Cook as directed on package, add rum and cool. Fold in pineapple and maraschino cherries and proceed with recipe.

Fresh Pineapple Sherbet

fruit from 1 fresh pineapple, coarsely grated
1 cup pineapple juice
2 tablespoons lemon juice
1 cup water
1 cup sugar
1 cup heavy cream whipped with 3 tablespoons light rum
6 maraschino cherries, stemmed

In a saucepan, combine all ingredients except whipped cream and cherries. Simmer for 15 minutes until thickened. Freeze in a shallow tray until edges are iced and mushy. Beat mixture with electric beater until fluffy. Freeze overnight. Several hours before serving, soften at room temperature and fold in whipped cream. Spoon into tall crystal sherbet glasses and top with cherries. Refrigerate. [Canned pineapple tidbits can be used also (30-ounce can).] Serves 6.

Pineapple Froth

1 can (30 oz.) crushed pineapple or fresh grated pineapple
2 tablespoons honey
1 tablespoon lemon juice
1 tablespoon rum or rum flavoring
1 slice fresh ginger (minced)
1 cup heavy cream, whipped and tinted light green
   with vegetable coloring

In a chilled pyrex bowl, combine all ingredients except whipped cream. Fold in whipped cream lightly. Freeze until edges are iced (4 to 5 hours). Remove and with electric mixer beat until fluffy. Spoon into your prettiest dessert dishes and refreeze. Remove from freezer 1 hour before serving and refrigerate. Garnish with shredded coconut, maraschino cherries or toasted almond slivers. Serves 6.

Kamailio:

1. You can turn the dessert into a mold if you wish. A half hour before serving, dip into warm water and turn over onto a pretty platter. Garnish as in recipe. Refrigerate until needed.

2. You may not believe this but we have used our best "whiskey sour" crystal stemware to freeze this dessert in, without damage to any of them. Try it!

3. You can also freeze dessert in a bowl. At least one hour before serving remove from freezer. When it becomes mushy, spoon into fancy dessert dishes and refrigerate.

Delicious Pineapple Sherbet

Sherbet embellished by chunks of fresh field-ripened Kawai pineapple.

Peel, core and cube a fresh pineapple (see index). Coat with honey. Place a large scoop of pineapple sherbet in a footed compote bowl and surround with honey-dipped pineapple cubes. Place a Denguri fan on the side of the bowl and serve with a fortune cookie.

Heavenly Pineapple Whip

4 egg yolks
2½ cups pineapple juice
2 envelopes unflavored gelatin
½ cup sugar
dash of salt
3 tablespoons lemon juice
1 can (13 oz.) pineapple tidbits, drained
10 maraschino cherries, cut into small pieces
2 cups heavy cream, whipped

In a saucepan, beat egg yolks with a whisk. Add 1 cup pineapple juice and whip until blended. Stir in gelatin, sugar and salt. Heat mixture slowly over medium heat, stirring constantly until just ready to boil. Remove from heat and add remaining pineapple juice and lemon juice. Chill mixture in refrigerator until it mounds when dropped from a spoon. Fold in pineapple tidbits, maraschino bits, and then the whipped cream. Pour into an 8- to 10-cup mold and chill until set. Before serving, unmold and garnish with additional maraschino cherries. Serves 8 to 10.

Hawaiian Pineapple Fritters

1 large pineapple, peeled, cored and cut into slices ¼-inch thick
　　or 1 can (16 oz.) pineapple slices, drained
3 tablespoons sugar
1 cup flour
½ teaspoon salt
2 eggs, beaten
1 tablespoon melted butter
1 tablespoon lemon juice
⅔ cup milk
dash of rum or sherry wine (optional)
2 inches oil for deep frying

Sprinkle fresh pineapple slices with sugar (not the canned) and let stand 30 minutes. Sift together flour and salt. To the beaten eggs add the melted butter and lemon juice and combine with flour. Add the milk (and sherry or rum if you wish) and stir until mixture is well blended and smooth. Let stand 30 minutes. Heat oil in a large skillet for deep frying. With tongs dip pineapple slices into batter and put a few at a time into hot oil. Do not crowd. Turn once and fry until delicately browned. Drain on absorbent paper and sprinkle with sugar. Glaze under broiler flame. Serves 6.

Liu Liu:

Fritters can be made in advance, but do not broil them. Before serving sprinkle with sugar and broil on both sides until glazed.

Exotic Pineapple Meringue

3 small pineapples, halved lengthwise (leaves intact)
6 scoops ice cream (any flavor)
4 egg whites
pinch of salt
¼ teaspoon cream of tartar
8 tablespoons sugar
1 tablespoon rum

Scoop pineapple out of shells (see index for procedure) and cut into small pieces. Replace in shell and sugar if necessary. Cover leaves with silver foil.

Preheat oven to 400° F. (this is important!). Place a large scoop of ice cream in pineapple center and cover with meringue (see below). Spread meringue to edge of pineapples, pulling it up in peaks and swirls. Place pineapples on a baking sheet and bake for 6 minutes. Remove foil and serve immediately on a bed of greens. Serves 6.

MERINGUE

Beat egg whites with salt and cream of tartar until soft peaks form. Gradually add the sugar, 2 tablespoons at a time, beating well after each addition. Add the rum and continue to beat until stiff peaks form when beater is raised. Pastry bag and #5 star tip can be used.

Aloha Pineapple and Banana

    1 can (30 oz.) pineapple slices
      or 1 large fresh pineapple, peeled, cored and cut into 10 slices
    2 bananas, cut into 10 pieces
    1 tablespoon lemon juice
    3 tablespoons cinnamon sugar
    4 egg whites (at room temperature)
    ¼ teaspoon cream of tartar
    ½ cup of sugar
    maraschino cherries (for garnish)

Aloha PINEAPPLE *and* BANANA

Drain pineapple slices and arrange on a greased baking sheet. Place banana pieces in center of pineapple. Sprinkle with lemon juice and ½ of the cinnamon sugar. Beat egg whites with cream of tartar until soft peaks form. Gradually add the sugar, 2 tablespoons at a time, beating well after each addition. Continue to beat until stiff peaks form when beater is raised. Spread meringue over the top of the pineapple slices, covering the banana, with a fluted or swirling design. Sprinkle remainder of cinnamon sugar over meringue, and bake in a preheated 400° F. oven for 10 minutes until meringue is golden brown. Garnish with maraschino cherries and serve warm or cold. Serves 10.

Island Fruits with Crème de Menthe Sauce

When fresh fruits are available they should be substituted for canned fruits. Use a large can or one pound of everything fresh.

> pineapple fingers or slices
> lichees
> kumquats
> melon balls
> mangoes
> grapes, seedless
> mandarin oranges
> peaches and pear halves
> lemon juice
> 1 small package lemon jello

Line a silver serving tray with ferns (real or artificial) or leaves. Arrange fruits attractively in a circle or in rows, with the fruit overlapping each other (keep colors and shape in mind). Sprinkle with lemon juice. Heat jello as per directions and cool. With a pastry brush, coat fruits. This will prevent discoloration and give a sheen to fruits (use the leftover jello for dessert at lunchtime for the family). Serve with a bowl of Crème de Menthe Sauce (below). Serves 12.

Kamailio:

Another way of serving the fruit salad is by halving small pineapples from crown to base. Core and scoop out fruit leaving a ½-inch shell. Cut fruit into chunks and combine with other colorful fruits. Heap the pineapple shell attractively with mixed fruits and coat with jello as recipe directs.

The fruit salad can also be arranged in individual coupettes, a large crystal bowl or brandy snifter.

Cut fresh fruit can also be kept from becoming discolored by being dipped into salted water (1 teaspoon salt per cup of cold water). This improves the flavor too.

Liu Liu:

Since jello is used to make this attractive fruit platter, you can easily prepare everything in advance.

CREME DE MENTHE SAUCE

1 pint commercial sour cream
1 cup honey
¼ cup Crème de Menthe (green) liqueur

Combine all ingredients well or use a beater. Refrigerate. If a darker tint is desirable, add a drop of green food coloring.

Luau Fruit Decoration

(It's edible and can be prepared 1 or 2 days in advance.)

1. Line the bottom of a large round tray with styrofoam floral blocks (each about 5″ x 4″ x 2″) leaving a two-inch empty border all around. Cover the blocks with silver foil.

2. Pile 3 or 4 blocks at one end of tray and skewer them well to the bottom blocks with heavy wooden picks. Conceal blocks with ferns or leaves (real or artificial); fasten in place with toothpicks. (Styrofoam and picks can be bought at dime stores or florist.)

3. Using same procedure as in making lemon rosettes (see page 170) cut 10 or 12 points through the center of a large melon. Remove seeds.

4. Secure the halves well with heavy wooden picks, one above the other, onto the raised blocks.

5. Now arrange fruits (see Island Fruits page 236) in overlapping sections, following the drawing. Start at one side and work clockwise, using toothpicks occasionally to hold fruit in place. Fruit should completely cover foil.

6. Around the two-inch border, arrange circles of pineapple, fresh orange slices, spiced apple rings, etc., overlapping slightly. In the center of each, insert a lychee; secure a green or red cherry with a fancy pick in each lychee.

7. Arrange two bunches of grapes to fall gracefully from sides of melon; fasten with picks; skewer a bright berry to each melon point with a fancy pick.

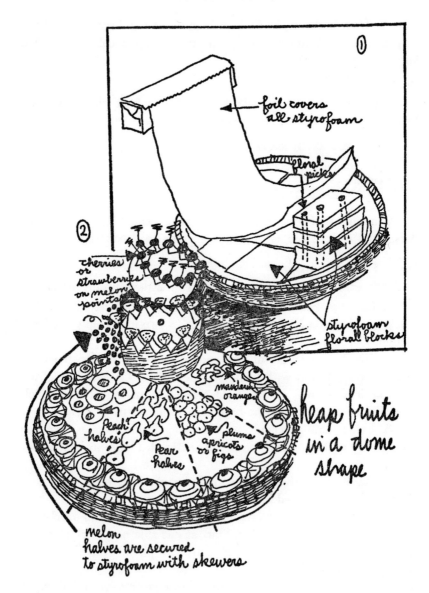

foil covers all styrofoam

floral picks

styrofoam floral blocks

cherries or strawberries on melon points

heap fruits in a dome shape

mandarin orange

Peach halves

Pear halves

plums apricots or figs

melon halves are secured to styrofoam with skewers

8. Follow procedure in previous recipe for sprinkling fruits with lemon juice and brushing with gelatin (see recipe above). This prevents discoloration and shrinking, so that fruits can be prepared 1 to 2 days in advance.

9. Just before serving, fill melon halves with cantaloupe or watermelon balls. Serve with crème de menthe sauce (see page 237).

Kona Koffee Parfait

Ice cream flavors with the haunting taste of Kona Koffee liqueur at its best.

Place coffee ice cream in a parfait glass. Combine 1 ounce Kona Koffee liqueur with ½ ounce grenadine and spoon over ice cream. Freeze overnight. Top with whipped cream (use pastry bag) and maraschino cherry. Place a Denguri fan into side of parfait glass. Serve with a fortune cookie.

Kona Coffee

The little known village of Kona is the home of the Kona coffee plantations—the only place in Hawaii and even the entire United States where coffee is grown commercially. The Hawaiians attribute the excellence of their Kona coffee to the fact that it is grown only along the coastline under ideal climate. Kona coffee can be purchased from Empire Coffee, 486 Ninth Avenue, New York 10018.

Iced Kona Coffee

Make coffee your favorite way and sweeten to taste. Chill. Fill a tall glass or mug with cracked ice and pour coffee over it. Add a dash (or more) of Kahlua liqueur. Top with a dollop of whipped cream.

Koko Palm Cakes

Triple tropical fruit layers, shredded fresh coconut and a splash of rum.

3 sponge cake layers
splash of rum
splash of maraschino cherry juice
#2 can (16 oz.) pineapple filling
3 ounces shredded coconut
1 pint whipped cream
1 tube (3 oz.) red piping jelly
1 tube (3 oz.) green piping jelly
1 miniature plastic palm tree

Spread pineapple filling thickly between sponge layers and splash rum over filling. Drizzle cherry juice over layers. Put layers together and spread whipped cream, ¼ inch thick, over entire exposed surface. Sprinkle shredded coconut liberally over whipped cream. With red piping jelly, write "Aloha" on center of top. Stick palm tree near letter "A". Pipe green jelly next to red for a two-tone effect.

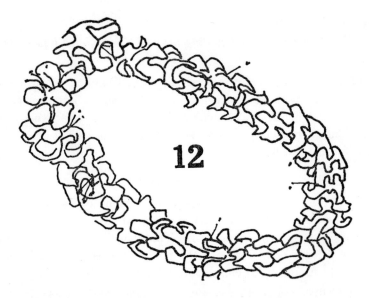

LET'S HAVE A LUAU

Take a birthday party with all its little goodies, add an elaborate wedding feast with singing and dancing, throw in a traditional Thanksgiving dinner with the trimmings, then top it off with an old-fashioned country supper; serve them all at the same time in the same gaily decorated room and you've got something like an authentic Hawaiian luau.

Actually, there's nothing that really compares to a genuine Hawaiian luau. At best, we can only imitate it. For, of all the festive events that Hawaiians are famous for, nothing is more symbolic of their culture and character than the traditional luau. Love, marriage, family, friendship, religion and prosperity are all celebrated in a joyous ritual that goes back to the very origins of tribal structure.

The ancient Hawaiian word for this glorious event was *Ahaaina*, or, "gathering of friends to partake of food". As time passed, the commonly used word *luau*, meaning "leaf of the taro" (the taro plant was and still is an important food source) became the accepted name for this happy occasion.

For the fun-loving people of the Islands, almost any occasion can be used as an excuse to give a luau—birthdays, national and religious holidays, visitors from other Islands, marriages and even divorces! Before and during the luau, which may take many days to prepare, there is much singing and dancing and frequently the natives from different villages will engage in friendly contests, with everyone winning the prize of added enjoyment.

Though the luau is essentially a happy event, it is also richly endowed with ancient tabus and religious ritual. It is these sacred laws and tribal customs that dictate not only the type of food that can be eaten but also how and when it can be eaten. But the prevailing mood and atmosphere is always one of relaxed contentment and contagious conviviality.

A "must" for any traditional luau is the decoratively displayed roast suckling pig. Though the little porker may occupy the place of honor at the luau table, a colorful panoply of assorted fruits, fishes, fowl, vegetables, and sweets are featured too. The cookables are placed in a huge, deep pit called an *imu* or underground oven which is heated by hot stones lined and covered with ti and banana leaves and insulated with handfuls of good clean earth. Here the food is cooked until the fragrant and tantalizing aromas permeate the air and herald the coming of a glorious feast. Now all one has to do is to eat, drink and be reminded in a hundred wonderful ways that "life can be beautiful . . . especially at a Hawaiian luau".

A Home Luau

Aloha! Here's your opportunity to give the most unforgettable party ever—a Hawaiian luau. Capture the romance and excitement of the Islands right in your own home or backyard, with a minimum of effort and expense.

It's easy to give a luau for 5 to 50 people because most of the exotic foods can be prepared in advance. Try it for any gala occasion, fund-raising functions, graduation party and just plain fun gatherings.

Hundreds of unusual materials for a luau, from invitations, records, table decorations, inexpensive costumes, party favors—everything from tiki gods to fresh Hawaiian foliage—many useful after the party for the bar, den or patio, are now easily obtainable (see Sources of Supply), and also easy to make.

Here are some tips for that unusual party.

Invitations

You can make your own invitations. For example, to notepaper on which date, time and place are printed or written, add the following:

Drawing of palm tree or a tiki god (copy ones in this book).

Make a montage of pineapple and other typical fruits cut from magazines.

Paste on a paper lei.

Cut straw mats into sections and use them as backing for the notepaper.

Starch a square of a splashy tropical print and paste down on cover of card.

Dress

The invitations can suggest that your guests come colorfully dressed for the occasion: grass skirts, aloha shirts, muumuus, sarongs, colorful shifts, and, for the young or daring, bare feet.

Decorations

In the Islands where the lush tropical foliage and flowers grow in profusion, a luau is not complete without a breathtaking display of greenery. To simulate this, fill baskets with lots of flowers and strongly patterned leaves that will not wilt easily; large-leaf philodendron pruned from a houseplant (you won't hurt the plant if you cut out a a few leaves), ivy, rhododendron, magnolia branches and ferns or juniper can be used. Hawaiian flowers and ti or croton leaves can be ordered (see Sources). If you are using foliage from your garden, cut the leaves 24 to 48 hours before you need them, and put them in a pail filled with water. Keep them in a cool dark place, perhaps a shower stall or guest room, until the morning of the party. Then arrange as needed.

For atmosphere, use dimmed lights, candlelight, paper lanterns and torches. Fishnets can be hung across ceilings and walls.

Gather every large bowl you can and fill them chock full with papayas, coconuts, pineapples, lemons, limes and entire hands of bananas. Place all around the room (plan on using them for dessert). Encircle bowls with flower leis. Hawaiian masks, tiki gods, thatching, and tapa-designed paper add to the luau mood (see Sources).

Tables

In keeping with the authentic mood of the Hawaiian luau we suggest that you serve your guests from low (knee-high) tables . . . a little difficult for those afflicted with rheumatism but they'll soon get the hang of it. If you're reluctant to cut off the legs of your Chippendale dining room table, you can improvise a very effective table with long wooden planks supported by bricks (table should be about sixteen inches from the floor). Forget the tablecloth. Cover the entire serving area instead with rose petals, greenery, flowers and of course, food. Forget about the chairs too . . . your guests will be more comfortable sitting on cushions or mats and if they should get a little uncomfortable from overeating, they can just roll under the table.

Serve food in coconut shells, large and small clam shells or pretty wooden bowls. Hawaiian designed paper goods are available also (see Sources of Supply).

To add a glow at the table, have your guests heat their puu puus over the open flame of a hibachi with bamboo skewers.

Entertainment

According to Hawaiian tradition, guests should bring a favorite dish of theirs to the luau. Another tradition is hula dancing contests for men and women. Prizes are awarded for the best ones. Singing contests can also be held. The music of the ukulele will add just the right note, but Hawaiian records are *da kine* (that way) too.

It is also customary for the hostess to give the guests a souvenir (see Sources of Supply).

As the guests enter, wish them *Aloha*, which means hello (as well as farewell). It's not a luau without the traditional "*Aloha*" greeting, a great big kiss and a flower lei placed around the neck of each guest by the host or hostess.

Planning ahead (Liu Liu)

After your guests have been invited, plan and write out your menu, shop, cook it over a period of 2 or 3 days, wrap carefully, and freeze it about two weeks before (we prefer short-term freezer storage). Forget everything until the day before the party.

The day before, check your store of soda, liquor and ice cubes; make your cocktail dips, marinate vegetables and prepare anything that could not be frozen. Foods that require complete thawing should be removed from the freezer and refrigerated.

The morning of the party, wash and dry thoroughly salad greens; wrap in Saran wrap. Refrigerate sodas and arrange leaves and flowers; set out cigarettes and candy. Take out trays and serving dishes to be used. Set the table.

About three hours before the great event, remove the food from the freezer and check the menu to be sure you haven't forgotten anything.

Just before you dress, turn on oven and start foods heating slowly. After you're dressed, put out the cold dips. While the person in charge of the bar (your husband? a guest?) is pouring the second round of drinks, get your vegetables heated, salad tossed, remove the heated food and garnish. And now—*e hoihoi,* enjoy!

Luau Language

Hawaiian is one of the world's most beautiful languages. It is a lilting, melodious tongue, rich in folklore and filled with humor. Even the names of its places, like Lanai or Mauna Loa, sing.

Remarkably, Hawaii did not have a written language as recently as 150 years ago. History was recorded in songs, poems and chants. The missionaries standardized the language—choosing the pronunciations that seemed to be the most common—and gave it an alphabet.

It is said that they had to choose between the letters R and L to denote a Hawaiian sound that comes roughly between the two. They wrote out the personal name of King Kamehameha II as both Liloliho and Rihoriho and asked him to choose. He liked the looks of the former —so Hawaiian has an L rather than an R. With a written language created so arbitrarily, everybody is an expert in pronunciation!

Hawaiian is as strange as it is beautiful. The name of one of the islands' smallest fishes is humuhumunukunukuapuaa, while some people have last names as simple as I. The word "no" means "yes, indeed". The word *aa,* which describes a kind of lava, has crept into our own scientific language and appears as the second word in our dictionary, after *a* but before *aardvark.*

Learn Hawaiian and you know parts of the world's leading languages: The tongue includes words from Chinese, Japanese, Korean, Portuguese, Spanish, a number of Philippine dialects—and several species of pidgin.

PRONOUNCING HAWAIIAN

It's easy to speak like a native. Hawaiian has only 12 letters: five vowels and seven consonants, and they most always sound the way they're supposed to.

One of the reasons why the language sounds so graceful is every word ends in a vowel and there is always a vowel between consonants. This also makes pronunciation easy.

Let's take the vowels first. They're A, E, I, O, U, like our own. Pronounce them this way:

A, as in far

E, as in they
I, as in machine
O, as in no
U, as in too

If you've ever studied Latin or any of the Romance languages, you'll recognize these vowel sounds as the same. The consonants—H, K, L, M, N, P and W—sound just like their English counterparts.

Which syllable of the word should you accent? It's always the next to the last one, which means that a two-syllable word has the accent on the first syllable.

See how easy? humuhumunukunukuapuaa, which looks like a jaw-breaker, rolls off the tongue. Say: hu-mu, repeat it, nu-ku, repeat it, a-pu-a-a. If you're pronouncing it right, it should come out as hoo-moo-hoo-moo-noo-koo-noo-koo-ah-poo-ah'ah.

Now, any language so simple deserves to have some exceptions to the rules for pronunciation, and here they are for Hawaiian.

The letter W is pronounced V when it comes just before the last syllable. The drink *awa*, for example, is pronounced *ava*. The W in Hawaii, on the other hand, is not before the last syllable if the word is properly pronounced Hawa-i so the W stays. Do the islanders a favor and refrain from calling it Ha-why, Ha-va-i or Ha-why-a.

There is also the matter of the "glottal stop" in Hawaiian which is like the sound before the second oh in the English expression oh, oh. Some Hawaiian words have a glottal stop and some don't—even though they're spelled the same. Uku with the glottal stop means louse; without, it means pay. Kau with the glottal stop means mine; without, it means yours.

You may not be exactly right unless you understand which words use the glottal stop. But then, again, Hawaiians are a very understanding people.

You already know quite a lot of luau language. For example, the ladies come wearing *muumuus, lavalavas* and *holokus*. The men and women are greeted with a kiss, an *Aloha* and a *lei* to wear around the neck. Here are some other phrases that will add charm to a romantic occasion.

Greetings

Greetings—Aloha
Come in and sit down—Komo mai e noho iho

The house is yours—Nou ka hale
How are you?—Pehea oe?
I am fine—Maikai
(When leaving, say *a hui hon kaua,* which means until we meet again.)

Toasts

Here's how—Kamau
Bottoms up—Okolemaluna
To happiness—Lea lea kakou
(The response to a toast can be *mahalo,* which means thank you, or *likepuoe,* same to you.)

Foods

Avocado—Pea
Baked food—Kalua
Baked food wrapped in ti leaves—Laulau
Banana—Maia
Bowl—Umeke
Chicken, fowl—Moa
Coconut—Niu
Coffee—Kope
Dish—Pa
Fish—Ia
Food; also, to eat—Kau Kau
Mango—Manako
Oven, underground—Imu
Paste of taro plant, traditionally eaten with the fingers—Poi
Pig, ham—Puaa
Pineapple—Halakahiki
Rice—Laiki
Salted salmon salad—Lomi Lomi
Shrimp—Opae
Sweet potato—Uala
Tea—Ki

Menus

1. NATIVE HAWAIIAN LUAU

Lomi Lomi Salmon   Poi   Laulaus
Roast Suckling Pig
Chicken Luau
Japanese Broiled Fish in Teriyaki Sauce
Fresh Pineapple Fingers   Haupia (Coconut Pudding)
Baked Bananas

2. GARDEN PARTY LUAU

Pina Passion Cocktails
Tahitian Fish   Chinese Chicken Wings with Plum Brandy Sauce
Barbecued Roast Pork   Pickled Mushrooms, Radishes and Turnips
Corn from the Islands
Island Mango Ice Cream
Kona Coffee
Kona Koffee Grog (After-Dinner Drink)

3. HOME LUAU FEATURING BEEF

Coco Loco Cocktails   Sashimi
Meat Balls Bali Bali   Korean Broiled Beef
Noodles Ono Loa   Cucumber Canoes
Mangoes in Honeyed Sauce
Kona Coffee
Tahitian Kooler (After-Dinner Drink)

4. INEXPENSIVE HOME LUAU

Hawaiian Fog Cutter Cocktails
Bean Curd Appetizer   Five-Spice Chicken Livers
Hawaiian Hamburgers
Sweet Potato Mock Poi
Spring Kim Chee
Red Oranges
Kona Coffee
King Ka-Meha-Meha (After-Dinner Drink)

5. HOOLAULEA (A GALA HOME PARTY)

Hawaii Kai Treasure Cocktails
Tahitian Tidbits   Lion's Head Shrimp Balls
Kona Cornish Hens on Pineapple Husks
Eggplant in Coconut Cream
Orange Sweet Potato Rosettes
Aloha Pineapple and Banana Meringue
Kona Coffee
Humuhumunukunukuapuaa (After-Dinner Drink)

6. CHRISTMAS DINNER MENU

Greet your guests by saying Mele Kalikimaki which means Merry Christmas.

Mai Tai Cocktails
Baked Clams Kai
Cucumber Soup
King Kaulooloo Duck   Ham Alii
Yams and Apples
Candied Tomatoes   Portuguese Fried Broccoli
Bean Sprouts Vinaigrette
Fresh Pineapple Sherbet
Kona Coffee
Hawaiian Russians (After-Dinner Drink)

7. HAWAIIAN CURRY PARTY FOR NEW YEAR'S

If you have been slowly working up to giving a real all-out Hawaiian luau but happen to be short on time, money or courage, you might try this for New Year's Eve. A curry party offers you many advantages. First you can achieve the festive air and appearance of a luau without the roast suckling pig. And that's a big savings right there. Second, you can make a little go a long way since the prime ingredient here will be rice. And finally you can provide your guests with a variety of dishes.

Seafood lovers will go for the shrimp curry, meat lovers can have their choice of beef or pork, and for those who favor the bird, there's always good old chicken curry. If you want to follow the traditional Hawaiian manner of making your curry by the layer, then you can come up with a splendid array of flavors and spiciness.

Hawaiians make a five-layer curry which they call "five-boy" curry, a name borrowed from the Pakistani of India. Traditionally, the Indians allowed each boy of the family the privilege of preparing and serving his own condiments. For real festive occasions, we recommend an eight- or even a ten-boy curry. Just make sure you have lots of fresh coconut, pineapple, chutney, nuts, chopped bacon, ginger root and yogurt.

Five-boy or ten-boy curry . . . take your pick. But if you're giving it on New Year's Eve, you'll have to say *Hauoli Makahihi Hau*—Happy New Year!

Sufferin' Bastard Cocktails
Chafing dishes of: Waikiki Wontons with Plum Brandy Sauce
and Lobster Coconut Curry (serve in individual coconut
shells; see index)
Rice   Assortment of Sambals
Heavenly Pineapple Whip
Kona Coffee
O'Brien Hawaiians (After-Dinner Drink)

8. PUU PUUS FOR COCKTAIL PARTIES

The Puu Puu party combines the mainland cocktail party custom of heavy drinking along with hors d'oeuvre and the Polynesian approach which places the greater emphasis on food. Drinks are used only to complement the excellent food. Here are five different groups. Use only one group if you're having a small party of say 6 or 8 people; two groups of *puu puus* for 12 or 16; and so on. Allow 3 *puu puus* for each guest.

(a) Assortment of Kumaki: Pineapple Kumaki, Oyster Kumaki, Chicken Kumaki, and Chicken Liver Kumaki.

(b) Hibachi Shrimp and Pineapple, Shrimp Fingers, and Tahitian Tidbits.

(c) Mushrooms Lelani, Spareribs Ali, and Chinese Chicken Wings with Plum Brandy Sauce.

(d) Fried Wontons, Korean Meatballs, and Chinese Chicken Wing Clubs.

(e) Coconut Shrimp, Teriyaki Beef, and Manu Chix.

9. BUFFET SUPPER MENU

Headhunter Zombie Cocktails
Polynesian Cocktail Dips with Shrimp Chips
Chafing Dishes of: Beef Mai Kai, Fried Rice,
and Sesame Tomatoes
Flaming Bananas, Apples, and Pineapples for Dessert
Kona Coffee
Kona Koffee Grog (After-Dinner Drink)

10. BUFFET SUPPER MENU

Waikiki Daiquiri Cocktails   Cocktail Dip with Shrimp Chips
Chafing Dishes of: Stuffed Fish Rolls, Spareribs with Black
Bean Sauce, and Kapaa Sesame Salad
Fresh Pineapple Sherbet   Kona Coffee
Waikiki Sunset (After-Dinner Drink)

11. DINNER MENU

Navy Grog Cocktails
Mushrooms Lelani
Bean Curd Soup
Steamed Fish, Chinese Style   Coconut Rice
Bean Sprouts and Peppers   Native Vinaigrette
Pineapple Soufflé
Kona Coffee
Tahitian Koolers (After-Dinner Drink)

12. FONDUE DINNER MENU

Tahitian Breeze Cocktails
Pineapple Kumaki
Passion Fruit Soup
Polynesian Shrimp Fondue
Cinnamon Rice   Sesame Tomatoes
Banana Cream Dessert
Kona Coffee
Waikiki Sunsets (After-Dinner Drink)

13. SWINGING SWEET SIXTEEN PARTY

Sweet Sixteen Birthday parties at the Hawaii Kai Restaurant are a tradition, but you can have a successful one in your home too.

About a month before the party, send out *Aloha* invitations or make your own (see A Home Luau). In a short time you'll know who's coming . . . how many chairs to borrow, how many party favors to buy, how much food to prepare (it can all be frozen) and how much money to ask your husband for. (This should be no problem; remember, it's *his* daughter too.)

For the actual party, follow the Sweet Sixteen Party procedure used at the Hawaii Kai (below) as closely as possible, improvising where necessary. Dad can be the M.C., introducing the games, contests and dances, or a professional can be hired. For music, a local "rock and roll" group supplemented by Hawaiian records can be used.

At the Hawaii Kai each birthday girl has her own "island" hut. The tables are bedecked with leaves and flowers (see A Home Luau). Each setting has an "*Aloha*" place card and a token gift for each guest from the "birthday girl" (small stuffed animals, seed necklaces, etc.).

The service plate is encircled by a lei and on each chair is a large coconut straw hat. Tiki mugs for the Tahitian Kooler drink add a decorative touch. As each guest arrives, a colorful lei is placed around her neck and she is greeted of course with *Aloha*.

Flaming puu puu hibachis loaded with hors d'oeuvre cast flickering lights on the palm-thatched Island huts, whose ceilings are hung with outrigger canoes and blowfish lamps. The walls are covered with tappa cloth and tiki gods. The birthday girl sits at the head of the table in a huge Island Queen chair.

The festivities begin with an *okole* (bottom) contest. This is the Island version of musical chairs. Of course, the word *okole* is bandied about, and the winner receives a prize.

Next is the Hat Contest. Each guest decorates her coconut straw hat with items found on the table (knives, forks, flowers, etc.), and then parades around the bandstand in her makeshift hat. The one with the most bizarre hat wins a gift.

The master of ceremonies then introduces the star of the show, Tiki, a handsome Hawaiian who dances with each birthday girl in a dance contest. The winner receives a gift from Tiki—a kiss.

A Hawaiian love song, "For You", is sung to each birthday girl.

Next comes the Bamboo Dance Contest—the Tuni Kling. Two Hawaiians hold the ends of two 10-foot poles in each hand, 2 inches from the floor. As they beat them together in time to the music, Tiki demonstrates how the dance is done. He dances in and out, between the poles as they are moved in and out (remember double-Dutch jumping rope?). He then dances with a partner. The music tempo increases gradually, and becomes faster and faster. The girl who survives without tripping the poles is the winner and receives a gift.

There are many other dances performed by entertainers at the Hawaii Kai. One dancer teaches the *Hukilau* dance to the graceful fathers. They must roll up their pants, put on grass *hula* skirts and as they sway and swing, they sing with hand movements, "Are you going to a *hukilau*?". (This dance creates pandemonium.)

Mothers don straw skirts and are taught the *hula*, with much chiding and taunting to "move the lazy motor".

The party is, of course, not complete without opening gifts; then the Birthday Cake Ceremony follows, with everyone singing "Happy Birthday" to the accompaniment of the band.

At home, or at the Hawaii Kai, the day will be one to remember— a sweet day for a Sweet Sixteen—*Hauoli La Hanau* (Happy birthday)!

Drink: Wahini Cooler

Flaming Puu Puu Platter: Shrimp Chips, Kumaki, Shrimp Nui, Tim Sans, Spareribs Ali, Egg Rolls Ami Ami

Entrée: Tahitian Chicken with Halakahiki Niu Sauce (Pineapple Coconut Sauce), Hawaiian Sweet Potato Casserole, and Patty Shell of Cherry Applesauce

Dessert: Aloha Birthday Cake and Kona Coffee or Coke

All foods can be prepared in advance and refrigerated or frozen. Pastry shells for cherry applesauce can be found in the frozen food department of your local supermarket. Plan on 2 each of the puu puus per person.

Hawaiian Sweet Potato Casserole is served with a 10-inch scoop. Or the ingredients in the recipe can be combined, put into a pastry bag with a #6 French tip and pressed out on a large flat baking tin into individual large rosettes and baked until lightly browned. Recipe is based on 6 portions, so multiply accordingly.

14. LUAU, HAWAII KAI STYLE

Coconut of Exotic Fruits—a halved coconut filled with seasonal fresh
    fruits
Puu Puu Tray—Shrimp Nui, Egg Rolls Ami Ami, Kumaki, Tim San
    and Spareribs Ali
Celestial Nani or *Tears of Snow Soup*
Choice of Island Entrees:
    Roast Suckling Pig Samoan—served the Honolulu way
    Lobster Aloha—the caress of the South Sea winds in a delectable dish
    Cornish Hen Miki Moko—Individual Rock Cornish hens with meat
        stuffing, a wine ginger sauce, and served with fried rice on a
        fresh pineapple husk
    Flaming Tahitian Beef Brochette—fantasy of prime filet, excitingly
        served aflame
    Shrimp Pacifica—A Waikiki Beach favorite of whole jumbo shrimps
        and chopped pork with rare spices and rich egg sauce
    Roast Pork Hawaii Kai—Barbecued lean pork, sliced and skill-
        fully blended with rare chestnut sticks, bamboo shoots, hearts
        of exotic greens, crested with blanched almonds
    Chestnut Duck—the epitome of Polynesian duck
Samoan Salad
Dessert Island:
    Ko Ko Nut Rum Cake
    Mango Macadamia Delight Sundae
    Kona Koffee Parfait
    Fresh Pineapple Nuggets with Kona Honey
    Ice Cream, Island Flavors
Kona Coffee or *Hibiscus Tea*

Ingredients and Sources

ABALONE: Available in cans in many supermarkets, frozen at fish stores, and fresh on the West Coast, this shellfish is used in soups, sautéed dishes and salads. Heat toughens abalone, so cooking time must be brief. Store in covered container for no more than one week in refrigerator. Rinse in fresh water. Add water to cover; change water occasionally.

ALMOND PASTE: This is made from ground almonds and sold canned in supermarkets and gourmet shops.

BAMBOO SHOOTS: Young, tender, ivory-colored shoots from the bamboo plant; can be purchased fresh in spring and winter in Chinatown or Oriental food shops, and canned in supermarkets. Always rinse this vegetable in cold water before using and store, covered with water, in a plastic container. Change water every other day. It will keep more than a week refrigerated. Substitutions which may be made are celery, green pepper, cabbage or rutabagas.

BEAN CURD (SAME AS BEAN CAKES OR TOFU): A bland, creamy white, custardy product made from soy beans, puréed and pressed into cakes about 3 inches square and 1 inch thick. The cakes can be kept in the refrigerator in a covered container filled with fresh water for 2 weeks if you change water daily. Best used immediately, however. Canned bean curd is also available. There is no substitute.

BEANS, BLACK FERMENTED (SOMETIMES CALLED SALTED BLACK BEANS): These small salty, black, preserved soybeans are sold in jars or in plastic bags. They are used as a seasoning for beef, pork, fish and shellfish, and chicken. Before using rinse off salt, soak for 5 to 10 minutes until softened, then drain and mash.

BEAN SAUCE, BROWN: A thick paste used as a seasoning; comes in cans or jars and lasts indefinitely even after it is opened. Fermented black beans can substitute.

BEAN SPROUTS: The sprouts of tiny mung beans, 1½ to 2 inches long, add texture and flavor to all foods. They are sold fresh and canned, and are easy to grow at home.

To use fresh: Wash and refrigerate in water in a covered container; change the water every day. They will keep up to a week— longer if parboiled first. Or parboil by putting beans in boiling water, let the water come back to the boiling point, and cook for 1 or 2 minutes; then drain and put in plastic container to freeze.

To use canned: Drain off the liquid, and rinse the sprouts well in cold water to crisp them; then drain again before using. You can keep them in the refrigerator for 2 or 3 days; just cover them with cold water; drain before using.

To grow your own: It's easy! All you need are a rack, an ordinary colander, or an old pan or coffee can with holes punched through the bottom. Buy ¼ pound of tiny dried mung beans in an Oriental grocery (or see Source List which follows). Wash the beans and soak overnight in warm water; they will double in size. Rinse until water is clear. Line the colander or pan with a double layer of cheesecloth which has been dampened with warm water. Place beans on cheesecloth in a single layer and cover with cheesecloth. Sprinkle cloth with warm water to dampen. Place a pan under colander to catch excess water. Place this in a dark cool place (a closet, basement, oven). Darkness keeps the sprouts young and tender. Water bean sprouts every 4 hours with half a cup of warm water. Check to see water drains into pan; when pan is full, pour off water or it will become stagnant and moldy.

BITTER MELON (FRESH VEGETABLE): Cucumber-type vegetable but very wrinkled. It has a mintlike, refreshing flavor. Bitter melon is best with meat and seafood or chicken, in soup, or steamed and baked. It is available fresh during summer months and can also be found in cans. Refrigerate it for no more than one week. Parboil it for 5 minutes before using. Cucumber can be used as a substitute.

BOKCHOY: A fresh vegetable (Chinese cabbage) that resembles thick, white celery with dark green leaves. It is sold fresh by weight and will keep one week. Green or white celery is a good substitute.

BUTTER, CLARIFIED: Good for frying, since it will not burn even at a temperature of 400° F. Clarified butter can be refrigerated for several weeks.

To clarify butter: Heat ½ pound (2 sticks) sweet butter slowly in a saucepan; when foam accumulates on top, skim it off. Sediment will fall to bottom of pan; what's left is clarified butter, which you strain into a jar. Sediment and foam can be used for vegetables.

CELERY CABBAGE: A fresh vegetable that grows tightly packed, 10 to 12 inches long, and firm. Leaves can range in color from yellow to green. It can be eaten raw, pickled or cooked with beef or pork. Celery cabbage will keep refrigerated for one week. You can buy it in most produce stores and many supermarkets. Celery is a good substitute.

CHESTNUTS (DRIED AND SHELLED): They add flavor to chicken, pork and duck dishes. Buy in Italian or Oriental groceries by weight; canned chestnuts can be substituted.

To use dried: Soak overnight in water and cook until tender. Drain to use, unless otherwise directed in your recipe.

To shell fresh chestnuts make an "X" on the flat side of each one with a sharp knife. Place in an oiled pan over high heat and shake to coat chestnuts. Then bake in 325° F. oven until shells loosen. Another way is to cover chestnuts with boiling water and cook for 5 minutes. Let stand covered in the water for about 10 minutes. Remove shells and inner membrane.

CORNSTARCH: This is used extensively as a thickener in Hawaiian sauces and soups, to dredge meats and fish, etc. It has a flavor more delicate than flour, and produces the shiny glaze which is typical of Oriental and Hawaiian food. Note that cornstarch is mixed with water before it is added to the dish, and must be added at the last minute; it waters out when reheated.

DAIKON: A fresh vegetable; carrot-shaped, large long, white radish with a sharp flavor. The vegetable is used for garnish, soup, salad, etc. White icicle radish can be substituted.

DUCK SAUCE: see Plum Sauce.

EGG ROLL SKINS OR WRAPPERS: Squares of egg dough rolled thinly, and sold ready-made in Oriental stores by weight. Since the skins should be kept refrigerated or frozen, they must be purchased directly and not by mail order.

FIVE SPICES: A combination of these spices—star anise, anise pepper, fennel, cloves and cinnamon. Delightfully fragrant and pungent. Use sparingly on meat or poultry. You can buy it ready-made almost anywhere or, if you feel so inclined, buy the spices individually and combine equal amounts of each.

FLOUR, WATER CHESTNUT: An expensive flour made from dried chestnuts and used in batters or as a thickener and binder. It gives a crisp coating to fried foods. Cornstarch can be used as a substitute. Water chestnut flour can be obtained by mail order or directly from Oriental food shops.

GARLIC: Widely used in Oriental and Polynesian cooking, this is a delightful seasoning for seafood, poultry, etc. Fresh garlic is best, but garlic powder can be substituted. Garlic buds last for months in a covered plastic or glass container. A garlic press is excellent for crushing and mincing. To remove the skin, tap the bud with the flat blade of a knife.

GINGER ROOT: Odd-shaped and gnarled, it comes with a brown side, is cream-colored inside, and resembles a potato. It has a marvelous fresh, spicy taste that cannot be duplicated in dry ginger. Scrape or peel skin before slicing it, or crush it in the garlic press. Available in Oriental, Greek and Spanish food stores. Fresh ginger can be stored in covered container, in refrigerator, for 2 to 3 weeks. When covered with sherry wine, it can stay indefinitely. Ginger can be frozen in plastic bag also. *Candied ginger* or canned ginger in syrup may be substituted if the sugar and syrup is rinsed off.

HOISIN SAUCE: This thick, reddish-brown sweet sauce, tasting of almonds, is used sparingly on spareribs, duck, etc. It will keep for a year in a tightly covered container in refrigerator. It can be bought from mail order suppliers.

KUMQUATS: Small oval-shaped orange citrus fruit with an orangy flavor. The fruit can be purchased fresh in Oriental shops but, more easily, packed in syrup in cans at many supermarkets.

LICHEES (LYCHEES): The fresh ones are covered with a rough red shell; the pulp is white and translucent and has a hard brown seed. Available fresh only in early summer and, even then, hard to come by. The canned are small, sweet and delicate, resembling a white cherry or grape and can be found in some supermarkets. After opening, refrigerate in a well-covered container for one week, or freeze.

LOTUS ROOT: This root of the water lily is reddish brown and resembles thin, long sweet potatoes. The fresh root should be soaked before using; it is also available canned, and can be kept for 3 weeks in the refrigerator.

MUSHROOMS (DRIED): These are blackish brown, large mushrooms that have been dried. They are expensive and are therefore used sparingly; Before using, rinse and soak until soft. The water in which they soaked can be used in broth. Some European mushrooms are less expensive than the Chinese kind, but taste differently. You can substitute *fresh* mushrooms.

NOODLES (RICE OR RICE FLOUR): These thin, brittle, long noodles are made from rice and resemble white, stiff thread. They are used as a garnish by deep frying until they are white and puffy; they keep indefinitely. Sometimes called Vermicelli.

OIL, COOKING AND DEEP FRYING: The Chinese prefer peanut oil, believing that it does not absorb cooking odors. But corn oil is chosen in many households because it is low in saturated fat and high in poly-unsaturates. Use a good brand whatever you select.

OIL, SESAME: It is made from toasted sesame seeds and has a nutty rice flavor; it can be bought mostly from Oriental food shops. Use sparingly.

ORGEAT: A non-alcoholic almondy flavoring used in drinks. It keeps indefinitely in refrigerator. Orgeat can be bought in specialty shops and pharmacies.

OYSTER SAUCE: A thick, brownish, richly flavored sauce made from oysters, soy sauce and brine. It is used as a seasoning or even as a table condiment. Oyster Sauce is sold in cans and bottles and keeps indefinitely without refrigeration.

PEPPER: Freshly ground is far superior to the prepared pepper. Treat yourself to a pepper mill.

PLUM SAUCE: Also called *Duck Sauce*, this is a sweet and pungent, thick sauce made from plums, apricots, chili, vinegar and sugar. Use it as a condiment. You can buy it by the jar in all supermarkets or in pound cans at Oriental stores. It can be kept for months in the refrigerator.

SESAME SEEDS (PULVERIZED): To prepare, toast seeds until golden brown, add a pinch of salt, and then pulverize with mortar and pestle, wooden potato masher, or blunt end of large knife.

SHERRY WINE: Use a good quality, not a cooking wine; it costs no more than the sherry sold in small bottles at the supermarket. Since sherry is a fortified wine, it will last indefinitely.

SHOYU SAUCE: see Soy Sauce.

SHRIMP, BUTTERFLIED: Large shrimp are butterflied so they appear twice their size and can be thoroughly cooked when dipped in butter.

To butterfly them: Shell and devein shrimp, leaving tail intact. With knife, cut gently into the inside curve, not all the way through, almost to the tail. Open carefully to lie flat as shown in drawing on page 73.

SHRIMP AND LOBSTER CHIPS: Similar to potato chips when deep fried, but they come in pastel colors of blue, pink, yellow, green, and taste faintly of shrimp and lobster; the chips are used as a snack and for dipping.

SNOW PEAS (FRESH VEGETABLE): These are flat, pale-green tender pea pods which require little cooking (a few minutes). They can be purchased fresh in Oriental stores all year round, and are available frozen in most supermarkets.

SOY SAUCE (SHOYU SAUCE): A salty, pungent brown sauce that has many uses—it brings out the flavor of foods, colors and enhance gravies, and is used in marinades and dips. It comes light, dark or thick. Light soy is used where flavor is wanted but not color; dark (commonest variety) is blacker and richer in flavor. Thick soy is made with molasses and is black and heavy. The dark is available in all supermarkets but the best quality imported soy is sold in Oriental food stores and can be purchased in large bottles. A good substitute for the thick sauce is Brown Gravy Sauce, bead molasses type, also to be found in most supermarkets.

TARO ROOT AND TARO LEAVES: A starchy plant about the size of a large potato, and a staple of the Hawaiians; it is baked or boiled and made into *poi*. Leaves, called *luau*, resemble spinach in texture and taste. Only the root is available in Oriental food shops.

TI LEAVES: These are used by Hawaiians to wrap foods for cooking, and as "plates" for serving foods. Use ti leaves also for decorating luau tables.

TOFU: See Bean Curd.

TOMATO COLORING: Restaurant chefs paint this bright red liquid on pork and spareribs to enhance their appearance. Red vegetable color (used for coloring icings) can be substituted, but use sparingly. Buy tomato coloring in Oriental groceries or by mail.

VERMICELLI: A thin, hard, transparent, white noodle made from mung peas. Soak in water for 30 minutes and then cut into 3-inch lengths. Vermicelli becomes translucent and absorbs the flavor of the ingredients it is cooked with. It keeps indefinitely and is sold in 1-pound packages in Oriental food shops.

WATER CHESTNUTS (FRESH OR CANNED VEGETABLE): When fresh, these small crispy white vegetables have a tough skin which must be peeled. Fresh ones are delicate and sweet. Canned ones are a good substitute; drain and rinse in cold water before using. Both require little cooking and both can be kept in refrigerator about 1 week if covered with water.

WONTON SKINS OR WRAPPERS: These 3-inch squares of flour-and-egg dough rolled paper thin (see index for recipe) can be bought fresh in Oriental food stores. They are sold by the pound, very inexpensively (there are close to 100 to the pound). Store in refrigerator or freezer. See page 93-94 for recipe.

SOURCES

Most department stores have gourmet departments where the ingredients used in Hawaiian cuisine can be ordered. The following will fill mail orders:

1. House of Hanna
   1468 T Street, N.W.
   Washington, D. C.   20009
2. Kam Shing Company
   2246 South Wentworth Avenue
   Chicago, Illinois   60616
3. Kwong On Lung Importers
   680 North Spring Street
   Los Angeles, California   90012
4. Mee Wah Lung Company
   608 H Street, N.W.
   Washington, D. C.   20001
5. Oriental Food Shops
   1302 Amsterdam Avenue
   New York, New York   10027
6. Mon Fong Wu
   36 Pell Street
   New York, New York   10013
   Attention: Mr. Suon Leong
7. Oriental Import and Export Co.
   2009 Polk Street
   Houston, Texas   77003
8. Shiroma (S and I Company)
   1058 West Argyle Street
   Chicago, Illinois   60640
9. Star Market
   3349 North Clark Street
   Chicago, Illinois   60657

Orchids of Hawaii
Division of Hawaii International
305 Seventh Avenue
New York, New York   10001

Everything Hawaiian—souvenirs, favors, decorations, costumes, tableware, paper goods, guidebook and even musicians and entertainers. Catalog available.

Colonial Gardens
270 West Merrick Road
Valley Stream, New York   11580

Sources for Hawaiian party supplies (catalog available).

B. Ivaldi Company, Inc.
68-70 Jay Street
Brooklyn, New York   11201

Flambée Fanfare for foolproof flambéeing.

Index